CRITICAL INSIGHTS

Twelfth Night, or What You Will

CRITICAL INSIGHTS

Twelfth Night, or What You Will

Editor
Robert C. Evans
Professor Emeritus
Auburn University at Montgomery

SALEM PRESS
A Division of EBSCO Information Services, Inc.
Ipswich, Massachusetts

GREY HOUSE PUBLISHING

Cover photo: Chronicle / Alamy Stock Photo

Critical Insights: Twelfth Night, or What You Will, published by Grey House Publishing, Inc., Amenia, NY, under exclusive license from EBSCO Information Services, Inc.

∞ The paper used in these volumes conforms to the American National Standard for Permanence of Paper for Printed Library Materials, Z39.48 1992 (R2009).

Publisher's Cataloging-in-Publication Data
(Prepared by Parlew Associates, LLC)

Names: Evans, Robert C., 1955- , editor. | Shakespeare, William, 1564-1616. Twelfth night.
Title: Critical insights : twelfth night, or what you will / editor Robert C. Evans.
Other titles: Twelfth night, or what you will.
Description: Ipswich, MA : Salem Press, a division of EBSCO Information Services, Inc. ; Amenia, NY : Grey House Publishing, 2024. | Series: Critical insights. | Includes 13 b&w photos. | Includes bibliographic references and index.
Identifiers: ISBN 9781637007280 (hardback)
Subjects: LCSH: Shakespeare, William, 1564-1616 - Biography. | Shakespeare, William, 1564-1616. Twelfth night - Criticism and interpretation | Twelfth night (Shakespeare, William) - Criticism and interpretation. | BISAC: LITERARY CRITICISM / Shakespeare. | LITERARY CRITICISM / European / English, Irish, Scottish, Welsh. | LITERARY CRITICISM / Modern / 17th Century.
Classification: LCC PR2837.C75 2024 | DDC 822.3/3--dc22

First Printing

PRINTED IN THE UNITED STATES OF AMERICA

To Marianne Novy
and
Michael Goldman
for warm encouragement
when it was most needed.

Contents

Critical Contexts

Critical Readings

Resources

About This Volume

Robert C. Evans

This volume, like all the others in the Critical Insights series, is divided into several distinct sections. It begins with several introductory essays (including this one), then presents four contextual essays, then offers ten individual "critical readings," and finally concludes with various "resources" designed to supply readers with further historical and bibliographical information. The volume next offers biographies of the editor and contributors and finally concludes with a comprehensive index of names, titles, and topics.

The present volume opens with an introductory essay by Nicolas Tredell, a distinguished British scholar, who examines Shakespeare's comedy *Twelfth Night* in terms of several different kinds of characters who appear within the play. These include women, tricksters, clod-poles, gulls, clowns, and lovers. In particular, Tredell's essay "explores key elements of humor and pathos in *Twelfth Night* as they emerge in its specific words, actions and situations and feed into its overall themes." He first focuses on the play's "wit and wordplay, as exemplified in the initial duel of wit and words between Maria and Feste, which Maria wins" and then goes on "to consider the kinship between the Fool and the Trickster" before finally exploring "pathos in the play as evoked through the figures of Sir Andrew Aguecheek, Malvolio, Antonio, and Feste."

Tredell's essay is followed by a deliberately brief biography of Shakespeare by the volume editor.

Critical Contexts

The "Critical Contexts" section offers four different *kinds* of essays: one discussing the play in historical terms; a second surveying some of the critical responses the drama has elicited; a third presenting a very specific "critical lens" useful in examining the work; and fourth and finally, an essay comparing and contrasting *Twelfth Night* with two other dramas by Shakespeare. The "historical" essay in this case is by Christopher Baker, who discusses several different filmed versions of the play, beginning in 1910 and ending in 2013. Baker concludes that the six important films he surveys "demonstrate that *Twelfth Night* is a play of contrasting currents that flow from the church year's celebration itself, for the event of Twelfth Night is a time of festivity as well as the regrettable finale of Christmas joy. Both moods," he continues, "are held in tension by the play: Illyria as a land of marriages and reunion as well as dark rooms and shipwrecks." He thinks the play evokes "the pleasure of the present moment with 'ginger hot i' the mouth" (2.3.121-22) over against Feste's reminder that "Youth's a stuff will not endure" (2.3.53) as well as "the spirit of *carpe diem* contending with the gloom of *memento mori.* Which of these poles of experience is dominant in the play is," according to Baker, "a conundrum Shakespeare leaves to his audiences and players to answer." It is a play of "What You Will," inviting new and creative replies to its own question: "What country, friends, is this?" (1.2.1).

In a survey of a different sort—this time offering an overview of various distinctive critical readings of the play—Melissa Anderson reports on the contents of a recent collection of essays edited by James Schiffer, which she says offers "a variety of contemporary critical perspectives on *Twelfth Night* and its production history." She asserts that these essays, "whether delving deep into the history of specific words, philosophies, and knowledge in Shakespeare's period, or examining recent innovative performances of his play," all "demonstrate the variety of interpretation and experiences to which the play and its productions lend themselves." Anderson finds that the "individual essays are organized in a logical order that allows themes such as masculinity or the existence of Illyria in the Renaissance imagination to be followed from one essay to another" but notes that although "the essays were collected in 2011, the theme of transgender identities is conspicuously absent even in essays that examine the work of gender in the play closely." But she concludes that although the "exploration of productions of the play outside England is confined to Europe," the "breadth and depth of the collection showcases the adaptability, richly evocative language, and genius of this remarkable play."

In the essay presenting a very specific "critical lens" through which the play can be examined, Edwin Wong explores different theories about the nature and effectiveness of humor while trying to determine how and why *Twelfth Night*, in particular, is such a genuinely funny play. He ties his own thoughts to recent ideas about evolutionary psychology, arguing that what he calls the "evolutionary-incongruity theory of laughter combines two promising strands" and "has the most fact-based support." He contends that because "evidence suggests that animals laugh, to understand human laughter, it makes sense to look at its origins because it is far simpler to analyze animal behaviors" than to examine those of humans. Although he concedes that "some—and perhaps many—elements of the evolutionary-incongruity theory will be debunked," he also concludes that for the time being, "even though some disagree and others scoff, it is the best thing going because it is consilient"—a term whose meaning and importance he explores in the final pages of his essay.

Finally, in the contextual essay involving comparison and contrast, Matthew M. Thiele explores the topic of "Tragicomic Juxtaposition in *Macbeth*, *Twelfth Night*, and *Much Ado About Nothing*." Examining, to some degree, some of the same issues concerning comedy raised by Wong, Thiele tries to imagine why and how Shakespeare's plays in various genres might have appealed to their very first audiences. "In Shakespeare's plays," he suggests, "the words 'comedy' and 'tragedy' seem to be more or less marketing tools." Thus, when the play's earliest producers labeled a play "*The Comedy of This* or *The Tragedy of That*," they "were developing expectations that they then managed, in various interesting ways, as the plays work themselves out. The point," Thiele concludes, "seems to be surprise. Shakespeare's plays are written with the courageous attitude that the customer is not always right, and that they only think that they know what they want. What most of them want is to be surprised. Shakespeare's plays," he contends, "give that gift constantly."

Critical Readings I

The contents of this volume now shift from different critical contexts to specific "critical readings"—that is, essays that examine *Twelfth Night* from deliberately various points of view. This section opens with a survey, by Robert Evans, of the introductions included in a wide variety of scholarly editions of the play—introductions that are themselves full of distinctive insights into the work from diverse points of view. Evans contends that some of the "most important work done on any Shakespeare play is the work done by specific editors. The people chosen to edit Shakespeare's works, or to comment on them in 'complete' collections, are usually top scholars. And when their work," he continues, "involves editing a single play, such as *Twelfth Night, or What You Will*, they are usually experts on that play in particular." Therefore, reading such introductions "is often a very good way to get a solid sense of 'the best that has been thought and said' about" a drama. "Moreover, by reading *numerous* introductions, one soon becomes familiar with the main issues and controversies associated with a given play. One hears an ongoing conversation in which different editors and scholars express their sometimes similar, sometimes varied opinions about the topics at hand and present a wide range of relevant evidence to support their views and conclusions."

Evans's essay is followed by a survey of a different kind—this one by Brandon Schneeberger, who offers a critical overview of numerous essays concerning "Religion in *Twelfth Night*." Focusing on ten essays from the 1970s to the 2020s, Schneeberger concludes that although "other topics have certainly been discussed regarding the play, religious commentary continues to shape much of the criticism, suggesting that a robust understanding of *Twelfth Night* should include a thorough understanding of the religious conversation both within the play and in Shakespeare's England." Schneeberger notes that although "critics may not agree on certain religious aspects of Shakespeare's play, we can be certain that critics, teachers, and directors will continue to consider how religion shapes one of Shakespeare's most enduring comedies."

Next, James Hirsh, in an essay on "The Puzzling Title of *Twelfth Night, or What You Will*," asserts that "in crafting a number of his plays Shakespeare adopted a subtle technique that elicits from playgoers empathy in regard to a character as no other technique can. Instead of simply telling or showing playgoers something about a character's situation and inviting them to imagine what it *might* be like to be in such a situation," Shakespeare, according to Hirsh, "constructed each of these plays in such a way that playgoers (merely by trying to respond appropriately to the play) are *in fact* placed in a situation that, however faintly, resembles the situation in which the character finds himself. This," he argues, "is one of Shakespeare's most original and inventive techniques," and his own essay explores "a particularly intriguing example of Shakespeare's employment of this technique" in *Twelfth Night*. In this case, "Instead of merely telling playgoers about the rewards and the risks of exercising one's imagination or merely depicting characters who are rewarded or punished for exercising their imaginations, Shakespeare places playgoers in situations that tempt them to exercise their own imaginations and thereby to run the risk of being foolish."

In another essay offering a distinctive critical approach, Matthew M. Thiele, exploring issues of "Government, Sovereignty, and the Unruly Household in Shakespeare's *Twelfth Night*," contends that the "disorder in Olivia's house reflects the disorder of the state and Orsino's abandonment of his official duties, which is evident in his single-minded and futile pursuit of Olivia's consent in love." According to Thiele, "Just as an absolute system of governance that has no real ability to check a ruler usually produces incompetent leaders who abuse authority and neglect their duties, an unregulated household provides the venue for various abuses if not checked and corrected by a competent head." He thinks that in the world of *Twelfth Night*, "Orsino needs Olivia more than Olivia needs Orsino, and that obviously has interesting and important political implications. For one, it suggests that Olivia should have the autonomy to choose a suitable partner, even if the one she chooses is a woman. It also suggests," in Thiele's opinion, "that government needs sovereign households more than sovereign households need government, and that rulers should tread lightly. The play reserves significant sovereignty over household affairs for the owner of the house, suggesting that a sovereign household is the foundation of civil order."

Critical Readings II

If the first half of the Critical Readings section deals with the various ways in which *Twelfth Night* has been interpreted by scholars, the second half deals with how the play has been interpreted both by illustrators of books and by directors and actors for the stage. Thus, in a pair of related essays, Robert Evans and Jordan Bailey look at the ways early illustrators, especially from the Victorian era (the heyday of illustrated editions of Shakespeare) imagined two key scenes from the play, both of which involved the comic players of this drama's riotous subplot. Evans's essay, for example, deals with the infamous "party" scene involving Sir Toby Belch, Sir Andrew Aguecheek, and Feste the Clown, on the one hand, and the censorious Maria and Malvolio on the other. When Malvolio, determined to quash the party, manages to offend everyone involved (including Maria), he suddenly finds himself the victim of Maria's plot to make him look ridiculous before Countess Olivia. Evans examines various illustrations of these key episodes.

Bailey, in a sense, picks up where Evans left off: she examines the scenes in which Malvolio does indeed make a fool of himself, not only before Maria and her friends but especially before Olivia. By getting Malvolio to dress in yellow, cross-gartered stockings, Maria's scheme takes revenge on Malvolio for his earlier, imperious behavior. Bailey ends by making points relevant to both of these essays. She argues that "illustrated editions of Shakespeare's plays occupy a sort of intriguing middle ground between what might be called a 'mere' reading edition (that is, one featuring nothing but text, pure and simple) and a live performance on the stage." She contends that "illustrated editions could help early readers (often physically distant from 'major' Shakespearean theaters and without access to modern-day films and television broadcasts) to visualize the appearance of important characters, the ways those characters might interact, and the over-all 'tone' of a key scene or episode."

Such editions "also allowed early readers to compare and contrast their own conceptions of a play's episodes with the conceptions of talented, imaginative artists who had obviously given serious thought to an episode before trying to render it visually." Finally, she asserts, "these kinds of editions, full of often very interesting drawings, also gave early readers extra value for their money, providing them with access not only to the works of the world's most famous playwright but also to the talents of skillful contemporary visual artists."

The final four essays of the "Critical Readings" section deal with several important "live" performances of the play—performances in which audiences' reactions to the comedy are visible and are part of the show. All the performances discussed in this section are still easily available for viewing, either on the Internet, or on DVD, or in both ways. Thus, Eric Sterling discusses the ways numerous critics responded to a 1998 production of the play at New York's Lincoln Center—a production that was broadcast nationally by PBS. This staging, directed by Nicholas Hytner, featured a number of "star" actors (including one Academy award winner) and was soon nominated for Tony Awards in various categories, including best revival of a play, best set design, best costume design, best lighting design, and best original score written for a theatrical production. Sterling reports, however, that "published reviews of the play were largely uneven" and that "even critics who admired the show usually found something to dislike, especially in the major performances, although performances in the comic subplot were widely admired and practically every reviewer praised the production's set." Sterling, nonetheless, contends that "the mere fact that the play was filmed and broadcast in front of a 'live' audience makes Hytner's production a significant event in the history of Shakespeare on film."

Robert Evans makes much the same argument about another major "live" production of *Twelfth Night*—this one originally staged in 2012 at "Shakespeare's Globe Theatre" in London before then moving to a major "West End" theater before moving again across the Atlantic for a major staging on Broadway in New York. This production, featuring an all-male cast led by Mark Rylance and Stephen

Fry, was enormously popular and praised wherever it was performed. It is widely regarded as one of the best and most successful stagings of *Twelfth Night* ever mounted, and the reviews Evans surveys support that conclusion. They tended to range from enthusiastic to highly enthusiastic both in London and in New York, and, in fact, in the United States the play was quickly nominated for various important Tony awards and won them in diverse categories. Evans surveys reviews of the staging at the Globe (which fortunately was filmed) and of the staging in New York (bits and pieces of which can be seen on YouTube, where audience members have posted a few illicit clips and where some clips from the Tony Awards show have also been posted).

Finally, in the collection's concluding essay, which deals with playing *Twelfth* Night "for laughs," Evans examines the two productions just discussed as well as two others (one from Canada's Stratford Festival and one from London's National Theatre). His purpose is to report how two key scenes from the play were greeted by audiences in all four venues. In particular, he examines when, why, and how audiences responded to laughter in the varied stagings of these scenes. Evans concludes that because Shakespeare's plays were created to be read but especially to be staged, reading his comedies "*in conjunction with* an essay such as this one can remind readers of how variously the dramas can be imagined by particular directors, how differently they can be brought to life by specific actors, and how distinctly they can provoke responses from specific audiences in specific performance spaces."

Resources

This volume concludes with a chronology of Shakespeare's life, a complex chronological listing of his works (with detailed indications of how differently various dates have been assigned to the composition and first performances of many of his writings), and a bibliography of secondary scholarship especially relevant to *Twelfth Night*. These resources are then followed by a biography of the editor, biographies of the contributors, and a comprehensive index.

Shakespeare's Sad Clowning: Humor and Pathos in *Twelfth Night*

Nicolas Tredell

Modern editions of *Twelfth Night* usually call the Fool in the play "Feste" in the cast list and the speech prefixes that identify the speakers of specific lines of dialogue. The name is appropriate as "Feste" means "revels" in Italian and, in Elizabethan pronunciation, rhymes with "jester." But in the dialogue itself, the name occurs only once, when Duke Orsino requests a song and Curio, one of his attendant gentlemen, replies "He is not here, so please your lordship, that should sing it." The duke asks who the absent singer is, and Curio names him: "Feste the jester, my lord, a fool that the Lady Olivia's father took much delight in" (2.4.8-12; 226-27; all Shakespeare quotes are from the editions in the Works Cited list at the end of this essay and follow this format: act number, scene number, line number[s] and, after the semi-colon, page number[s]). Elsewhere in the dialogue, the other characters, and on occasion Feste himself, refer to him as "fool." In the original text of the play in the 1623 First Folio, however, the stage directions and speech prefixes call him "Clo," an abbreviation of "Clown." Although this essay will style him "Feste" in accordance with critical convention, it will begin by locating him within the history of the development of the figure of the clown, to which Shakespeare makes a major contribution.

Prior to the turn of the sixteenth century, the primary meaning of "clown," according to the online *Oxford English Dictionary*, had been that of "[a] countryman, rustic, or peasant," with implications of "ignorance, crassness, or rude [rough] manners." Such people might inadvertently have been figures of comedy and/or pathos, at least to patronizing courtly or urban eyes, like the "rude mechanicals" in *A Midsummer Night's Dream* [1595] (3.2.9; 63), especially when they tried to be serious; but they did not intentionally set out to be funny and/or pathetic. Around 1601-02, however, the time to which *Twelfth Night* is usually dated, the word "clown" was acquiring an important new meaning: "A fool or jester, as a stage character (originally representing a rustic buffoon), or (in Shakespeare) a retainer of a court or great house" (online *OED*). The Clown in *Twelfth Night* combines both these characteristics; Feste is a "fool or jester, as a stage character" and "a retainer of a [. . .] great house," that of Lady Olivia. The Clown we see in the play is, of course, no rustic buffoon, whatever his social origins may have been, but a highly intelligent, verbally agile, quick-thinking, sophisticated, and industrious performer, as Viola, in her guise as Cesario, recognizes after a clash of verbal swords with him:

> This fellow is wise enough to play the fool,
> And to do that well craves a kind of wit.
> He must observe their mood on whom he jests,
> The quality of persons and the time,
> And, like the haggard [wild (female) hawk], check at every
>   feather
> That comes before his eye. This is a practice
> As full of labour as a wise man's art [.]
>
> (3.1.58-64; 254-55)

Viola's observations imply the insecure position of the Fool—any Fool—who is "a retainer of a court or great house;" he has to be aware of and adjust to the mood and character ("quality") of his audience. and the timing of his jests is vital. For such a figure, "play[ing] the fool" is no ludic self-indulgence but a performance that, if it inadvertently offends those who have power over him, could result in dismissal, whipping, or worse. Viola's use of the noun "labour" here emphasizes that the Clown is a kind of professional who must *work* as hard as a scholar or a schoolteacher.

The idea of the "wise fool" was an Elizabethan commonplace, reflecting the reality of real-life fools in the royal and noble courts of the medieval and Renaissance periods, but Shakespeare, characteristically, particularizes, enriches and develops it by his distinctive language and by weaving the Fool into a substantial strand of the whole fabric of his drama. In *Twelfth Night*, Feste is the sad clown who focuses the humor and pathos that the play evokes, but the work's sad clowning is not confined to him: in varying proportions, it spreads across the play and its characters. This essay will explore key elements of humor and pathos in *Twelfth Night* as they emerge in its specific words, actions, and situations and feed into its overall themes. We first focus on the key elements of humor in *Twelfth Night*, wit and wordplay, as exemplified in the initial duel of wit and words between Maria and Feste, which Maria wins; we go on to consider the kinship between the Fool and the Trickster; and we then explore pathos in the play as evoked through the figures of Sir Andrew Aguecheek, Malvolio, Antonio, and Feste.

The Woman's Part

Feste first appears in *Twelfth Night* with Maria, and their verbal swords clash immediately in a contest of wits between doughty duellists. It is worth examining their duel in some detail as it exemplifies how wit and wordplay work in *Twelfth Night,* and how they are evident not only in Feste but also, and sometimes more strongly, in other characters, especially the female ones.

Maria starts to speak to Feste in a paradoxical way by saying she will *not* speak to him unless he tells her where he has been, thereby implicitly reproaching him for being away from Olivia's house, although he is one of her retainers, and thus neglecting his duties. She threatens him with retribution for this: "My lady [Olivia] will hang thee for thy absence" (1.5.3; 184). Although this threat is exaggerated, it highlights Feste's subordinate status in the household; whatever license he may enjoy as a Fool, he is still subject to summary dismissal and possibly to corporal if not capital punishment. But Feste turns the threat into an occasion for gallows humor, effectively saying "So what?"—"Let her hang me"—and stressing the upside of being dead: "He that is well hanged in this world needs to fear no colours" (1.5.4-5; 184). Here "colours" means the colored flags of military regiments, but perhaps also includes a bawdy pun on "well-hung" in the sense of having a large masculine endowment. Maria demands that Feste prove his statement about a hanged man fearing no colors, and he at once ripostes: "He shall see none to fear"

(1.5.7; 184)—that is, a dead man need not fear the battlefield and neither should a living man with ample masculine equipment. A little later Feste supplies another possible post-hanging benefit: "Many a good hanging prevents a bad marriage" (1.5.18; 185). This may be a proverb that he adapts to the situation and that incorporates a further possible bawdy pun, with its implication that a well-endowed man should prove a virile husband and thus conduce to a good marriage.

When Feste says he is "resolved on two points" (1.5.21; 185), it is Maria who plays the Fool, in the sense of both assuming the punning role of a jester and "playing," or manipulating Feste. She does so through wordplay, taking "two points," which Feste uses to mean "two resolutions," in one of its other possible meanings at the time, the tagged laces that fixed breeches to a doublet (in modern parlance, suspenders or, in the United Kingdom, braces). Maria says, "That if one [of your two points] break the other will hold; or if both break your gaskins [wide breeches] fall" (1.5.21, 22-23; 185). Falling pants can be a moment of purely visual humor but Maria evokes it verbally: Feste's pants, or in Elizabethan terms his hose, do not actually fall down, but Maria has conjured up, through quick and clever wordplay, the image of them doing so and thus rendered him momentarily ludicrous in the inward eyes of the audience members or the readers of the text, and perhaps in his own, for after this he effectively concedes defeat in his verbal duel with Maria and compliments her intellectual and verbal agility: "Apt in good faith, very apt" (1.5.24; 185).

Feste dismisses her with a further compliment: "If Sir Toby would leave drinking, thou wert as witty a piece of Eve's flesh as any in Illyria" (1.5.24-26; 185). It is notable that he avoids the most obvious adjective to commend her as a potential wife for Sir Toby, "pretty," which is more often used of women than men although it is not exclusively female in its application. Instead, he uses an adjective that could apply to either gender, though it was probably perceived in Shakespeare's era as a male rather than female faculty; he commends her for her wit, her sharp intelligence, rather than her physical good looks. This is appropriate in relation to Sir Toby who, for all his dissolute drunkenness, is himself sharply intelligent, and it anticipates his offstage marriage to Maria near the end of the play, which Fabian reports when confessing the plot against Malvolio to Olivia and presents as a "recompense" for Maria's penning of the letter that ensnares the steward (5.1.356-58; 350). Her combat with Feste immediately establishes her as a person of wit who can not only hold her own with but also triumph over a professional Fool and could doubtless take on other Witsters. In this respect, she ranks with Viola and Olivia (although her social status is lower than theirs), and, indeed, with other notable Shakespearean women such as Beatrice in *Much Ado About Nothing* (1598) and Rosalind in *As You Like it* (1599-1600). Moreover, Maria is not only a wily Witster but an ace Trickster.

The Trickster's Part

There is a close kinship between the figure of the Fool and the figure of the Trickster who features in many ancient mythologies and persists in later literature and culture in various guises—for example, in Autolycus, the "snapper-up of unconsidered trifles" in Shakespeare's *The Winter's Tale* [1609] (4.3.26; 252), who takes his name from Odysseus's maternal grandfather, described in Homer's *Odyssey* as "the most accomplished liar and thief / in all the world, for he had been given these talents / by Hermes himself" (*Odyssey* (19.447-9; Mitchell 396-98; 262). Hermes was the ancient Greek God of, among other things, thieves and liars; the ancient Romans called him Mercury and the latter name features at one significant moment in *Twelfth Night*, when Olivia defends Feste against Malvolio's animadversions and the Clown thanks her with an invocation of this god: "Now Mercury endue thee with leasing [lying], for thou speak'st well of fools" (1.5.93-94; 190).

In *Twelfth Night*, the most obvious Trickster is Sir Toby Belch, who also displays some of the characteristics of the Fool in his verbal agility and capacity for repartee—most famously in his riposte to Malvolio when the latter reprobates his unruly nocturnal behavior: "Dost thou think because thou art virtuous there shall be no more cakes and ale?" (2.3.112-13; 220). This is an informed response on

Sir Toby's part because it references the food and drink employed in traditional church festivities, which Puritans—of whom Malvolio is, in part, a satirical embodiment—particularly condemned because it could lead to unruly behavior. It thus skillfully links Sir Toby's own drunken disorderliness, which might otherwise seem merely debauched and disruptive, with religious devotion and casts Puritanism as repressive. Sir Toby's riposte also raises a general ethical issue: does one have the right to impose one's own definition of virtue on others who may not share it? It is significant that the phrase "cakes and ale" has become proverbial as an assertion of the right to have a good time—or, in the words of the American Declaration of Independence (1776), the right to "the pursuit of happiness."

To highlight Sir Toby's capacity to focus general ethical issues is not, however, to deny his boorish behavior or his identity as a Trickster, a con artist whose mark, or intended victim, is initially Sir Andrew Aguecheek, whose unearned income amounts to "three thousand ducats a year" (1.3.20; 171) and who would benefit financially from marrying Olivia. But after the run-in with Malvolio, a different mark takes precedence: the self-loving steward himself; and the aim is not to appropriate his money but his *amour-propre*, to take him down a peg or two—or several pegs. In this enterprise, however, it is Maria, not Sir Toby, who assumes the lead, who is the Trickster-in-Chief. As she tells Sir Toby: "For Monsieur Malvolio, let me alone with him. If I do not gull him into a nayword and make him a common recreation, do not think I have wit enough to lie straight in my bed" (2.3.130-33; 222).

Maria certainly does have wit enough to gull Malvolio, indeed more wit than Sir Toby possesses. It is a commonplace of confidence-trickery that marks can only be conned if they want to be; and Maria focuses unerringly on the weakness that will make Malvolio want to be conned. In her view, this is not primarily his perceived Puritanism but the fault Olivia has already diagnosed: "O, you are sick of self-love, Malvolio" (1.5.86; 190). Maria puts it this way:

> The devil a Puritan that he is, or anything constantly but a time-pleaser; an affectioned ass [. . .]; the best persuaded of

himself, so crammed, as he thinks, with excellencies that it is his grounds of faith that all that look on him love him, and on that vice in him will my revenge find notable cause to work.

(2.3.142-48; 223)

Maria's phrase "grounds of faith" might in other contexts mean "grounds of religious faith," the basis of a commitment to a particular set of religious beliefs and practices such as Puritanism; but Maria subverts this meaning to apply it to Malvolio's vanity. It is that "vice" of vanity that Maria will use to gull, or dupe, Malvolio, by her ingenious plot or "device" (2.3.152; 2.5.176; 224, 249). It is worth noting here, however, that the motive she ascribes to herself for hatching and pursuing her plot might itself seem vicious: the desire for "revenge." This desire distorts and taints what could otherwise seem a salutary moral lesson that might teach Malvolio to be less vain in future. We shall pursue this matter later in this essay.

The nature of Maria's "device" to gull Malvolio is further proof of her intelligence and innovativeness. She will "drop in his way some obscure epistles of love" (2.3.150-151; 223)—that is, love letters (although in the event we hear only of one). The key adjective here is "obscure." As the epistle Maria does pen proves, she is highly literate and her calligraphy is that of an aristocrat, above her servile station, because it is very difficult to distinguish from that of her mistress, the Countess Olivia; given this, she could write a letter that would unequivocally look as if it came from Olivia and in which Malvolio was explicitly named. But this might be too obvious and would also appeal less to Malvolio's intellectual vanity than an "obscure" letter whose meaning he would have to work out. Instead of naming Malvolio directly in the forged epistle, she plans to adopt the rhetorical technique of synecdoche, a figure of speech in which a part is used to refer to a whole, or vice versa. The letter will refer to "the colour of [Malvolio's] beard, the shape of his leg, the manner of his gait, the expressure [expression] of his eye, forehead and complexion" and by means of such synecdoches, "he shall find himself most feelingly personated." (2.3.151-54; 223-24).

Manipulated by Maria's pen, Malvolio will become a man of parts rather than a coherent whole. Her letter will include three more items, two of which are not original body parts, and one of which is a bodily expression that is, for him, unusual and inappropriate. Malvolio exhibits these items because he thinks Olivia wants him to—even though, as Maria points out after he has taken the bait, they consist of "a colour [Olivia] abhors" (yellow), "a fashion she detests" (cross-gartering), and "a smile" that suggests a levity wholly unsuited to a person who is "addicted to a melancholy" (2.5.193, 194, 195, 196; 250), as Olivia currently is. These additional parts will effectively take Malvolio apart when he assumes them, reduce him to a set of bizarre, disjointed fragments in Olivia's eyes that can only be held together by interpreting them as signs of madness.

The scene in which Malvolio appears before Olivia yellow-stockinged, cross-gartered and smiling, is very funny and understandably loved by actors and audiences. They turn a character with no sense of humor into an unwitting source of humor, make the sober steward a clown in both the original meaning of the word—an inadvertently uncouth person whose appearance and behavior are inappropriate to the situation—and in the later sense, which developed from the eighteenth century, in which a clown is a figure who, as in a circus or pantomime, adopts strange clothing and facial expressions to arouse laughter without any words. But although the key elements of humor in this scene are visual, they have been generated by verbal means, by the words in Maria's forged letter, as she herself remarks: "He does obey every point of the letter that I dropped to betray him" (3.2.73-74; 268). We may recall here Maria's play on "points" (suspenders/braces) and the visual image this conjures up of Feste's pants, or hose, falling down; here the "points" in Maria's letter have likewise become, metaphorically, suspenders that Malvolio himself slashes so that Malvolio's figurative pants fall down, revealing his yellow-stockinged cross-gartered legs and turning him, in all eyes except his own, into a grotesque embarrassment and then into an image of insanity. But Maria's ingenious trick works too well, lurching into overkill and, in its consequences, shifting the mood from humor to pathos. It is to the pathos in the play that we now turn as it is embodied in Sir Andrew Aguecheek, in Malvolio when he is confined as a madman and in Antonio in his thwarted love for Sebastian. We conclude with the pathos expressed in Feste's final song.

The Clod-pole's Part

Chris Baldick's *Concise Oxford Dictionary of Literary Terms* (1992) defines "pathos" as "the emotionally moving quality or power of a literary [or dramatic] work or of particular passages within it, appealing especially to our feelings of sorrow, pity, and compassionate sympathy" (163). The adjective deriving from "pathos" is "pathetic," but in modern colloquial English "pathetic" is usually a dismissive term that means "pitiably inadequate." In *Twelfth Night*, this modern meaning seems applicable for most of the play to Sir Andrew Aguecheek. Through his knighthood, Sir Andrew is a member of the lesser nobility (Olivia, as a countess, ranks higher and Orsino, as a duke, is in the top echelon below royalty); he should, therefore, be able to comport himself in a courtly manner; but his attempts at knightly airs and graces and at showing a knight's valor almost always flounder, generating laughter and (in Maria and Sir Toby) strengthening their contempt for him. Indeed, Sir Andrew is often close to a clown in the original sense of the term—an uncouth rustic; at one point Sir Toby calls him "a clod-pole" (3.4.185; 285), a term that equates Sir Andrew's head ("poll") with a lump of earth ("clod") and that might, in Shakespeare's time, have been applied insultingly to a countryman close to the soil.

Maria quickly enumerates Sir Andrew's failings in her exchange with Sir Toby before the clod-pole knight's first appearance; Sir Toby tries to talk him up but Maria is having none of it, calling Sir Andrew "a fool" in the fully pejorative sense (in contrast to the "wise fool" exemplified by Feste), "almost natural" (where "natural" has the sense of "intellectually challenged"), " a great quarreller," and "a coward" as well as being, in Sir Toby's company, "drunk nightly" (1.3.22, 27, 28, 29, 34; 172, 173), where the adverb is an ironic pun on "knightly."

All the negative qualities Maria identifies will be exemplified in *Twelfth Night,* and some are immediately evident on his first appearance. When he initially encounters Maria he says, "Bless you, fair shrew" (1.3.45; 173), apparently intending "shrew" as a compliment (possibly meaning "shrew-mouse"); but its primary meaning is that of an ill-tempered woman (as in *The Taming of the Shrew* [1590-91]). Toby then urges him to "Accost" Maria and Sir Andrew, apparently in all seriousness, takes this imperative to be her surname: "Good Mistress Accost, I desire better acquaintance." When Maria says, "My name is Mary," Sir Andrew changes his form of address but perpetrates a further error, addressing her as "Good Mistress Mary Accost" (1.3.47, 50-51, 52, 53; 174). Although Sir Toby has claimed, in his exchange with Maria before Sir Andrew's entrance, that his knightly guest "speaks three or four languages" fluently (1.3.24; 172), Sir Andrew is baffled when, a little later, Sir Toby uses the common French interrogative pronoun "*Pourquoi* [...]?" ["Why?"]: (1.3.88; 176).

For much of the play, Sir Andrew is "pathetic" in the more modern sense of the term; hopelessly inadequate in all the activities in which a knight might be expected to acquit himself well. But there are moments of pathos in the more traditional sense of the term: for instance, when Sir Toby affirms that Maria "adores" him, Sir Andrew says, poignantly and wistfully: "I was adored once too" (2.3.174, 176; 225)—and this does not seem like a boastful and possibly false self-boosting claim but a genuine memory of a time when he might really have been an object of adoration. As the play progresses, Sir Toby's exploitation of Sir Andrew, mixed with his increasingly prominent contempt for him, makes the hapless knight an object more of pathos than of humor, even if, as with Malvolio, his own character flaws make him an easy victim. This is particularly the case when Sir Toby eggs Sir Andrew on to challenge Cesario (who is, of course, Viola in male disguise). Here Sir Toby makes use of two of the flaws Maria diagnosed at the outset: Sir Andrew's readiness to quarrel and his cowardice. Sir Andrew drafts a challenge that Sir Toby claims he will deliver but after Sir Andrew's exit, he makes it clear he will not do so because the letter is "so excellently ignorant" that it will "breed no terror in the youth" (3.4.183,184; 285).

When Sir Andrew and Cesario/Viola finally face each other with swords, Sir Toby and Fabian have already made them thoroughly afraid of each other, and both have determined that they will not harm their opponent. At that moment, however, Antonio, thinking that Viola/Cesario is Sebastian, intervenes. Sir Toby, who is not a physical coward like Sir Andrew, draws his sword, but at that point officers intervene to arrest Antonio. Sir Toby then eggs Sir Andrew on to confront and challenge Cesario/Viola again, but this time Sir Andrew unknowingly challenges her twin brother, Sebastian, who, in contrast to his sister, lacks nothing of a man, and gives both Sir Andrew and Sir Toby "bloody coxcomb[s]" (5.1.172, 185, 186; 335, 336). Afterwards, when Sir Andrew, with apparently sincere sympathy, offers to help Sir Toby and seems to seeks a camaraderie arising from their joint status as casualties by saying that they will have their wounds "dressed together" (5.1.201; 337), Sir Toby gives a scathing response in which, for the first time, he tells his fellow-knight to his face what he thinks of him: "Will you help? An ass-head and a coxcomb and a knave, a thin-faced knave, a gull?" (5.1.202-03; 337). Sir Andrew makes no reply and after Olivia has said "Get him to bed, and let his hurt be looked to" (5.1.204; 337), he exits with Sir Toby, Fabian, and Feste, and never reappears. But it seems likely that such a quick succession of insults would hit home like rapid punches in the solar plexus. In this moment, Sir Andrew becomes pathetic not only in the sense of seeming hopelessly inadequate but also in the sense of arousing pity and sympathy: a true figure of pathos. Malvolio likewise becomes a true figure of pathos, but only after he has been taken apart and reassembled as a madman by Maria's stratagem and his own gullibility.

The Gull's Part

Malvolio is the prize gull, or dupe, of *Twelfth Night*, and his misfortunes, like those of Sir Andrew, result from the fusion of his own character flaws with the stratagems of Tricksters. The results are initially comic; but when Sir Toby, Maria, and Fabian conspire, as Sir

Toby puts it, to "have him in a dark room and bound" (3.4.131; 282), the humorous element starts to fade. It should be said that binding and confinement in darkness were the standard treatment for perceived insanity at the time and that the more callous or coarse of the play's contemporary spectators (and some in subsequent centuries) would still see Malvolio's maltreatment as funny and perhaps feel that it "serves him right."

There have also been more sophisticated arguments by critics and editors that have sought to deny Malvolio his share of pathos. C. L. Barber, for example, in his influential *Shakespeare's Festive Comedy* (1959), contends that "[t]o play the dark-house scene for pathos, instead of making fun out of the pathos, or at any rate out of most of the pathos, is to ignore the dry comic light which shows up Malvolio's virtuousness as a self-limiting automatism" (256). T. W. Craik, in his notes in the 1975 Arden edition of *Twelfth Night*, argues that Olivia's remark, immediately after Malvolio's exit, that [h]e "hath been most notoriously abused" (5.1.372; 351) "can hardly be spoken with complete seriousness, still less with positive anger" (152). Today, these remarks look like examples of gaslighting that attempt to obscure the experiential pain of abuse. If we link *Twelfth Night* with a later play that also prominently features a Fool, *King Lear* (1605-06), we can see the maltreatment of Malvolio as another harrowing spectacle in a Shakespearean theatre of cruelty that includes, at the lesser end of the sadistic spectrum, the confinement of Kent in the stocks (2.2.123-49; 233-35) and, at the greater, the blinding of Gloucester (3.7.66-86; 300-01). In all these cases, the most spontaneous emotional and ethical response seems to be that of pity for the suffering victims, whatever their faults and/or functions in the overall pattern of the play.

We may compare the response the incarceration of Malvolio invites with an exchange in *The Tempest* when Ariel describes the plight of Prospero's brother and his followers, whom Prospero's magic has paralyzed and imprisoned in a grove. Ariel concludes: "if you now beheld them, your affections / Would become tender," and Prospero asks: "Dost thou think so, spirit?" Ariel replies: "Mine would, sir, were I human" and Prospero responds: "And mine shall"

(5.1.18-20; 113). Although Prospero has good reason to continue to wreak vengeance on his brother, who has usurped his dukedom and driven him from Milan, he nonetheless yields to Ariel's plea for tenderness.

There is no similar access of tenderness in *Twelfth Night*. The conspirators against Malvolio know that he is not mad, and there is a strong streak of sadism in their explicit desire to prolong his agony. In this respect, they change positions with Malvolio, incarnating malevolence, ill-will, as he once did. As Sir Toby says when they plan to confine the steward in a dark room and bind him: "We may carry it thus for our pleasure and his penance till our very pastime, tired out of breath, prompt us to have mercy on him" (3.4.132-35; 282). Although Sir Toby attributes moral and religious motives to the false imprisonment of Malvolio and factors in his eventual release—it will be a "penance" for him and in time the conspirators will "have mercy on him"—these seem perfunctory justifications that are outweighed by the motives implied in the words "pleasure" and "pastime," which suggest that the conspirators see it as primarily a means of self-gratification and of passing the time. As we have already indicated, Maria also sees it as revenge—and so, it finally seems, does Feste.

The Clown's Part

The role of Feste in the gulling and incarceration of Malvolio is especially intriguing. Early in the play, before Maria conceives the plot, Malvolio, asked by Olivia to respond to Feste, refuses to play the repartee game—perhaps through incapacity or pride—and instead denounces the fool as "a barren rascal" whom he saw "put down the other day" by "an ordinary fool" and who now seems, under Malvolio's verbal onslaught, "out of his guard," without defense. Malvolio goes on to offer a potentially penetrating analysis: "Unless you laugh and minister occasion to him, he is gagged [silenced]" (1.5.79-81, 82-83; 189). Feste's immediate silence appears to prove Malvolio's point; he does not respond directly to the steward's strictures and only speaks again after Olivia has rebuked Malvolio; and then he addresses Olivia rather than Malvolio himself, invoking

Mercury as we saw above. Feste's silence suggests that Malvolio may be on to something here that applies not only to this Fool but also, and more generally, to jesters, clowns, and comedians: that their identity depends on responsive audiences and a failure to arouse fitting responses diminishes them not only professionally but also, and more profoundly, existentially. It may be because Malvolio has hit on this nerve that Feste—as we see near the end of the play—seems to nurse a grudge against him.

Once Maria has hatched the plot, she makes it clear that she sees Feste, along with herself, Sir Toby, and Sir Andrew, as a co-conspirator who will covertly observe Malvolio's finding of the forged epistle: "I will plant you two—and let the fool make a third—where he shall find the letter" (2.3.168-69; 224). In the event, however, the Fool is absent from the surveillance team; the "third" proves to be Fabian, whose status and function are uncertain—he may be a member of Olivia's household and/or possibly a law student—but who is also motivated by the desire for revenge because Malvolio put him at least temporarily out of Olivia's favor by reporting his interest in a bearbaiting (a target of Puritan disapproval because of its perceived potential for disorderliness rather than its cruelty to animals, which might be the primary objection today). Feste's absence at this point is unexplained: it might suggest that he is less culpable than the other conspirators, but it could also be that his feelings against Malvolio are so intense that he fears he might betray their hidden presence. Feste does participate in the plot later, however, by playing the role of Sir Topas when Malvolio is still confined, then reassuming the role of Fool and taking delivery of Malvolio's letter to Olivia. He delays giving the letter to her, however; only when she commands that Malvolio be brought to her from his confinement does Feste hand it over, excusing his delay on the grounds that Malvolio is mad—which he knows to be untrue: "I should have given't you today morning, but, as a madman's epistles are no gospels, so it skills [matters] not much when [at what time of the day] they are delivered" (5.1.282-84; 345).

When Malvolio is brought to them and Fabian confesses to the plot, pleading that it should provoke "laughter [rather] than revenge" when "the injuries [. . .] on both sides" are "justly weighed" in the balance (5.1.360, 361-62, 363; 350), Feste admits his own role as Sir Topas "in this interlude" and reiterates the gist of the injurious words that Malvolio directed against him early in the play: "Madam, why laugh you at such a barren rascal, an you smile not, he's gagged" (5.1.366, 368-69; 350, 351). This echoes, even if it does not exactly reproduce, Malvolio's remarks back in act one: "I marvel your ladyship takes delight in such a barren rascal [. . . .] Unless you laugh and minister occasion to him, he is gagged" (1.5.79-80, 82-83; 189). Feste's recollection of Malvolio's words, even if imperfect, does reinforce the idea, as we suggested above, that these observations had bitten deep, threatening not only Feste's professional identity as a fluent fool but also, and more deeply, his existential identity, which depended on people responding to him with laughter and giving him opportunities to jest. In this context, the proper name "Feste," especially in its Elizabethan pronunciations, may suggest the verb "fester" and recall the striking final line of Shakespeare's Sonnet 94: "Lilies that fester smell far worse than weeds" (94). We could adapt this to Feste and say: "Jesters that fester smell far worse than weeds." It could be that Feste has allowed his grudge against Malvolio to fester and to turn the Fool from a figure of mirth to a figure of malevolence, not a sad clown but a sadistic clown, a genre-bender who threatens to turn a comedy into a revenge tragedy; Feste concludes his reminder of Malvolio's existential insult by saying: "And thus the whirligig of time brings in his revenges." This provokes Malvolio to declare "I'll be revenged on the whole pack of you!," after which he abruptly exits (5.1.369-70, 371; 351). Orsino tells Fabian to "[p]ursue him and entreat him to a peace," but given that he has, as Olivia acknowledges, "been most notoriously abused" (and Fabian has been one of his abusers), it is difficult to see how he could be adequately pacified (5.1.369-73; 351). At the end of *Twelfth Night*, Malvolio remains an outsider, a figure of pathos as well as of potential vengeance, unassimilated into the harmonious resolution that is supposed to conclude a comedy, and thus perturbing and subverting the dominant genre of the play.

Along with Malvolio and Sir Andrew, a third figure of pathos remains unassimilated, on the outside of the comic resolution, at the end of *Twelfth Night*: Antonio, the sea-captain who rescued Sebastian from drowning and risks his life and liberty in Illyria for him.

The Lover's Part

In contrast to the other figures of pathos in *Twelfth Night*, Malvolio and Sir Andrew, Antonio seems a largely admirable character; where Malvolio is mean-spirited, Antonio is generous; where Sir Andrew is cowardly, Antonio is brave. Each of his appearances is significant in conveying his character and his plight and in contributing to a pattern that works against a harmonious resolution of the comedy. We first see him in Illyria after he has recently rescued Sebastian from drowning; strong bonds have formed between them, and both use the language of courtly love in expressing their affection for each other; but Antonio's feelings for Sebastian seem especially intense. His first words are "Will you stay no longer, nor will you not that I go with you?" (2.1.1-2; 205). But Sebastian is determined to set out on a journey alone and, although initially reluctant to disclose his destination, he finally reveals that he is bound for Orsino's court and exits. In a brief soliloquy, Antonio says that he has "many enemies in Orsino's court" but, addressing the absent Sebastian, declares: "come what may I do adore thee so / That danger shall seem sport, and I will go" (2.1.41, 43-44; 207).

When we next see Antonio, he is trying to act as a kind of minder to Sebastian, concerned to use his knowledge of Illyria to protect the man he adores, who is a stranger in a strange land. When Sebastian declares that he would not willingly have asked him to assume this role, but that he accepts it since he "make[s] pleasure of [his] pains," Antonio says he can do no other—"My desire, / More sharp than filed steel, did spur me forth"—and claims that his "willing love" made him all the more ready to act as Sebastian's protector (3.3.4-5, 11; 269). But he acknowledges his own peril to Sebastian: "I do not without danger walk these streets" (3.3.25; 271). In a sea-battle against Orsino's fleet, as he tells Sebastian, he held out against returning goods seized from Illyria during a trade war, and he would be apprehended if he were now discovered in Illyrian territory. He, therefore, gives Sebastian his purse and goes to lie low.

He does not lie low for long, however; he reappears in the next scene when, mistaking Viola, in male attire for Sebastian, he intervenes to protect him/her as she is, very reluctantly, about to clash swords of steel rather than words with Sir Andrew. When Sir Toby indignantly asks Antonio who he is, the latter's reply again stresses his love for Sebastian: "One, sir, that for his love dares yet do more / Than you have heard him brag to you he will" (3.4.311-12; 294). As we mentioned earlier, Sir Toby is no coward whatever his other failings, and draws his sword; but at that point Orsino's officers identify and arrest Antonio.

Then comes a moment of high pathos: Antonio, impelled by necessity, asks Viola (whom he still thinks is Sebastian) to return his purse. but she does not do so because she cannot—she does not have it. He charges "Sebastian" with ingratitude, showing the bitterness of a rejected lover as he recalls how he "[r]elieved him [Sebastian] with such sanctity of love, / And to his image, which methought did promise / Most venerable worth, did I devotion"; he goes on to denounce him as a "beauteous evil" (3.4.358-60, 366; 297). Even though audience members or readers of the text know that Antonio is mistaken, they can, prompted by the poetic force of Shakespeare's language and the poignancy of the dramatic situation, nonetheless empathize imaginatively with his feelings at this point and feel pity and sympathy for him, responding to him as a figure of pathos. Significantly at this point, the first of the two officers who have arrested Antonio think he "grows mad" (3.4.368; 297), the same diagnosis made of Malvolio's behavior. In both cases their apparent madness is the result of a cognitive error, though Antonio's is less egregious, given the comedy convention of "identical twins" that *Twelfth Night* deploys, which entails that one twin cannot be distinguished from the other when they are apart. The most significant difference between Malvolio's error and Antonio's, however, is that the former results from vanity and the latter from love.

Antonio makes his final appearance in the last long scene of *Twelfth Night* when the officers lead him out to confront Orsino. The duke asks him why he endangered himself by staying in Illyria and Antonio's reply once more emphasizes his primary motivation: his "love" for Sebastian, which he gave "without retention or restraint, / All his in dedication"; he reiterates that his self-endangerment was "pure[ly] for his love" (5.1.77-78, 79; 326). He also expresses once more his bitterness at Sebastian's supposed self-distancing from the man who loves him and helped him but whose purse he refused to return, recalling the pathos of that moment even as the true facts of the situation are starting to emerge.

After that, however, Antonio speaks only once more in the play, when Sebastian enters, with Viola already on stage. Sebastian does then reciprocate some of Antonio's affection, calling him "my dear" and declaring "[h]ow have the hours racked and tortured me / Since I have lost thee!" (5.1.214-16; 338). Antonio does not directly respond to these terms of endearment and his last words in the play express an almost philosophical wonderment at the likeness of the twins more than any personal anguish: "How have you made division of yourself? / An apple cleft in two is not more twin / Than these two creatures. Which is Sebastian?" (5.1.218-20; 339). The pathos of Antonio at this stage of the play emerges, not only from this moment itself, but also from his subsequent silence and inaction, though it may be easy to lose sight of it in the flurry of revelation, reconciliation and resolution that follows and that, in a sense, sharpens the pathos; for Antonio the reconciliation and resolution go no further than this initial encounter with the real Sebastian. The restoration of gender norms in the heterosexual marriages of Sebastian and Olivia and Viola and Orsino, and even of Sir Toby and Maria, are happy endings for them but not for Antonio. Like Malvolio, he is unassimilated into the concluding formal pattern of the comedy, left on the outside, a man apart.

The fourth figure who remains isolated at the end of the play is the Clown, Feste, the singing jester, and we will conclude with a consideration of his last song.

Conclusion

Pathos comes to the fore at the end of *Twelfth Night*, in the song that Feste sings. Its second line, "With hey, ho, the wind and the rain," features in all five of its stanzas and its fourth line, "[f]or the rain it raineth every day," ends four of them. Take the second stanza, for instance:

> But when I came to man's estate,
> With hey, ho, the wind and the rain,
> 'Gainst knaves and thieves men shut their gate,
> For the rain it raineth every day.
>
> (5.1.386-89; 353)

Although "hey, ho" may have a buoyant sound, like the refrain of an upbeat song or a jig, the phrases "the wind and the rain" and "the rain" that "raineth every day" seem like images of sadness, given the close metaphorical link between "rain" and "tears," as in *King Lear*, when a Gentleman compares Cordelia's mixture of "smiles and tears" to "[s]unshine and rain at once" (4.3.18; 318). Feste's song conveys the sense that "man's estate," or women's—more generally, the state of adulthood—is a state of sadness. This does not mean that the Clown is primarily sad for himself, that he is indulging in self-pity; rather he is sad for the world and his final song concentrates the sad clowning, the inextricable mixture of humor and pathos that pervades *Twelfth Night* and constitutes a crucial element of Shakespeare's view of the human condition.

Works Cited

Baldick, Chris. *The Concise Oxford Dictionary of Literary Terms*. 1990. Oxford UP, 1992.

Barber, C. L. *Shakespeare's Festive Comedy: A Study of Dramatic Form and Its Relation to Social Custom*. 1959. Princeton UP, 1972.

Craik, T. W. *Introduction and Notes to Twelfth Night*. Edited by J. M. Lothian and T. W. Craik. The Arden Shakespeare, Second Series. 1975. Thomson Learning, 2001.

Declaration of Independence: A Transcription. 4 July 1776. National Archives, www.archives.gov/founding-docs/declaration-transcript.

Homer. *The Odyssey*. 2 vols. Greek text with an English translation and an introduction by A. T. Murray. The Loeb Classical Library, 1919, Harvard UP, William Heinemann. 1960.

Mitchell, Stephen, translator. *Homer: The Odyssey*. 2013. Weidenfeld & Nicolson, 2014.

Shakespeare, William. *King Lear*. Edited by R. A. Foakes. *The Arden Shakespeare*, Third Series, 1997, Bloomsbury, 2013.

_____. *A Midsummer Night's Dream*. Edited by Harold F. Brooks. *The Arden Shakespeare*, Second Series. 1979, Thomson Learning, 2001.

_____. *Shakespeare's Sonnets*. Edited by Katherine Duncan-Jones. *The Arden Shakespeare*, Third Series, 1997, Thomson Learning, 2007.

_____. *The Tempest*. Edited by Frank Kermode. *The Arden Shakespeare*, Second Series. 1954; sixth edition 1958, University Paperbacks series, Routledge, 1990.

_____. *Twelfth Night*. Edited by Keir Elam. *The Arden Shakespeare*, Third Series, Bloomsbury, 2008.

_____. *The Winter's Tale*. Edited by John Pitcher. *The Arden Shakespeare*, Third Series, Bloomsbury, 2010.

Biography of William Shakespeare

Robert C. Evans

William Shakespeare, who has become perhaps the world's most celebrated writer, was born sometime in late April, 1564, in the small market town of Stratford-upon-Avon, about a hundred miles northwest of England's capital city of London. He was christened on April 26, in the local parish church, and it is customary to assume that he was born three days earlier, on April 23. This is not only the exact day on which he would die fifty-two years later; it is also the day devoted to the celebration of Saint George, England's patron saint. (These facts, like most of the others in this essay, are drawn from the splendid chronology of Shakespeare's life and times compiled by G. Blakemore Evans with the assistance of J. J. M. Tobin. The Evans/Tobin's edition of Shakespeare's works contains (especially in its appendices) massive documentation of practically every aspect of the playwright's life.)

William's parents were John and Mary Shakespeare; they had married in 1557, when John was already one of Stratford's four constables. They eventually had eight children in all (the first was born in 1558). William was their first son. Local records indicate that John, a successful glove-maker, was elected and/or appointed to various civic offices in 1559, 1561, 1562, 1565, 1568, and 1571. His selection in 1568 as bailiff meant that he occupied the town's key office. William, then, was born into a prominent, respected middle-class family.

Shakespeare probably attended the local grammar school, where he would have received a solid education emphasizing mastery of the Latin language and Latin classical literature. Stratford was also a town sometimes visited by traveling theatrical troupes patronized by various aristocrats. Such visits occurred, for instance, in 1568, 1572, 1574, 1576, 1578, 1579, 1580, 1581, 1582, 1583, 1586, and so on. Thus, although Stratford was somewhat distant from London geographically (four days by foot; two days by horseback), it did have some experience of the growing interest in dramatic performance that was becoming increasingly popular in the English capital in the late sixteenth century. In 1576, James Burbage built "The Theatre," London's "first regular playhouse" (Greenblatt 3371) and in 1577 "The Curtain Theatre" also opened in the capital. Other theaters soon followed. By 1581, drama and theaters had become so important that the government issued a decree to make sure they were regulated.

Meanwhile, on November 27, 1582, a license was issued for the marriage of William Shakespeare and Anne Hathaway, the daughter of a prominent local farmer. Shakespeare was eighteen (and, thus, legally a minor) at the time; his bride was eight years older and was already pregnant. Their first child (Susanna) was christened on May 26, 1583. The birth of two more children came in 1585: the twins Hamnet and Judith (who were christened on February 2). In that same year, Shakespeare's father was fined for not attending church. His financial fortunes had begun to decline in 1577, when he began increasingly to be "cited for various debts" (Evans 1990). In 1578, Shakespeare's mother had to pawn various properties to help raise money. Her husband's attempt, in 1580, to redeem the pawned property was unsuccessful. In 1587, John was "ejected by the Stratford Corporation as an alderman for failing, for some years, to attend . . . officially called meetings" (Evans 1996). Thus, as William entered official adulthood, his family's status was no longer as secure as it had been when he was born.

Sometime in 1586 (or 1585), Shakespeare may have left Stratford, perhaps to become a schoolmaster somewhere. (Recent theories assume that he may have taken a position, as tutor and amateur actor, with a prominent Catholic family in Lancashire.) Evans suggests that sometime around 1589 he became associated with a prominent troupe of actors and may have written his first play (Part One of *Henry VI* [later revised]). In ensuing years he may have written or contributed to other works, such as Part Two of *Henry VI* (1590-91?). (Suggested dates of composition of Shakespeare's writings are often highly conjectural; for alternative datings, which sometimes vary greatly, see the Chronology of his works at the end of this volume.) In 1592 Shakespeare had become prominent enough on the London literary scene to be attacked by another professional writer, Robert Greene, who seems to have been bothered by the success of this so-called "vpstart Crow" (Evans 1959). Meanwhile, back in Stratford, Shakespeare's father was "cited [in 1592] for failing to attend monthly church services, as the law required, for fear of being arrested for debt" (Evans 1998). Thus, as the son's fortunes were rising, the father's were in even greater decline.

Shakespeare now became an increasingly prolific and successful writer. Evans attributes his great play *Richard III* to the years 1592-93, years that also saw the composition of his immensely popular narrative poem *Venus and Adonis*, which he dedicated to the Earl of Southampton in 1593. In these early years of the new decade, he may also have been working on *The Comedy of Errors*, his *Sonnets*, a narrative poem titled *The Rape of Lucrece*, the bloody tragedy titled *Titus Andronicus*, and his inventive comedy *The Taming of the Shrew*. Evans dates all these works—so varied in genre—as being composed between 1592 and 1594. Shakespeare's 1594 dedication of *Lucrece* to the Earl of Southampton suggests, again, that he was making valuable contacts among the English aristocracy.

In the middle years of the 1590s, the flood of new works (at least according to Evans's datings) continued: the comedy *The Two Gentlemen of Verona* (1594); the comedy *Love's Labor's Lost* (1594-95); and the history play *King John* (1594-96). In 1595, Shakespeare was paid "for the performance of two comedies at [the royal] court" in late December 1594 (Evans 2002). By 1595 he also seems to have become a "sharer" (or investor) in his acting company, the Lord Chamberlain's Men (so called because their official patron was one of the chief figures of the court). It was as a "sharer" that Shakespeare earned the money that would eventually make him a rich man. Writing plays was not especially lucrative, but owning a right to part of the profits of ticket sales definitely was.

Evans dates the composition of the history play *Richard II* to 1595. He dates both *Romeo and Juliet* and *A Midsummer Night's Dream* to 1595-96. He dates *The Merchant of Venice* to 1596-97 and the First Part of *Henry IV* to that same period. But 1596 also, unfortunately, saw the death of Shakespeare's young son Hamnet, at age eleven. During this period, Shakespeare was also involved in various minor legal troubles. But he continued to write. Evans dates the comedy *The Merry Wives of Windsor* to 1597. (This was the year Shakespeare purchased a substantial home in Stratford called "New Place.") Evans notes that Shakespeare was listed as a comic actor in 1598, and he reports that twelve of Shakespeare's plays were commended by Francis Meres in that same year—a year that also saw the composition of the Second Part of *Henry IV* and (in 1598-99) the composition of the comedy *Much Ado about Nothing*. Evans dates three plays to 1599: *Henry V*, *Julius Caesar*, and *As You Like It*. It was also in 1599 that the almost circular-shaped Globe Theatre—the famous structure so long associated with the glories of the period's drama—was opened in Southwark, on the southern bank of the River Thames.

Evans dates Shakespeare's most famous play—*Hamlet*— to the years 1600-01. It was in the early autumn of 1601 that Shakespeare's father died (perhaps as a Catholic during a time when England was officially a Protestant country). Evans dates the poem "The Phoenix and the Turtle" to around 1601 and dates both *Twelfth Night* and *Troilus and Cressida* to 1601-02. He dates *All's Well That Ends Well* to 1602-03. It was in late March of 1603 that Queen Elizabeth I finally died after forty-five years as one of the most successful monarchs in English history. She was succeeded by King James VI of Scotland, who now also became King James I of England. James's intense interest in literature led him to take over the patronage of Shakespeare's acting company, which now became known as "the King's Men."

During the new "Jacobean" period, Shakespeare produced some of his greatest works, and his plays were now increasingly performed at the royal court. Evans dates the composition of both *Measure for Measure* and *Othello* to 1604, the composition of *King Lear* to 1605, and the composition of *Macbeth* to 1606. He dates the composition of *Antony and Cleopatra* to 1606-07 and the composition of three other plays to 1607-08: *Coriolanus*, *Timon of Athens*, and *Pericles*. In 1607, Shakespeare's daughter Susanna married a man named

John Hall, and Evans notes the intriguing fact that in that same year both *Hamlet* and *Richard II* were "acted on board Captain William Keeling's ship, the *Dragon*, off Sierra Leone [Africa], 'which I permit to keepe my people from idlenes [sic] and vnlawful games, or sleepe.'" Evans reports that *Hamlet* was performed again on the *Dragon* in March 1608.

In the autumn of 1608, Shakespeare's mother died, but the same year saw some good fortune as well: he now became a "sharer" in an indoor, more elite theater opened within the city of London itself. The year1609 saw the unauthorized publication of his *Sonnets*, and Evans dates the composition of the play *Cymbeline* to 1609-10. He also suggests that it was around 1610 that "Shakespeare is believed to have returned to Stratford to live" (2012). Evans dates the composition of *The Winter's Tale* to 1610-11, and he notes that *The Tempest*—often considered Shakespeare's last great play—was acted at court on November 1, 1611, the presumed year of its composition. Evans dates the composition of *Henry VIII* (co-written with John Fletcher) to 1612-13, the same years during which Shakespeare seems to have co-written (with Fletcher) a now-lost play called *Cardenio*. The year 1613 also saw the composition, with Fletcher, of the play *The Two Noble Kinsmen*.

But 1613 also witnessed the accidental burning and destruction of The Globe Theatre. Its thatched roof caught fire during a performance of *Henry VIII*. According to a contemporary source, special pyrotechnic effects designed to enhance the authenticity of the performance "did light on the thatch, where being thought at first but an idle smoak, and their eyes more attentive to the show, it kindled inwardly, and ran round like a train, consuming within less then [sic] an hour the whole house to the very grounds" (Evans 1968). Although the famous playhouse was quickly rebuilt and the new version opened in 1614, an era had ended. Soon the Globe's beloved chief playwright would also be gone.

In February 1616, Shakespeare's daughter Judith married a man named Thomas Quiney. Judith gave birth in November 1617 to a son whom she and her husband named "Shaksper." Unfortunately, his namesake, the great dramatist, had already passed away. Having redrawn his will on March 25, 1616, William Shakespeare died less than a month later, on April 23. This, supposedly, was the very day on which he had been born fifty-two years earlier. He was buried, on April 25, in the same church in which he had long ago been christened. In a life that lasted little more than half a century he had produced some of the greatest literature ever written. Most of his texts were eventually collected and published in 1623 (the same year his widow died) in a massive "folio" (or large-sized) edition compiled by friends and former colleagues. It is a beautifully fitting monument to the treasures it contains.

Works Cited

Evans, G. Blakemore, editor. *The Riverside Shakespeare*. 2nd ed., Houghton Mifflin, 1997.

Greenblatt, Stephen, editor. *The Norton Shakespeare: Based on the Oxford Edition: Comedies*. Norton, 1997.

CRITICAL CONTEXTS

Twelfth Night on Film

Christopher Baker

The perennial appeal of *Twelfth Night* is rooted in its full array of the plot devices typical of many of Shakespeare's comedies: confused twins, ring giving, disguising, mistaken identity, a shipwreck in a strange land, a forged letter, the reunion of separated siblings, the verbal antics of a clown, a story ending in marriages. These features can also be mingled with a comic judgment upon the extreme attitudes of certain characters—in this play notably Olivia's pompous steward Malvolio (who, she says, is "sick of ill-will" [1. 5. 93])—figures whose behavior is unsociable enough to demand they undergo a punitive and possibly rehabilitating trick. Orsino, the duke of Illyria (where twins Viola and Sebastian have been shipwrecked and separated) is in his own way as subject to an exaggerated outlook as Malvolio, being enthralled by the excessive passions of love he feels for the countess Olivia who disdains his affection, herself immured in mourning for seven long years over the death of her brother. But Viola quickly punctures her excessive sorrow, saying, "I see you what you are; you are too proud" (1.5.251). Permeating the whole play is Shakespeare's concern for characters who must overcome such skewed outlooks to find and enjoy a healthy love, one that transcends gender or social rank, enabling them to flourish in the company of each other rather than languish in the solitude of their personal egoisms. Unlike his tragedies, in Shakespeare's *Twelfth Night* and his other romantic comedies conflicts are resolved without the theatrical reality of death, and characters are typically returned to more fulfilling, socially harmonious lives in the communal world of the play.

The International Movie Database (IMDb) currently lists 19 filmed versions (not counting animations) of *Twelfth Night* since its first screen appearance in 1910. This amounts to about one filmed adaptation every six years for over a century, a remarkable feat of theatrical longevity that is quite likely to continue. This essay offers brief critical considerations of a representative variety of these productions (listed by director and year, including films of some staged versions) as a way of demonstrating the vitality of the play and the creativity that numerous actors and directors have brought to their renditions of it.

Eugene Mullin and Charles Kent (1910)

Film historian Robert Hamilton Ball notes that between 1908 and 1911 "almost fifty new productions of Shakespeare were on the screen in America" and Europe (Ball 38), owing to producers' need for new storylines to film and the fact that Shakespeare was a respected author of works conveniently in the public domain. In 1910, the Vitagraph Company of America released a one-reel, 11-minute short film of *Twelfth Night* (available on YouTube). "Originally of 970 feet it has dwindled to 743; there is no title; parts are missing at the beginning, the ending, and no doubt elsewhere, and the sequences are not always in the proper order" (Ball 56). Co-directed by Eugene Mullin and Charles Kent, the film starred Julia Swayne Gordon as Olivia, Charles Kent as Malvolio, Florence Turner as Viola, and Tefft Johnson as Orsino. Ten title-cards highlight the film, starting with the rescue of Sebastian. The opening shipwreck, in which an actual beached ship is seen offshore as Sebastian (played by Edith Story) is pulled from the surf, was likely filmed "somewhere on the coast of Brooklyn," perhaps Bayshore (Ball 314). Other cards note the loves of Orsino for Olivia and Olivia for Viola in disguise (Cesario is not named); the forged letter of Maria (Marin Sais), Sir Toby Belch (William Humphrey), and Sir Andrew Aguecheek (James Young); and the angry departure of Malvolio as the true lovers unite at the end. No effort is made to capture any of Shakespeare's witty dialogue.

The film's stage flats and props are ornate and lush, with gilded furniture, abundant scenery foliage, and even a glimmering pool in the background of Olivia's palace. The costuming is rich and Elizabethan to the hilt: doublet and hose plus ruffed collars for Orsino's courtiers and velvet gowns with gauzy veils for Olivia's ladies-in-waiting. Florence Turner is a sprightly, energetic Viola who deserved a few more title-cards for her own dialogue. Charles Kent, his height accented by the tall staff of office he carries, is a suitably haughty Malvolio. In a character-revealing gesture, he hands Viola Olivia's ring after first fussily placing it on the end of his staff for her to take, rather than risk touching her himself. Sir Toby Belch, short, round, and boisterous, rollicks across the stage like a hyperactive understudy for Falstaff. At the conclusion, Orsino and Viola lovingly embrace in a matter of seconds, as do Olivia and Sebastian (after he enjoys a bit of angry swordplay with the duke), and Malvolio tears up the forged letter and stalks offstage in a huff. Even for those that did not know Shakespeare's play, there is enough stage business onscreen to keep a pre-World War I audience attentive for less than a quarter of an hour.

John Sichel (1968)

John Sichel's television adaptation is a heavily cut version of the play that runs just under two hours (an hour less than Tim Carroll's Globe staging [discussed later in this essay]). One of its most striking features appears immediately: a huge, painted screen depicting a stylized image of Orsino's turreted castle in Illyria, as if to answer Viola's opening question, "What country, friends, is this?" (1.2.1; like many directors, Sichel reverses the order of the first two scenes). Sichel offers us crowded sets filled with period details and props: street scenes; housefronts; interiors (Orsino's bedroom is large enough to contain a musical ensemble, and Malvolio's dark room hides under a flight of stairs); and Olivia's enclosed garden boasts hedges, a mullioned window, and a nude statue. The variety of locales is visually impressive, but it compels the actors to perform in a rather cluttered mise-en-scène.

Joan Plowright offers us a plucky, adventurous sibling rather than the attractive heroine—that role is suggested by the more photogenic Adrienne Corri as Olivia. Plowright, Corri, and Gary Raymond (as Orsino) speak their lines more as poetical statements than as dialogue; the dramatic action slows down markedly as they declaim their parts. Plowright tends to gaze off camera as she speaks, as if to emphasize that she is deep in thought. Several times Sichel replaces her actual soliloquies (especially in act two, scene two) with voiceovers of her reading her own lines while she "thinks" them, a needless bit of overstaging. Plowright plays both Viola and Sebastian (with darker makeup, a lower voice, and different costume), the camera alternating between them in reverse shots when they are meant to appear onstage simultaneously but are not seen together. Although Orsino claims that he is "unstaid and skittish in all motions" 2.4.18) when not focused on the beauty of his beloved, Gary Raymond plays him as a *miles gloriosus* of love, overly assertive and boldly confident in his black wig seemingly stolen from Laurence Olivier's portrayal of Richard III. Sheila Reid as Maria is a bubbly blonde who appears more interested in besting Malvolio for the sake of a jolly prank than for exposing him as the repressive, class-conscious social influence he is. Cuts made to the play removed references to her "revenge" and to her famous description of him as a "Puritan [...and] a time pleaser, an affection'd ass" (2.3.145, 153). Likewise gone from the play is her chilling comment, "I have dogged him like his murtherer" (3. 2. 75–76), a telling hint of underclass tension. A fortunate bit of casting was the English pop singer of the sixties Tommy Steele as Feste the Clown; in his peppermint-striped tights he sings prettily and handles Shakespeare's witty one-liners with sly aplomb and little of the melancholy that colors the performances of Anton Lesser or Ben Kingsley in the same part. When he disguises himself as the priest Sir Topas, everyone seems to enjoy pronouncing his name as "Top-ass."

Alec Guinness's Malvolio is, as most reviewers note, a masterpiece of comic acting. Though not as tall as many Malvolios, he is every bit as punctilious and smug, a kind of Shakespearean Uriah Heep whose obsequiousness to Olivia barely hides his own sense of false superiority. He is never without his gold chain of office, a symbol that ironically points to how far from genuine respectability he has fallen. His lines, too, suffer from cutting: his off-color joke about Olivia's "C's, her U's, and her T's" (2.5.91) has been bowdlerized from the play (as it is from Trevor Nunn's production, perhaps to earn a PG rating). Guinness enlivens the garden scene with comical business, physically turning around as he reads in Maria's letter, "If this fall into thy hand, revolve [consider]" (2. 5. 143). But beneath such silliness lurks a genuine malcontent, and we are taken aback when Guinness viciously shouts at Maria and her friends, "Go hang yourselves all. You are idle shallow things. I am not of your element" (3.4.128–29). Malvolio the malcontent and Jaques the satirist of *As You Like It* are intransigent cousins of a sort; the first refuses to change his ways and return to Illyria, and the second refuses to change his ways and leave the Forest of Arden. Kenneth Rothwell concludes that "As Malvolio, Alec Guinness is a marvel of subtle restraint, a fussy, ridiculous but nevertheless forlorn creature, the embodiment of one of Shakespeare's roster of lost souls" (Rothwell 109). We find Malvolio's hauteur insufferable but Guinness's performance of it impeccable.

Neil Armfield (1986)

Neil Armfield's stage version of *Twelfth Night* (available on YouTube) fared poorly at the box office, earning back less than half of its budgeted cost. Its filmed version is a televised production based upon the stage play put on at the State Theatre of South Australia. Armfield takes his cue from the holiday of *Twelfth Night* as a festive occasion to set the play in a Caribbean Illyria where Orsino (Ivar Kants) lords it over a crowd of tipsy revellers partying on a painted beach beside a painted ocean. This guiding conception of the play is certainly arresting, but none of the cast members—including Geoffrey Rush early in his career—rises to a truly memorable performance.

The film opens with several black and white title cards announcing that the play is about the "confusions of love" set in the "remote and exotic country of Illyria." This nod to silent-screen versions of Shakespeare jars anachronistically with the contemporary beachside setting. Orsino suddenly appears at the back of the stage, framed in a backlit doorway, and orders the beach band to "play on" (1.1.1). Dressed in a sport coat and slacks with slicked-back hair, Kants almost has the louche air of a petty mobster. He indulges in thoughts of love convincingly but is more dynamic when he returns in act five to angrily accuse Olivia of being a "marble-breasted tyrant"

(5.1.123). The red-haired Olivia (Jacqui Phillips), wearing a customary dark gown and peevishly smoking a cigarette, seems more overcome by boredom than by grief. A believable spark of loosely gendered affection ignites despite Viola's disguise when Olivia declares her love to her, suddenly embracing her in a hammock so intensely that both nearly fall to the floor (3.1.148–59).

With short, blonde hair, Gillian Jones plays Viola in a jacket and slacks that have somehow remained perfectly white despite having been through a shipwreck. (Armfield here may be borrowing a detail from *The Tempest*, whose stranded but fortunate travellers wash ashore on Prospero's magical island, "on their sustaining garments not a blemish, / But fresher than before" [1.2.218–19]). She is cautious and unsure at the start but grows gradually more mature until finally marrying, but Jones's slight frame and high-pitched voice fail to convey the feisty resourcefulness of a Shakespearean comic heroine like Rosalind in *As You Like It* or Beatrice in *Much Ado About Nothing*. With a striped shirt and blonde stubble of a beard, Jones also plays Sebastian, with Armfield using reverse camera shots to suggest the presence of two separate actors (for one brief moment a third actor is, in fact, used, facing away from us).

John Wood's Sir Toby Belch is unfortunately little more than the play's paunchy "drunk uncle," a one-dimensional figure rarely seen without a flask or bottle and lacking the crafty intelligence of John Saxon's portrayal. As Sir Andrew Aguecheek, a lanky Geoffrey Rush is his goofy, addled sidekick rather than introspective lost soul and drinking companion. Rush plays his zany part to the full, at one point appearing on the beach wearing mirrored sunglasses, zinc-white on his nose, and a pair of skimpy bathing trunks under a sun shirt. The offstage beach band occasionally adds drum rim shots that punctuate his gags and give the beach scenes a vaudevillian echo. Maria (Tracy Harvey) is dressed in a tan business outfit, with large spectacles and her hair in a bun. Despite granting Sir Toby a lingering kiss, she gives the impression of a prim librarian who has wandered onto the set by mistake, hardly the scheming and revenge-seeking tavern wench who has forged a letter from Olivia.

As Feste, Kerry Walker was nominated for best actress in a supporting role by the Australian Film Institute. In her sad-sack manner, with pork pie hat, bow tie, and pants hiked up with suspenders, her smiles are always ironic, and her songs are heartfelt and plaintive. John Cummins's Malvolio, in ruffled shirt and black bow tie, resembles a frustrated maître d' more than an imperious household steward. His fussy irritation at Maria and her gang seems too shallow for the disruption they are causing him. But when he sashays across the stage toward Olivia wearing not just cross-gartered yellow stockings but bright yellow Bermuda shorts as well, the result is the funniest moment in the play. Armfield's conception for a seaside *Twelfth Night* is nothing if not inventive, but the production has the feel of a shtick with a few too many gimmicks (such as Toby and Sir Andrew being inexplicably hoisted into the air on a bench) to blend harmoniously with the spirit of the play as Shakespearean comedy.

Kenneth Branagh (1987)

In act three, scene four as Sir Andrew Aguecheek enters, Fabian says, "More matter for a May morning" (line 147), a comment that for most directors warrants setting the play in the springtime. Not so for Kenneth Branagh, however, who, taking his cue from the play's title, places the entire production in Olivia's snow-coated garden. (Twelfth Night is the evening of January 5, the day before the church feast of Epiphany that ends the Christmas season.) The wintry setting underscores a melancholy, "Chekhovian" theme that Branagh believes runs through the play, a motif he discusses briefly in the play's DVD version. His concept raised eyebrows from some critics, but the show ran to packed houses after it opened in London in December, 1987. The DVD version presents its televised format as produced and directed by Paul Kafno in 1988.

Most notable in advancing the pensive element in this production is Feste as acted by Anton Lesser, whose clown is a hollow-eyed minstrel with unkempt hair and a fondness for the bottle we usually associate with Sir Toby Belch. His songs, often rendered as bright and lively melodies, are here transposed into testaments of regret and resignation, especially in "When that I was and a little tiny boy" (5. 1. 388–407) that closes the play. Lesser delivers most of his lines in a flat, affectless tone that sets an existential angst against the merry mayhem of the other minor figures. He can relate well to Malvolio in his dark room because he recognizes the darkness that affects everyone: "I say there is no darkness but ignorance, in which thou art more puzzl'd than the Egyptians in their fog" (4.2.44). This Feste is an effective contrast to Sir Toby Belch, played by James Saxon. Wearing a snappy hat, gold watch fob, and furred coat, he appears more like a prosperous merchant than a boisterous barfly. A shrewd conniver and even a decent singer, he is never so drunk that he cannot foment some new mayhem or enjoy bossing around the forlorn Sir Andrew Aguecheek (James Simmons), boasting "Marry, I'll ride your horse as well as I ride you" (3.4.298–99).

Feste's brooding manner is enhanced in a different key by the bitter meanness of Richard Briers, who brings to the role of Malvolio a frantic obsessiveness when he declares, "Nothing that can be can come between me and the full prospect of my hopes" (3.4.85–87). When he declares "Jove, I thank thee" (2.5.179), we hear a momentary echo of the gospel pharisee: "God, I thank thee that I am not as other men are" (Luke 18:11). But Briers produces belly-laughs too when he appears in his yellow stockings with two spit curls plastered to his forehead and offers Olivia a disturbingly bizarre, toothy grin. Comic details like this almost make us forget that Malvolio—and the overbearing attitude he represents—is, as Toby says, "an enemy to mankind" (3.4.103). Throughout Malvolio's megalomaniac outburst, Fabian, Toby, and Sir Andrew observe him from behind a spindly Christmas tree that is barely big enough to hide one of them, let alone all three. When he emerges from his dark room and staggers offstage in a torn and filthy nightgown, we are torn between Maria's desire for justice and Olivia's expression of compassion: "He hath been most notoriously abused", she says (5.1.378).

The two female leads are well balanced. Olivia (Caroline Langrishe) is cooly reserved at first and dedicated only to mourning (as her black gown suggests), but she is convincingly surprised that her love for Cesario (and, later, Sebastian) is an emotion she cannot control: "I love thee so," she tells Cesario, "that maugre all thy pride, / Nor wit nor reason can my passion hide" (3.1.152–53). Frances Barber, a brunette to Olivia's blonde, speaks her lines with engaging immediacy, unlike the more stiffly poetical style of Joan Plowright; her reunion with her brother prompts tears of joy. As Orsino, Christopher Ravenscroft is almost a spent force, a brooding, meditative presence worn out by coping with the "shapes" of "fancy" (1. 1. 14), not at all like the angry, defiant Liam Brennan we meet in Tim Carroll's production or Gary Raymond in John Sichel's adaptation. He, Feste, and Malvolio do most to give Branagh's production its minor key of a "dying fall" (1.1.4).

Trevor Nunn (1996)

For Shakespeare films 1996 was a banner year, offering us not only Trevor Nunn's *Twelfth Night* but also Kenneth Branagh's *Hamlet,* Adrian Noble's *A Midsummer Night's Dream*, and Baz Luhrmann's *William Shakespeare's Romeo + Juliet* as well. Budgeted at $5 million (with box office receipts over six times that amount) and with evocative locations on the coast of Cornwall and at the country estate of Lanhydrock House, it is unlikely that we will see a more visually impressive film of *Twelfth Night* than Nunn's. Nunn clearly views the text of Shakespeare's comedy not as a sacrosanct artifact that must not be modified, but rather as raw material for his own artistic conception of the play or what film critic Laurie Osborne calls his "auteur's vision." "In Nunn's *Twelfth Night,* twentieth-century constructions of character emerge from within ideologies of romantic love and gender; moreover, these constructions thrive through film cuts rather than the textual cuts used in earlier centuries" (Osborne 91). This is not to suggest that Nunn approaches changes to the text of the play casually, however. As Stephen M. Buhler comments, "the most transgressive elements in the resulting film involve Nunn's own anxiety about rearranging Shakespeare's materials; only [Orson] Welles has been more daring in restructuring the plays" (Buhler 156).

We meet such daring changes immediately. The film opens with an added voiceover by Feste (Ben Kingsley), establishing his brooding presence throughout the story and giving us a backstory of conflict between the Illyrians and the Messalines that renders the storm survivors a group of refugees being hunted by the men of Duke Orsino (Toby Stephens). The stormy shipwreck itself is graphically depicted in a long sequence that recalls the opening of *The Tempest*. Another alteration of the text moves the duke's speech at act one, scene 1, lines 33–41 to much later in the play where he recites it while being given a steaming sponge bath by Cesario, lending a potent sexuality to his mention of Cupid's "rich golden shaft" (1.1.35). Nunn's vision of love in this play is anything but exclusively Platonic or heterosexual. As he has said, *Twelfth Night* is "the most fundamental Shakespearean play about sexuality and gender" (qtd. Rothwell 239), and, therefore, its characters interact on, and lead us through, multiple levels of gender simultaneously.

In a brief interview on the film's DVD, Nunn states his view that the play is "more emotional" than most of Shakespeare's comedies, comparing it to Chekov's plays *Uncle Vanya* or *The Cherry Orchard*. More than most productions, with perhaps the exception of Kenneth Branagh's, Nunn's version has a strain of melancholy that is fed by the role of Feste. Ben Kingsley's portrayal of the clown is subdued, at times even morose, and his songs are delivered in the plaintive tones of a sad loner who comments wryly on the action as a marginal observer, as when he scans the beach of shipwreck survivors from atop a cliff. His final song is delivered looking into the camera as he walks off-screen alone, promising "I'll strive to please you every day" (5.1.407) and repeating "every day" with a sardonic, almost sinister chuckle. "Kingsley's somber tone reflects a major streak of sobriety in *Twelfth Night*, which the late Harry Levin once encapsulated in the remark that 'the cakes and ale of Illyria are consumed in a house of mourning'" (Rothwell 240).

The theme of melancholy is further enhanced by Nigel Hawthorne's Malvolio, who, the actor notes in his DVD commentary, is "quite a sad character, ludicrous." Though a figure of fun, his comedy springs from his utter devotion to an inflated sense of himself that isolates him from others, leading Fabian to say, "Look how imagination blows him" (2.5.43–44). When we see him among the cooks and maids in the kitchen, he becomes the Shakespearean ancestor of Carson, the imperious butler of *Downton Abbey*. His attraction to Olivia is also fed by his own ambition, and Hawthorne practically swoons as he hopes one day "To be Count Malvolio" (2.5.36). He reads Maria's forged letter with crazed intensity, announcing that he "will wash off gross acquaintance" (2.5.163–64) as he embraces a nude female statue in Olivia's garden, barely able to control his sudden rush of libido. Hawthorne does arouse our sympathy as a victim of the vindictive Maria. She is played well by Imelda Staunton as the conniving inspiration of the plot against him, a role that suits Staunton who also played the devious Dolores Umbridge in the *Harry Potter* films. When she declares, "For Monsieur Malvolio, let me alone with him.... I know I can do it" (2.3.137, 141), we sense there will be pleasure for her in inflicting pain upon him. Douglas Brode notes that "the nastiness of the plot against Malvolio violates the celebratory comedic climate, moving into a predecessor of the comedy of cruelty" (Brode 97). Mel Smith offers us a satisfyingly boozy and rambunctious Sir Toby, but Richard E. Grant excels in his physical comedy as the slow-witted Sir Andrew Aguecheek. Whether dancing a wild coranto or defending himself in the trumped-up swordfight with Viola, he is indeed, as he says of himself, "a fellow o' th' strangest mind i' th' world" (1.3.11–12).

The three principals play out Nunn's gyrations of gender well. Toby Stephens as Orsino, with a neat Van Dyke mustache and a matinee-idol smirk, is both a military martinet and a vulnerable lover kept busy in managing his emotions within the triangle of himself, Olivia, and Viola. In his bathtub scene with Viola or with her in the billiard room when they almost, but-not-quite kiss, Orsino seems momentarily oblivious as to just which gender he is reacting to, concerned only that it be a heart responding in kind to his. His definition of masculinity announces that men are superior to women in being more fundamentally unstable: "Our fancies are more giddy and unfirm, / More longing, wavering, sooner lost and worn, / Than women's are" (2.4.33–35). Nevertheless, he is more a man of action than the moony romantic as played by Christopher Ravenscroft. Helena Bonham Carter as Olivia gradually emerges from her mourning mood, shifting from her sorrowing self to love for Viola as Cesario, a process underscored by her change of costume from black to lighter blue when she declares her love while winsomely twirling a lock of her hair. She is exasperated at having to deal with her household of comic figures but has a compassionate heart, defending Feste as an "allowed fool" and showing concern for the humiliated Malvolio. Her face is always expressive; when she finally sees Viola and Sebastian together, she exclaims "Most wonderful" with wide-eyed amazement. Imogen Stubbs (at that time Trevor Nunn's wife) gets great comic mileage out of the effort she makes to be an accomplished Viola at masculine activities, whether it be horse jumping, card playing, cigar smoking, sword fighting, or billiards playing. She never hesitates to speak up, reminding Olivia not to be proud and shouting Olivia's name so loudly that it echoes from the hills (1.5.275). Together, Carter and Stubbs are a pair of energetic, forthright comic heroines whose energy helps to propel the production. Nunn's vision of the play is a major achievement in the stage history of this romantic comedy.

Tim Carroll (2013)

Tim Carroll first directed *Twelfth Night* in 2013 at the Globe Theatre, later receiving the 2014 New York Drama Desk Award for Outstanding Director of a Play and for Outstanding Revival of a Play for this production. This rendition, known as an "original practice" version, is as close as we will come to an original Elizabethan performance of the play (minus the use of original pronunciation). The stage is bare of nonessential furniture or props, the scenes change with a smooth fluidity, the women's roles are played by men, Malvolio's dark prison employs the under stage space through a trap in the floor, and the play ends with a high-stepping jig danced by the cast. The pacing of dialogue, especially by Feste the Clown (Peter Hamilton Dyer), is crisp and energetic, and there is plenty of deft stage business with occasional comments by the actors to the groundlings at the edge of the stage.

The use of men to play women is expertly managed. At times we forget we are seeing men in drag and easily accept that we are watching actors playing characters playing disguised roles. There are also, however, moments in which we are purposely made aware of the device of cross-dressing, as in the smirks and giggles of Maria (Paul Chahidi, sometimes in a clearly male voice) or when the duke, grasping Cesario's hand, suddenly seems unsure of whether he is not, in fact, really in love with Viola's alter ego, played by Johnny Flynn. Orsino's confusion here is emphasized by Feste's song "Come away death" (2.4.51–66). When Viola declares to Malvolio, "I am the man" (2.2.25) the mingled levels of gender behind her remark arouse a good laugh from the Globe audience. Mark Rylance lends to the character of Olivia a thin, reedy voice conveying a faded sense of authority but more often a bemused and slightly dotty frailty. Rylance also gives her a unique style of walking, composed of short, rapid steps under her black, floor-length gown so that she appears to be gliding across the stage on a hidden Segway scooter, producing a hilarious, robotic effect. According to Stephen Fry, Rylance's facial makeup of stark white with red lips and darkened eyebrows is based upon period portraits of Elizabeth I, a well as on Viola's comment that Olivia's face is "beauty truly blent, [both] red and white" (1.5.240; Fry).

Duke Orsino (Liam Brennan) enters the play like a combative, disgusted Lycidas, ripping a leaf from the overhead foliage. For him love is aggravatingly fragile; it is "high fantastical" but also a mood that can "sicken and so die" (1.1.15, 3), as the melancholy musical accompaniment to his speech suggests. He longs for the absent Olivia in true Petrarchan anguish, and his angry frustration over the pangs of disappointed love offer an emotional counterpoint to the high jinks of the low-comedy characters. The helplessness of those caught up in the web of love or time is a recurring theme. Olivia laments, "Fate, show thy force: ourselves we do not owe [control]" (1.5.311), while Viola complains, "O Time, thou must untangle this, not I; / It is too hard a knot for me to untie" (2.2.40–41), and Feste reflects that, "the whirligig of Time brings in his revenges" (5.1.375–76).

Revenge is, of course, the purpose of Maria's plot against Olivia's steward Malvolio, who wishes to subject all he sees to his "austere regard of control" (2.5.67). He is played with a fine condescension by Stephen Fry that marks Malvolio as someone who—as H. L. Mencken defined Puritanism—is haunted by the fear "that someone, somewhere, may be happy" (Daintith 258). Malvolio is intelligent enough to have risen to the rank of steward but not smart enough to realize his own myopic pride. His "cross-garter'd stockings" visually display just how strait-laced he is. A hilarious bit of stage folly ensues when Toby Belch, Sir Andrew Aguecheek, and Fabian all crowd into the "box-tree" (2.5.16), literally a leaf-covered box with windows through which they can watch Malvolio demonstrate that he is, indeed, "a contemplative idiot" (2.5.20). Significantly, Malvolio is not around to hear Antonio capture the essence of the steward's flaw: "In Nature there's no blemish but the mind. / None can be called deform'd but the unkind. / Virtue is beauty" (3.4.375–77). (How like Shakespeare to have a sea captain utter moral philosophy!) Malvolio leaves the play with his hubris bloody but unbowed, unwilling to humble himself to rejoin the Illyrians (even when the duke "[entreats] him to a peace" [5.1.379]), a populace who accept that "Nothing that is so is so" and that love alone is "high fantastical." This production of *Twelfth Night* is a most endearing and historically accurate realization of the play.

The six productions considered in this essay demonstrate that *Twelfth Night* is a play of contrasting currents that flow from the church year's celebration itself, for the event of Twelfth Night is a time of festivity as well as the regrettable finale of Christmas joy. Both moods are held in tension by the play: Illyria as a land of marriages and reunion as well as dark rooms and shipwrecks; the pleasure of the present moment with "ginger hot i' the mouth" (2.3.121–22) over against Feste's reminder that "Youth's a stuff will not endure" (2.3.53); the spirit of *carpe diem* contending with the gloom of *memento mori.* Which of these poles of experience is dominant in the play is a conundrum Shakespeare leaves to his audiences and players to answer. It is a play of "What You Will," inviting new and creative replies to its own question: "What country, friends, is this?" (1.2.1).

Works Cited

Ball, Robert Hamilton. *Shakespeare on Silent Film: A Strange Eventful History*. Theatre Arts Books, 1968.

Brode, Douglas. *Shakespeare in the Movies: From the Silent Era to Shakespeare in Love*. Oxford UP, 2000.

Buhler, Stephen M. *Shakespeare in the Cinema: Ocular Proof*. State U of New York P, 2002.

Daintith, John, et. al., eds. *Bloomsbury Dictionary of Quotations*. Bloomsbury Publishing, 1988.

Fry, Stephen. "Stephen Fry on *Twelfth Night*." Interview by Susan Haskins and Michael Ridel of *Theater Talk*. YouTube, 28 Dec. 2013, www.youtube.com/watch?v=iDBvX6fTW00.

Osborne, Laurie. "Cutting up Characters: The Erotic Politics of Trevor Nunn's Twelfth Night." *Spectacular Shakespeare: Critical Theory and Popular Cinema*. Edited by Courtney Lehmann and Lisa S. Starks. Fairleigh Dickinson UP, 2002, pp. 89–109.

Rothwell, Kenneth S. *A History of Shakespeare on Screen: A Century of Film and Television*. Cambridge UP, 1999.

Shakespeare, William. *Twelfth Night*. Edited by William P. Holden. The Yale Shakespeare. New Yale UP, 1954.

_____. The *Tempest*. Edited by David Horne. The Yale Shakespeare. Yale UP, 1955.

Twelfth Night. Directed by Eugene Mullen and Charles Kent, Vitagraph, 1910.

Twelfth Night. Directed by John Sichel, ITV, 1968.

Twelfth Night. Directed by Neil Armfield, Roadshow Television, 1986.

Twelfth Night. Directed by Kenneth Branagh, 1987, Thames Television.

Twelfth Night. Directed by Trevor Nunn, 1996, BBC Films.

Twelfth Night. Directed by Tim Carroll, 2013, Globe Theatre.

Twelfth Night: Recent Critical Perspectives

Melissa Anderson

Introduction

Twelfth Night: New Critical Essays, edited by James Schiffer and first published in 2011, is the most recent book-length collection of essays by contemporary Shakespeare scholars devoted to *Twelfth Night*. Part of Routledge's Shakespeare Criticism series, which aims to bring together exceptional works from leading scholars representing multiple critical approaches, the volume explores critical reception and performance history, historical and cultural context, and readings of the play through various critical lenses. The introductory essay by Schiffer sets the stage for the following essays with the history of performance and criticism of this beloved comedy.

Noting that the complicated double plot of the play has influenced interpretations both on the stage and by critics and precludes any "unanimous criticism on the genre of the work as a whole or about how the two strands of action affect and reflect one another" (2), Schiffer mentions the publication history, sources, and first performances before delving into four hundred years of criticism and performance. Early appreciation of Malvolio's comic downfall led to virtual neglect of the play from critics and companies when tastes ran more to Shakespeare's tragedies than to his comedies. Nineteenth-century interpretations of the play, influenced by the critical trends of the day, explored the more tragic aspects of the primary characters while performances often emphasized song and spectacle. Twentieth-century interpretations focused on that noted duality of the play while also recognizing the significance of the ensemble on the play's impact. Character studies have been common in the critical history of the work, and debates over the ending persist throughout the history of the play's reception. Postmodern critics have employed psychoanalytic, new historicist, and post-structuralist criticism in their interpretations and have suggested readings that recognize same-sex desire and the influence of class.

After briefly discussing recent staging history of the play, Schiffer turns to the essays included in the volume and notes how they contribute to the critical history of the play he has outlined.

Patricia Parker, "*Twelfth Night*: Editing Puzzles and Eunuchs of All Kinds"

Patricia Parker's essay traces the textual alterations that have been made by Twelfth Night's editors since the publication of the First Folio and explores how significantly those changes have affected our interpretation and understanding of the text. Editors have erased puns and wordplay, "corrected" portmanteaus, and otherwise elided the layers of meaning potentially present in one ostensibly misspelled word in the First Folio in favor of more recognizably, and reductively, correct spellings and usages. For example, the eighteenth-century editor Lewis Theobald changed a line reading "coole my nature" in the Folio to "curl by nature" in his edition, a correction that not only lacked historical plausibility, but also hid a probable reference to gender reversal, a central theme of the play (49). Changes such as these persisted in future editions, which effaced ambiguities in the Folio that actually contribute to the overall atmosphere of bafflement and misunderstanding that reign in Illyria and that is necessary for the narrative to function. Post-Folio editorial corrections to punctuation and to stage directions have similarly reduced confusion created by the Folio text that may have been essential to the theme and meaning of the play, central as misprision is to the plot.

In addition to noting the perhaps erroneous corrections made by editors after the publication of the Folio, Parker also highlights a reference surprisingly missed by editors of *Twelfth Night*: a reference to the eunuch flute, a musical instrument not only well-known in Shakespeare's day but also recognized by editors of *Coriolanus* who remark upon its significance in that play. This editorial oversight has had an effect similar to that of the corrections identified earlier in the essay; it reduces the multiple layers of meaning inherent in a line of Viola's speech in the Folio text to a simpler, and less interesting reference, while also contributing to a now-discredited theory that the play had been revised after Viola's line was written. Instead of reading Viola's declaration that she will become a eunuch for Orsino as a mistake, the multiple references to eunuchry in the play support a reading of that word as intended, and the possibility of a reference also to the eunuch flute is even more evidence for this reading. Parker explains that it is "crucially important" to understand that the eunuch flute is an instrument that transmits the sound of another instrument or voice, something that Viola does, in fact, undertake to do as Orsino's messenger (57). Again, what later editors appear to miss is the way that Shakespeare's text works synergistically to express many ideas simultaneously.

By correcting or simplifying these meanings, editors have effaced the complexity, and also the genius of the play. By reintroducing the unedited text of the Folio, Parker reveals layers of meaning hidden by editorial revision of this rich and multifaceted work.

Bruce R. Smith, "'His fancy's queen': Sensing Sexual Strangeness in *Twelfth Night*"

Like Parker, Bruce R. Smith also identifies important meanings ignored by most editors of *Twelfth Night*. Editors have mostly defined Shakespeare's use of "fancy" as a type of imagination or love-longing but have overlooked seventeenth-century meanings of the word that aligned it with sense experience. Parker explains, "[fancy] was a factor in early modern psychology, in the story that early modern men and women told themselves about what was happening inside as they perceived something and spoke, to themselves or to others, about what they were perceiving" (65–66). Drawing on both post-structuralist literary theory and early modern philosophy, Smith claims that "fancy" links the body to language and allows us to better understand gender and sexuality in the play. As in other Shakespeare comedies, "fancy" is linked inextricably with erotic desire in *Twelfth Night*.

Smith undergirds his argument about the multiple meanings of fancy in *Twelfth Night* and other Shakespeare plays with an explanation of how sense experience and knowledge were inseparable for Shakespeare and his contemporaries. Citing seventeenth-century philosophers such as Thomas Wright, Edward Reynolds, and others, Smith describes the role of imagination, and of fancy, fantasy, and *phantasmata*—all related terms—in the epistemology of the period. Smith then demonstrates that, often, sixteenth- and seventeenth-century products of fancy—such as decorative arts in the playhouses themselves—had a decidedly sensuous or even erotic component. The visual experience of *Twelfth Night*, then, itself a play rich in visual detail, would be especially dense in fanciful sense experience. And the language of *Twelfth Night* is suggestive of fancy, too, with its alliterations and musicality.

Once the term "fancy" is definitively linked with perception, the physical body, and the production of knowledge, then Smith is able to show how the term works to complicate perceptions of sexuality and gender in the text, particularly when the term is applied to what others imagine they are experiencing in the presence of the disguised characters Viola and Sebastian. The combination of "strange," which for Shakespeare's contemporaries could mean unfamiliar, outlandish, or singular, with fancy in many formulations in the play then seems to allow for a complicated perception of gender and sexuality that resists easy classification and definition. For Smith, the identification of the many layers of meaning in these terms, usually ignored by editors, creates a space of play in gender identities in *Twelfth Night* that is more accurate for the period than is usually recognized. "With respect to other people," he writes, "as with respect to all objects of sense experience, fancy is always in play: it functions as an essential factor in *every* act of perception, not just whimsy and dreaming" (78).

David Schalkwyk, "Music, Food, and Love in the Affective Landscapes of *Twelfth Night*"

Like Smith, David Schalkwyk also examines the ways that imagination and bodily experience are explored in *Twelfth Night,* this time through the role of music in the play. His essay begins by contextualizing the workings of music on the individual within early modern conceptions of the passions. Schalkwyk's examination of the famous opening lines, "If music be the food of love, play on...," reveals that what is at stake in the play is the nature of love and its relation to desire, something not easily settled in Renaissance or Classical philosophy. In Platonic philosophy, love and desire are linked, but many of the philosophers of Shakespeare's day viewed them as different things, with love existing as a more disinterested, idealized concept and desire being more firmly rooted in the physical realm. *Twelfth Night* explores these possibilities without staking a clear claim for either a love separate from or identical with desire.

Schalkwyk notes that throughout the play, Shakespeare invokes music's relation to love and desire; like food it has the ability to satisfy appetites, if only temporarily. Music also can reflect the internal emotions of the lovesick individual; in a sense, it can express unspoken feelings. The suggestion that music allays desire and/or expresses emotion is evident in several of Orsino's speeches, but Schalkwyk shows that Orsino's own conception of love is problematic in the worldview of the play. Orsino claims that the reliability of internal feelings, and whether or not they are akin to love or more correctly identified with desire, is based on gender, which of course makes it deeply complicated in a play in which gender is unstable. If women are less capable of deep, lasting love, and are linked more to physical desire, then what of the woman—Viola—perceived as a man and the love s/he is currently experiencing? Orsino's theory is based on theories of the humours common in Shakespeare's day; the play refutes this reductionist theory in part through its destabilizing of the gender binary but also by Viola's actions as a lover throughout. Schalkwyk writes, "Viola as Cesario calls into question the very basis for distinguishing between men and women on the basis of an intrinsic difference in humoral fluids and temperatures. She unmasks the ridiculous misogyny that denies women the 'retention' required for constant affection" (89).

The conflation of music, food, and love is also apparent in what Schalkwyk categorizes as "the central comic scene of *Twelfth Night*" (92), when Feste sings of love for Sir Andrew and Sir Toby. Love, food, time, and music come together in the scene that displays the complex relationships between the characters and their notions of friendship at the same time that it dissolves in joking revelry. Explaining Renaissance views on friendship, Schalkwyk claims that it is Viola who exemplifies loving friendship and erotic devotion even though women were deemed incapable of both; Viola's temporary status as both man and woman allows her a fuller emotional existence. Schalkwyk also claims that by predicating love on actions, which the language of the play does, Shakespeare demonstrates that we can evaluate its validity in the behavior of lovers. But even if actions are evidence of love, Shakespeare still allows for the internal experience of love. The music of the play is what allows for an expression of what is happening internally for those in love. Schalkwyk explains that "[m]usic both stands for and, in its operation on the senses, feeds and manipulates the affective soul of audience and character alike" (96). Thus, *Twelfth Night* is able to present a view of love that is physical and active while also working within; embodied and also experienced as an internal state.

Laurie E. Osborne, "'The marriage of true minds': Amity, Twinning, and Comic Closure in *Twelfth Night*"

Laurie E. Osborne begins her essay by contextualizing *Twelfth Night* in the history of male friendship and its conflictual relationship with heterosexual marriage, noting that the friction between these relationships shows up frequently as a theme in both the poetry and comedy of Shakespeare. In Osborne's formulation, it is the role of twinning in the play that allows Shakespeare to somewhat resolve the conflict between marital love and male friendship.

In a review of Shakespeare criticism examining amity, Osborne notes the relative lack of articles on the topic of amity exploring *Twelfth Night*; those that do mention the play often, surprisingly, focus on characters other than Viola, who for much of the play is posed as a page and male friend to Orsino. Viola is also a twin, both literally as the twin sister of Sebastian, and also figuratively, as she inhabits the identities of both Viola and Cesario in the play. Osborne explains, "In Cesario's twinning and unusual status as both male and female, *Twelfth Night* offers an alternative model of the true friend —a hero who is also a heroine...who can literally wed his friend" (100). Early modern notions of friendship based on likeness also underscore the importance of twinning in *Twelfth Night* in its study of amity.

Invoking the problems critics and directors have had making both the friendship between Cesario and Orsino and the engagement of Viola and Orsino believable, Osborne suggests that early modern audiences would not have questioned these relationships in the same way because they would see them both rooted in loving friendship as described by Renaissance philosophy. In fact, Cesario acts much less like the page or servant he is purported to be than like a true friend; he challenges Orsino far more than would be proper for a servant, and Orsino takes the advice of his servant far more seriously than one in his position normally would. And the deep amity experienced by Viola while disguised as Cesario provides a foundation for romantic love. Too often, when women play the role of Viola/Cesario, this double experience of amity/romantic love is hidden, and only the heterosexual desire between Orsino and Viola is visible. For early modern audiences seeing a boy play the role, however, the emphasis on friendship would be much more obvious. That the figure of Viola/Cesario is both male and female simultaneously is essential to the resolution of the central conflict of the play; as Osborne states, "[b]y claiming both genders, Cesario makes a crucial move toward resolving Orsino's doubled and therefore static loves—for his friend and for a woman" (109).

The relationship between Antonio and Sebastian also reinforces the message about amity that the play is communicating. The threat to that relationship that is created when Antonio takes Cesario for Sebastian is resolved when Viola's true identity is revealed. Similarly, the threat to the friendship between Cesario and Orsino that is created by Olivia's marriage to Cesario/Sebastian is also neatly resolved with the revelation of Viola's identity. The play imaginatively explores and tests what constitutes true friendship by means of twinning and doubled identities and suggests more complex possibilities for relationships between men and women. As Osborne concludes, "[i]n *Twelfth Night*, the best male friend is a woman and the most desirable wife is the loving male friend" (112).

Goran V. Stanivuković, "Masculine Plots in *Twelfth Night*"

Goran V. Stanivuković regards *Twelfth Night* as "one of Shakespeare's most masculinist plays" (114) because he sees much of the play as exploring what does and does not make a man. Unlike many critics who examine the play in light of early modern medical definitions of gender, Stanivuković claims that the depictions of masculinity in the play owe more to romance literature than they do to Renaissance medicine. In particular, he links the depiction of masculinity in *Twelfth Night* to popular plays and prose romances widely known in the period by all, and not just by the educated elite. These texts presented a masculinity based on the chivalric ideal that runs counter to what is evident in Shakespeare's comedy. Recent critics and editors have noted that some of these texts, particularly *Parismus* by Emanuel Forde, may have been among the sources for Shakespeare's play, but they have overlooked the way Shakespeare may have consciously rewritten the plot of such romances in order to comment on contemporary models of masculinity.

For Stanivuković, the chivalric masculinity on display in popular prose such as *Parismus* is made comic in *Twelfth Night,* since "[h]umorous heroic masculinity suited better the entertainment quality of dramatic romances, while the nostalgic re-imagining of chivalry was better adapted to the printed book and reading whose purpose was both instruction and entertainment" (119). To accomplish this parody, Shakespeare restages classic scenes from *Parismus,* such as a scene in which the hero fights a duel with the primary villain and promotes chivalric values. In *Twelfth Night,* however, the parallel scene is satirical, with Sir Andrew fighting Viola, provoking questions about the value of such violence and the masculinity that supports it.

The questioning of gender brought on by Viola's disguise is frequently discussed in *Twelfth Night* criticism, and Stanivuković notes that *Parismus*'s Violetta also disguises herself as a male page. The effect of the disguise in the earlier text is different, however, since in *Parismus* the stability of gender is never interrogated the way it is in Shakespeare's play and the disguise serves merely as a trick that helps along the plot. Male desire is equally untroubled in *Parismus,* because the romantic constancy of the hero is seen as constitutive of his masculinity. In *Twelfth Night*, however, Orsino is not constant; his desire for Cesario calls into question his stated love for Olivia. In fact, it is Viola, not Orsino, that exhibits the determination, energy, and constancy of idealized masculinity in the play.

Stanivuković argues that *Twelfth Night* uses satire to overturn the heroic ideal of masculinity, and that this move is based on a cultural shift from chivalric to romantic masculinity. In the romantic version, the importance of desire, class, and merit is privileged in a courtship narrative that is resolved in marriage. The character of Antonio, who throughout the play has exhibited a romantic form of masculinity but does not find a mate in the plot's resolution, offers a slight challenge to the neatness of this model by showing that it does not function equally well for all men.

Marcela Kostihová, "Post-Communist Nights: Shakespeare, Essential Masculinity, and Western Citizenship"

Like Stanivuković, Marcela Kostihová also examines the depiction of masculinity in *Twelfth Night*, but she focuses on the way it has been interpreted in post-communist Czech productions of the play. In particular, Kostihová looks at the portrayals of Antonio and Sebastian on the stage, because in her mind these two characters both embody models of masculinity and friendship valued in Renaissance culture. However, in the modern Czech Republic, their relationship is read as potentially same-sex sexuality and, therefore, controversial as a depiction of masculinity. For Kostihová, the conflicts attendant on staging this controversial masculinity are tied up with questions of identity emerging from the post-communist socio-political context in the Czech Republic. Looking at two particular productions as exemplars, she states, "[t]hese *Twelfth Night* productions betray a deep ambivalence about accepting homosexuality as one of the natural variants of human behavior and identity" (132).

Kostihová situates her analysis of these productions within the history of post-communist culture in the Czech Republic. According to her, the country saw a rejection of communist-era gender equality and a "return" to more traditional "Western" ideas of gender and sexuality. These roles were being redefined at the same time that Czech people were trying to determine what a Czech national identity should look like. This conflation of gender roles and citizenship is important, because Kostihová sees the embracing of a "Western" Czech identity at the same time that "Western" ideas of gender equality, multiculturalism, feminism, and so on are resisted as resulting from a desire to affirm a somewhat confused notion of nationality typical of countries emerging from a period of ideological domination. The refusal of many Czech women to embrace new roles in a more patriarchal post-communist society has led to fears about the future of Czech society, widespread frustration among Czech men, and uncertainty about the status of masculinity in the culture.

In post-communist Czech theater, there have been few productions of Shakespeare's works that question gender and sexuality, even if stagings of some contemporary American musicals have done just that. And stagings of *Twelfth Night,* with its notorious questioning and confusion of gender and sexuality throughout the play, have tended to downplay any content that could be read as affirming same-sex sexuality or interrogating traditional masculinity. The trouble is that most of the characters in *Twelfth Night* fail to live up to the standards of traditional masculinity such as swordsmanship, devotion to honor, and protection of others. The characters of Antonio and Sebastian, however, do live up to these standards, but their passionate and professed love for each other also evokes potential same-sex sexuality for contemporary audiences, even if it would not do so for audiences in Shakespeare's day.

The decisions made by contemporary directors in stagings of the play in the Czech Republic reveal the inherent politics of the male identities on the stage. Kostihová notes that one director, Eniko Esenyi, chose to emphasize the heterosexual content of the play. She explains, "[a]lmost every instance of Shakespeare's sexual innuendo seems to have been not only duly noted, but also transformed into a corresponding (mostly non-verbal) stage action" (138), and yet "[t]he only sexual innuendos that are conveniently omitted are those suggested between the potential same-sex couples, Olivia and Cesario and Antonio and Sebastian" (138–39). In this production, Antonio was portrayed as hypermasculine, and there was no real significance to the relationship between him and Sebastian, who embodied little more than a heterosexual lover in this version of the play. These choices, which fail to create the rich, multilayered portrayals of Shakespeare's characters you might expect at a National Theater performance, reflect for Kostihová a fragmented male identity and Czech nationality.

Kostihová also analyzes a 2005 Summer Shakespeare performance of *Twelfth Night* in Prague. In this performance, directed by Viktor Polesný, a more complex notion of masculinity *was* presented on the stage. In particular, Polesný explored different models of masculinity through the characters of Sir Andrew, Antonio, Sebastian, and even Cesario. What is more, he also allowed Olivia's desire for Cesario to persist even after Viola's identity was revealed. The fact that the play was part of the "relaxed" Summer Shakespeare Festival, and that an atmosphere of play and frivolity was emphasized, however, allowed the questions raised by the director's choices to remain in the realm of fantasy and fun and outside any political discourse.

Kostihová ends her essay by musing that these Czech stagings of *Twelfth Night* and their presentations of masculinity are always inherently political. Furthermore, they reveal both the importance of Shakespeare to the Czech national identity and also how unacceptable same-sex sexuality currently is in constructions of Czech masculinity.

Elizabeth Pentland, "Beyond the 'Lyric' in Illyricum"

Elizabeth Pentland claims that instead of seeing the setting of *Twelfth Night*, Illyria, as a mythical place, as many critics have done, Shakespeare's audiences would have seen it as a recognizable place with its own historical and political associations. Some recent scholars have identified Illyria from classical works of history known in Renaissance England, and contemporary audiences would have been aware of Illyria from geographical works and travel narratives. Because it was located in the eastern Adriatic, English audiences would not have been terribly familiar with Illyria, but they would have known it to be in a relatively dangerous region famous for storms, pirates, and trade.

Pentland lists the many contemporary documents referring to Illyria as proof of its associations for Shakespeare's audiences, noting that Antonio's depiction as a pirate also reinforces the idea that the region was prone to acts of piracy. The wealth and rich trade of the region is also well documented in the literature of the period, all of which make it unlikely that Shakespeare chose the setting arbitrarily.

The character of the Illyrians themselves in early modern texts also has parallels to that of the different personalities in *Twelfth Night*. In contrast to their more warlike neighbors, the Illyrians were seen as especially fond of revelry, and Sir Andrew and Sir Toby do seem to embody the Illyrian stereotype. Contemporary texts also suggest an independent mindedness in Illyrian women we can see demonstrated in Olivia throughout the play.

Pentland cautions that critics have highlighted the status of Illyria as a place of fantasy within the comedy of *Twelfth Night*, ignoring its real identity for Shakespeare's contemporary viewers. "We should not forget," she states, that "Illyria was also famous to Elizabethans as a commercial and cultural crossroads where Italian, Turkish, and Greek practices mingled with local custom, and as an ancient kingdom with a long and fascinating history of piracy, resistance to Rome, and female rule" (163).

Catherine Lisak, "Domesticating Strangeness in *Twelfth Night*"

In contrast to Pentland, Catherine Lisak suggests that an examination of what Illyria actually represents in *Twelfth Night* reveals that the country and its residents are anything but foreign. Lisak explores the origins and various meanings of the word "stranger" in the early sixteenth century, noting its difference yet relationship to terms like "foreigner" that were less common in the period and also delineated specific rights or lack thereof for the individual in question. This linguistic history is important, because she sees *Twelfth Night* as playing with notions of "strangeness," challenging who or what really qualifies as a stranger and allowing characters to slip into and out of "strange" identities. Although the introduction of the stranger to a domestic situation was a common plot device in sixteenth-century comedies, Lisak contends that "*Twelfth Night* portrays strangers in a remarkably original light, by conjuring dramatic stereotypes while blurring national distinctions" (169). In doing so, the play allows for questioning of the meaning of strangeness and investigation of how identities are constructed.

Lisak notes that unlike typical travelers experiencing a catastrophic disruption to their plans, neither Viola nor Sebastian appear to have any destination in mind or any serious anxiety about the way their voyage has been redirected. Instead, they both seem to be pursuing a more emotional or developmental journey, and the mythic qualities of Illyria add to this impression. Viola and Sebastian may actually be less strangers to their new acquaintances than they are to themselves. Additionally, as newcomers to Illyria, they are able to identify the strangeness of the inhabitants of the place and reveal it to the audience. Some of that strangeness lies in the behavior and romantic excesses of those at court. Viola, in her role as page, uncovers the "emotional deadlock" of the existing relationship between Olivia and Orsino (171), and, by the end of the play, resolves it by marrying Orsino herself and enabling Olivia's marriage to Sebastian.

The idea of travel to faraway lands would have had instant associations for the first audiences of *Twelfth Night,* who would have been aware of New World discoveries and travel narratives full of strange people and their ways. The play does not, however, simply recreate one of these narratives on stage unquestioned. "Shakespeare's handling of new world discoveries is double-edged," writes Lisak, "because he exploits their wondrous effect on the crowd while toning down, through clownish smiles, their potential to interpellate existing assumptions" (174).

If Illyria is a foreign or strange place in *Twelfth Night,* we can read its residents as exploring strangeness through their language and behavior. Lisak notes the foreign words frequently used by Sir Toby and identifies Malvolio as another character who evokes the strange in a sense. In his attempt to woo Olivia, Malvolio wears strange, old-fashioned garb which, unfortunately for him, just makes a mockery of his desires and marks him as a "parody of a pedantic Puritan" (177) and hopelessly antiquated. By using Malvolio as the embodiment of strangeness, and linking him to religious conflicts in England, Lisak claims, Shakespeare is able to separate the concepts of "strange" and "foreign," allowing the foreigners, Viola and Sebastian, to become part of the local domestic scene, and Malvolio, the local resident, to be the "strange" character whose ideas and behavior are thoroughly rejected.

Lisak sees *Twelfth Night* as part of a sixteenth-century trend to use foreign characters to reveal truths about the character of English citizens. Foreign drunkenness, madness, and other traits are evident in the Illyrians and yet are so markedly English that the foreign locale is, in effect, domesticated. The result is that the audience members themselves feel challenged by the way the comedy plays with identity and suggests that what is strange is English and that Illyria is actually an England made strange.

Nathalie Rivère de Carles, "Staging the Exotic in *Twelfth Night*"

Following both Pentland and Lisak, Nathalie Rivère de Carles attempts to capture what the land of Illyria actually signifies in *Twelfth Night*, determining that it is a land of unclear geography representing ultimately "the exotic" on the stage. What is read as exotic has changed in different historical periods, but the flexibility of Illyria to encompass many different conceptions of the exotic has made *Twelfth Night* open to richly creative and evocative stagings.

Historically, productions of the play have often chosen to play up the indeterminacy of Illyria's actual location, sometimes using costume and set design to evoke exoticism and other times editing the text and language of the play to emphasize exotic elements. Rivère de Carles examines closely what is known of specific stagings of the play in France in the late nineteenth and early twentieth centuries; these stagings invoked the pastoral tradition or Elizabethan drama, to evoke a sense of the exotic predicated on a sort of travel in time for their audiences. More recent stagings have similarly used a confusion of space, time, and identity to convey the exotic. As an example, Rivère de Carles references a 2004 production by Antonio Latella that used an all-female cast, a mix of musical styles, and a setting reminiscent of the commedia dell'arte. What is common in all these stagings is that "the awkward sense of an indeterminate space is the real source of the exotic.... The play's exoticism lies in the dream-like quality of the performance of a script detached from its time and space" (190). Other contemporary directors on the continent have, like Latella, also chosen to relocate the play to other, recognizable, theatrical settings in order to achieve this effect.

Rivère de Carles sees the foregrounding of the exotic in these stagings of *Twelfth Night* as metatheatrical; they confront the audience with their status by referring regularly to the theatricality of these exotic settings. Contemporary directors have often achieved this by defying the audience's expectations for what they see on stage whether it be through stage architecture, setting, choreography, or other aspects of the production. With these metatheatrical moves, there is some risk of "shift[ing] the focus from the content of the play to its form" (196); some productions have focused intentionally on this type of formalism. In any case, Rivère de Carles suggests that "when working in full collaboration with the text, dramaturgy helps the spectators questioning their own time, place, and identity" (198).

Christa Jansohn, "'The text remains for another attempt': *Twelfth Night or What You Will* on the German Stage"

Christa Jansohn, like Rivère de Carles, also examines continental stagings of *Twelfth Night*, but her focus is on Germany; she provides an abbreviated production history of German versions of *Twelfth Night*, examining the directorial choices made and how they have influenced the performance of the play.

Nineteenth-century productions of *Twelfth Night* in Germany, using August Wilhelm Schlegel's translation, tended to focus on the romance and lyrical aspects of the play; in some of these, music was foregrounded to increase this emphasis. Successful productions staged in the Weimar and Third Reich periods were similar, avoiding political references and focusing on the poetry of Schlegel's translation. Although interest in the play remained after the war, the most popular productions were those that featured new translations, new interpretations of character, and new settings.

More recently, "radically modernized" versions of the translated text of the play have been used in settings vastly different from the dreamy or fantastical Illyria of the past. Instead, desolation, fatigue, and hopelessness seemed to be the reigning themes of many of the late-twentieth-century productions. Others opted for the eclectic and the surreal, staging interpretations that only hinted at Illyria as a specific place, or which relocated the play to imaginary locations such as a giant library.

German directors have played with the age of characters to convey their interpretation of the text, ignoring inconvenient lines that compete with their vision. Costumes (or lack thereof) have also been used to play with aspects of character in ways not directly evident in the text, suggesting wealth or poverty, historical period, or sexual emancipation.

Overall, Jansohn's history of the production of *Twelfth Night* in Germany demonstrates how the adaptability of Shakespeare's text is a large part of its timeless appeal. In Germany, productions of the play have been limited only by the imagination of its directors and the indulgence of its audiences.

Alan W. Powers, "'What he wills': Early Modern Rings and Vows in *Twelfth Night*"

Alan W. Powers examines the role of rings and love tokens in Shakespeare's day and their signification in *Twelfth Night.* In a culture in which not everyone was literate, rings held an important role as symbols of a vow or oral contract. Observing that rings are common throughout Shakespeare's work, Powers notes that "in no other comedy is one character, Viola/Cesario[,] offered so many gems" (219), supporting the notion that rings and tokens play a substantial role in *Twelfth Night* by symbolizing bonds and promises between characters.

According to Powers, rings were particularly important in Tudor culture as symbols sent by male suitors to their beloveds, as signs of engagement, much as they are today. By whom these symbols were sent is important, as often messengers ferried the rings between lovers, in life as on the stage. Malvolio delivers a ring from Olivia to Cesario, who, to Malvolio's surprise, refuses it, though he leaves it with him. It is then Cesario's turn to send a ring to Olivia, on behalf of Orsino, also refused. Viola/Cesario is thus at the center of a criss-crossed pattern of vows and rings, only resolved once the arrival of Sebastian allows Viola to inhabit a single identity.

Powers lists other love tokens exchanged in the play—a miniature (a piece of jewelry with Olivia's picture on it), a poem, a puzzle, as well as the ring exchanged between Olivia and Sebastian when they marry. These other love tokens also were common across Shakespeare's canon and in Elizabethan popular culture as well. The oral culture of Shakespeare's day required symbols to prove veracity and memorialize events, and rings and tokens served that function well. Powers notes that Shakespeare himself left money in his will to provide memorial rings for his colleagues and neighbors, thereby confirming the symbolic importance of the ring in the culture.

Ivo Kamps, "Madness and Social Mobility in *Twelfth Night*"

Contextualizing *Twelfth Night* within the early modern discourse of mental illness, Kamps examines the themes of diagnosis, madness, and cure in the Malvolio/Maria/Sir Toby plot of the play. For Kamps, it is the performances of madness and of identity that are central to this plot. Noting that in the period madness was usually believed to have a physical cause, Kamps finds that illusions and deceit are used in the play to trick Malvolio into displaying mad behavior. Seeing an analog in the way that Judith Butler describes the performance of gender, Kamps suggests that in other Shakespeare plays, the performance of identity is something that is read or recognized by others, and the diagnosis of madness applies when that performance becomes unintelligible. What is different in *Twelfth Night* is that Malvolio is "diagnosed" only after his peers have encouraged behavior they know will be seen as mad.

Maria and Sir Toby bamboozle Malvolio in revenge for what they consider behavior that transgresses his proper role as a steward in the household and also for his desire for upward mobility; the goal is to see his purported madness punished until he is forced back into his proper, subordinate role. Their plot succeeds, and Malvolio humiliates himself in front of Olivia, is deemed mad, and then suffers through imprisonment and torture. Kamps suggests that with Malvolio's vow of revenge, "Shakespeare insinuates that the ending of the play may not be the ending of the story" (237), perhaps an implication that the upward mobility for which Malvolio strives is already taking place in Elizabethan society.

Malvolio, who stands for puritanical values in the play, ironically ends up representing misrule in the text due to the madness plot; not only does he desire to upend class distinctions in his courtship of Olivia, but he also, in his anger at the end, disrupts the household by leaving the role he has played throughout most of the play. This sort of mad misrule infects other characters, too, as Olivia and Orsino both desire inappropriate mates, although the resolution of the play stops them short of actually consummating those desires.

In the end, Shakespeare does not explicitly endorse Malvolio's desire for upward mobility, but the ending of the play, which sees a righteous Malvolio declaring he will be avenged, suggests that the desire itself is not mad, and it is not easily extinguished, either.

Jennifer C. Vaught, "*Twelfth Night* and the New Orleans Twelfth Night Revelers"

Tracing Carnival and Twelfth Night traditions across England, Europe, and America, Jennifer C. Vaught notes that Mardi Gras participants such as the Twelfth Night Revelers perform similar functions to those in Shakespeare's play. Vaught writes, "Shakespeare's *Twelfth Night,* a play about aristocratic reactions to the rising middle ranks, and the Twelfth Night Revelers thereby expose the potentially conservative and violent underbelly of literary and cultural celebrations of the Feast of the Epiphany" (245).

After tracing similarities in Twelfth Night traditions in Louisiana and in fifteenth- and sixteenth-century England, Vaught notes the history of social unrest accompanying Twelfth Night celebrations. As a Lord of Misrule in this context, however, Shakespeare's Sir Toby has no intention of upending the social order. Instead, his role is to reinforce it by punishing, through a spiteful prank, the person seeking to disrupt it in earnest. Similarly, the Twelfth Night Revelers looked not to overthrow the social order but to validate a more conservative and hierarchical society of the past.

The New Orleans Twelfth Night Revelers emerged in the post-Civil War period amidst numerous class and race tensions. The group was formed by White supremacists immediately after Louisiana was forced to prohibit discrimination against African Americans, to desegregate schools, and to grant former slaves the right to vote. Instead of inverting the social order, the Twelfth Night Revelers "reinforced rather than diminished nineteenth-century class, gender, and racial inequalities" (252), often embracing violent imagery associated with armed rebellion against Reconstruction-era policies. Although the potential for Twelfth Night festivals and traditions to empower those of the lower social and economic classes has existed since medieval times, the history of the Twelfth Night Revelers in Louisiana shows that revels and misrule can also be used to validate regressive ideas and hierarchies.

Cynthia Lewis, "Whodunit? Plot, Plotting, and Detection in *Twelfth Night*"

Cynthia Lewis claims that *Twelfth Night* contains elements contemporary readers and audiences recognize from detective fiction. The play itself, she contends, contains numerous unsolved mysteries that cast the viewer into something resembling a detective role. She sees similarity in the way the detective story rewards the reader with a correct solution to the mystery and the way romantic comedies reward the audience with the resolution of "rampant confusion" (261). However, as much as viewers appreciate the skill with which a playwright such as Shakespeare resolves the highly complicated situation in which his characters find themselves, Lewis posits a rebuttal to this resolution in the way that multiple interpretations persist at the end of plays such as *Twelfth Night*.

Lewis examines the inconsistencies in Antonio's character, which account for several of the unsolved mysteries of the play and that resist complete closure of the narrative. She also explores the role of the riddle in Shakespeare's work. Riddles, she suggests, are often used to reveal identities, as they do in *Merchant of Venice* and *All's Well That Ends Well*. Some of the riddles in *Twelfth Night* are similarly resolved, and yet the important riddle at the core of Malvolio's story is never solved. Lewis suggests that using unsolved mysteries and riddles may be a way for the playwright to "retain control over the audience rather than surrender or share it at the play's end" (267). Alternatively, refusing complete closure of the narrative may be the playwright's way of exhibiting humility, acknowledging the human impossibility of perfect knowledge. Although contemporary readers may see "postmodern chaos" in the number of unsolved mysteries at the end of the play, Lewis states that, in fact, those mysteries may "posit early modern faith in perfect revelation whose time has simply not arrived" (269).

Conclusion

The essays in this volume represent a variety of contemporary critical perspectives on *Twelfth Night* and its production history. Whether delving deep into the history of specific words, philosophies, and knowledge in Shakespeare's period, or examining recent innovative performances of his play, the essays demonstrate the variety of interpretation and experiences to which the play and its productions lend themselves. The individual essays are organized in a logical order that allows themes such as masculinity or the existence of Illyria in the Renaissance imagination to be followed from one essay to another. Although the essays were collected in 2011, the theme of transgender identities is conspicuously absent even in essays that examine the work of gender in the play closely; more recent stagings of the play have addressed this theme more directly. The exploration of productions of the play outside England is confined to Europe; since the volume's publication, productions in other parts of the world have received critical attention. Nevertheless, the breadth and depth of the collection displays the adaptability, richly evocative language, and genius of this remarkable play.

Works Cited

Schiffer, James, editor. Twelfth Night*: New Critical Essays*. Shakespeare Criticism, Vol. 34. Routledge, 2011.

Why Are Malvolio's Cross-Gartered Yellow Stockings Funny? Showing the Sun with a Lamp on Shakespeare's *Twelfth Night*

Edwin Wong

Like knights and tights, nothing is intrinsically funny about cross-gartered yellow stockings. They are as funny as blue jeans and belts. Before Shakespeare's *Twelfth Night* begins, Malvolio received compliments for wearing them (2.5.137–38). When the play debuted, stockings were part of the court fashion (Linthicum 87–89).[1] Garters were necessary because those were the days before elastic fabrics. Cross-gartering involves wrapping the garter below the knee, crossing it behind the knee, and tying it above the knee in a bow. In the sixteenth and seventeenth centuries, from attendants to footmen, courtiers, gallants, lovers, Puritans, and pedants, any "persons who desired to present an especially neat appearance" wore them (92).

Despite garters tied cross being a commonplace of clothing, they make the show. They make the show because they are at the end of a long garden path down which Shakespeare has led the audience. With misprision in the highest degree, Shakespeare gets the audience to believe Malvolio is who he is not. Hook, line, and sinker, they take the bait. When they see Malvolio gartered, they realize that—never mind Malvolio—*they* have been taken for a ride. As a result, the audience experiences an involuntary physiological response in which they furrow their brows, draw up the corners of their mouths, and release a series of staccato, vowellike aspirations in a decrescendo pattern having a duration of 1/15 second spaced at intervals of 1/5 second from onset to onset (Provine 57). Laughter is an automatic reaction to incongruity.

Getting the audience to believe one thing and then pulling the rug out from under them is the kernel of comedy. Comedy is the art of the long joke. Consider the one about the girl and her mother:

> A little girl asked her mother for a dollar to give to an old lady in the park. Her mother was touched by the child's kindness and gave her the money.
> "There you are, my dear," said the mother. "But, tell me, isn't the lady able to work any more?"
> "Oh yes," came the reply. "She sells candy." (Hurley et al. 151)

Like dramatic comedy, the joke begins with red herrings. The adjective "little" and the mother's reaction bait the audience. More false pretenses follow in the description of the lady. The mind creates a probable image of a sweet child helping an elderly homeless person. But the audience is in for a rude awakening: the only thing sweet about the child is her tooth. In the same way as jokes create expectations to cast them down, Shakespeare typecasts Malvolio as a trusty Puritan steward and then exposes his sham front to be "only a screen image that masks his desire to have greatness thrust upon him" (Bloom 238).

Thinking Fast and Thinking Slow—First Impressions—Setting Traps

The mind, according to psychologists Daniel Kahneman and Amos Tversky, operates in two modes: it thinks fast or it thinks slow. When thinking slow, it multiplies double-digit numbers, fills out tax forms, or validates complex logical arguments. Slow thinking is laborious. When thinking fast, however, the mind analyzes facial expressions, determines the origins of a sudden sound, or completes the phrase "bread and..." (Kahneman 20–22). Fast thinking happens automatically with little voluntary sense of control. When thinking fast, the mind uses heuristic shortcuts. Thinking fast, however, is error-prone. To illustrate its pitfalls, Kahneman and Tversky devised a series of word problems resembling jokes. Consider their most famous example:

> Linda is thirty-one years old, single, outspoken, and very bright. She majored in philosophy. As a student, she was deeply concerned with issues of discrimination and social justice, and also participated in antinuclear demonstrations. (156)

When they asked students which is more probable, that Linda is a bank teller or that Linda is a feminist bank teller, over 85 percent got it wrong. They got it wrong because they were thinking fast. If they had thought slow, they would have realized that the subset of tellers who are feminists must be smaller than the number of tellers.

When told their error, few students found the Linda problem funny. Their responses ranged from an indignant "So what?" to a defensive "I thought you just asked for my opinion" (158). Indignation turns to laughter, however, when heuristics ("bread and....") are exploited *in a playful setting*:

> A: What is the most popular drinking soda?
> B: Coke
> A: What's something that's funny?
> B: A joke
> A: What's the word for the white part of an egg?
> B: The yolk. What, no! It's the.... (Hurley et al. 266)

The discovery of comedy is that people will pay money to be waylaid. In *Twelfth Night*, Shakespeare fills seats by deliberately sabotaging the heuristic generating first impressions.

Moments before Malvolio makes his entrance, two of Countess Olivia's retainers enter: Feste, her fool and Maria, her chambermaid. Feste is in trouble. He has been surreptitiously moonlighting at Duke Orsino's. He stands in danger of going from a housed fool into a homeless fool. Maria warns him. Then Olivia enters, attended by Malvolio. Olivia shows Feste the door: he has done wrong by being gone so long. Feste, however, tells a joke. Olivia laughs. Her train laughs. Everybody laughs except Malvolio. From his silence, spectators begin forming impressions. Perhaps he got up on the wrong side of bed. Perhaps he has a sour disposition. Maybe he is hard of hearing. Drama is a cat-and-mouse game between dramatist and audience. The dramatist drops clues and telegraphs outcomes while the audience tries to figure things out.

Clues follow when Olivia regains her composure:

> OLIVIA. What think you of this fool, Malvolio? Doth he not mend?
>
> MALVOLIO. Yes, and shall do, till the pangs of death shake him; infirmity, that decays the wise, doth ever make the better fool. (1.5.60–62)

According to M. M. Mahood's commentary on this episode, "The bitterness of Malvolio's reply is due to his realization that Olivia has forgiven Feste and is not going to turn him away" (1.5.71–72). For tantalizingly unknown reasons, although Maria warns Feste, Malvolio kicks the clown when he is down. Names provide an additional clue. "Malvolio" means "ill-will" from Italian *mal* "bad" and *voglia* "desire" and stands in contrast to "Feste" which means "feast" or "festival" from the Latin or Italian *festa*. Even without Italian, the audience would have picked up on the ill-sounding "mal-" prefix (think *malediction* or *malevolent* and contrast his name with "Benvolio" from *Romeo and Juliet*, formed, like *benevolent* or *benediction*, from Latin *bene* "well"). New data invalidates the initial conjectures that he slept poorly or has hearing issues. The conjecture that he is sour, however, gains credence. In a play named after a merry winter holiday filled with music, mead, masked balls, and misrule, Malvolio must be the odd man out. If Feste represents mirth and mayhem, Malvolio is his antitype. Spectators' intuitions are confirmed when Malvolio, having rebuked Olivia for taking "delight in such a barren rascal," declares that "I take these wise men that crow so [laugh uproariously] at these set kind of fools no better than the fools' zanies" (1.5.67, 71–72). In the seconds it takes the actor to deliver Malvolio's first eight lines, the audience, without conscious effort, has put together two and two: Malvolio is a stern and strict killjoy.

Jokes, such as the one about the girl and her mother, misdirect by encouraging stereotypes. Shakespeare pursues a similar strategy by typecasting Malvolio as a Puritan. It is an easy sell. Puritans were originally Protestants who fled during the reign of the Catholic Queen Mary (reigned 1553–58). Having been radicalized on the continent, when they returned during the reign of Queen Elizabeth (reigned 1558–1603), they brought back holy zeal to return to the true Christianity. As a result, they lived austerely and rejected Catholic pomp and festival such as Twelfth Night, the final day of the Christmas celebrations. Puritans were a small but influential minority. Like fringe groups today, they were making headlines; then, as now, minorities rather than majorities shape the course of history. Malvolio qua Puritan is an easy sell, because, Puritans, being the natural-born enemies of entertainment, were frequently caricatured on stage.[2] Shakespeare typecasts Malvolio by having Feste continually calling Olivia "madonna": "Feste is the only character in Shakespeare to use the word," writes Roger Warren, "he surely chooses it because its Catholic overtones—referring to the Virgin Mary—will antagonize the puritan Malvolio" (1.5.38). That Malvolio is a Puritan is Shakespeare's first trap.

Having set his first trap, Shakespeare baits his second trap. After Malvolio upbraids Feste, Olivia makes peace between them:

> OLIVIA. O you are sick of self-love, Malvolio, and taste with a distempered appetite. To be generous, guiltless, and of free disposition is to take those things for bird-bolts that you deem cannon bullets. There is no slander in an allowed fool though he do nothing but rail; nor no railing in a known discreet man though he do nothing but reprove.
> (1.5.73–78)

The second trap is that Malvolio is "a known discreet man." Although he reproves others and rails against foolery, this behavior is allowed because, as Olivia's trusty steward, his job is to uphold decorum and propriety. By having Olivia praise his discretion, "Shakespeare establishes Malvolio as a reliable, even essential steward in a great household; his repressiveness and lack of generosity need not interfere with his efficient discharge of duties, and may even help them" (Warren 46–47). Olivia's judgement of Malvolio, like the mother's judgment of her child in the joke, presumably can be trusted.

The Garden Path—Red Herrings—Two Malvolios

Once the traps are set, Shakespeare leads the audience down the garden path. On the path, the audience tests and verifies their suppositions. This process begins when Viola, disguised as Cesario, arrives at Olivia's. Viola comes to woo Olivia on behalf of the Duke (and sometimes Count) Orsino. As Olivia is mourning, his advances are unwelcome: "Go you, Malvolio," says Olivia, "If it be a suit from the count, I am sick, or not at home—what you will to dismiss it" (1.5.89–90). Her command "Go you" conveys his subservience. At the same time, however, "what you will" (the play's subtitle) conveys the esteem in which she holds him. All indications point to Malvolio being a known discreet man and loyal steward.

Having established his trustworthiness, Shakespeare begins, in the kitchen scene, to reinforce his Puritan credentials. It is after midnight. Sir Toby Belch, Sir Andrew Aguecheek, Maria, and Feste are carousing: "Marian, I say," says Sir Toby, "a stoup of wine!" (2.3.11–12). The allusion to "Maid Marian" is "a reference to the disreputable character who led morris dances and May games, popular diversions opposed by the puritans" (Donno 2.3.11). On cue, Malvolio enters:

> MALVOLIO. My masters, are you mad? Or what are you? Have you no wit, manners, nor honesty but to gabble like tinkers at this time of night? Do ye make an alehouse of my lady's house, that ye squeak out your cozers' catches without any mitigation or remorse of voice? Is there no respect of place, persons, nor time in you? (2.3.75–79)

The revelers strike back with two Puritan insults:

> SIR TOBY. Dost thou think because thou art virtuous there shall be no more cakes and ale?
> FESTE. Yes, by St Anne, and ginger shall be hot i'th'mouth too.
> (2.3.97–100)

Cakes and ale were associated with weddings, saints' days, holydays, and Catholic feasts. As a result, they were "repugnant to

Puritans" (Mahood 2.3.112). As well, Saint Anne, the mother of the Virgin, "was venerated in the Middle Ages but her cult was derided by Luther and later reformers; thus Feste's asseveration is a further dig at Malvolio's would-be puritan tendencies" (Donno 2.3.100). Unless Malvolio is a true-blue Puritan, why else would he swear by "Jove" instead of by "God" and find offence in the Madonna, Maid Marian, cakes and ale, Saint Anne, revelry, and other things hateful to Puritans (Davies 96, 104)?

Shakespeare insinuates but does not say Malvolio is a Puritan because jokes work when the audience, by thinking fast, fool themselves. Consider the joke about the bear Dolly Parton tells Jimmy Fallon:

> PARTON. In Pigeon Forge many years ago, back when I was a kid, they had a bear in a cage. You know, we're famous for bears in the Smokies. And they had a bear in a big cage up there and people would stop at this market and they would buy Cokes for this bear that was in the cage. And tourists would take pictures, 'cause it was Gatlinburg and that whole area. For years, you know, they would put Cokes and peanuts in the Coca-Cola cans or whatever the bottled Cokes were then. So, anyway, this bear was just getting bigger and bigger. But they were doing that and they were just selling all kinds of stuff at this market. And this poor bear was just drinking them all. And one day, some redneck put—[laughter from audience]. No, seriously, they put gasoline in a Coke can ["Awws" from audience]. Can you believe how bad people are? And the poor thing just went crazy. And it broke out of the pen. And it started towards Sevierville, because Pigeon Forge is about eight miles from Sevierville. And it just ran all the way down there. And it was just going down there. Then all of a sudden [shaking her head], it just fell over [*audience reacts*].
>
> FALLON. Oh.
>
> PARTON. I know.
>
> FALLON. Dead?

PARTON. No, it was outta gas.

[*Drum roll as laughter erupts. Fallon cannot believe it. He gets up from his desk, crumples the script, walks upstage, and falls to his knees*]

FALLON. I love you! I love you so much! (7:55–11:37)

For the joke to work, Parton cannot say the bear is dead. When Fallon asks, *then* she knows it is time to deliver the punchline. When he hears the punchline, he realizes he is caught: the redneck is a decoy drawing his attention from the comic fulcrum of gasoline being either a poison or a fuel. Fallon and the audience laugh because laughter is a knee-jerk reaction to the failure of fast thinking.

Only after Shakespeare is certain that the audience has committed does he suggest that Malvolio is a Puritan. When the revelers plot their revenge on Malvolio, he has Maria say: "Marry, sir, sometimes he is a kind of puritan" (2.3.119). Her statement finally confirms what everyone knows. In fact, only the daft Sir Andrew fails to see. He responds with the counterfactual: "O if I thought that I'd beat him like a dog!" [with the unspoken apodosis and protasis "But because I did not think he was a Puritan, I did not beat him like a dog"]. Because he is a dolt, his failure to get it signals to the audience that Malvolio *must* be a Puritan.

Note, however, that Maria hedges her remark. Malvolio is not "a puritan," but "a *kind* of puritan." He is a *kind* of Puritan because he only *appears* to be a Puritan: "The devil a puritan that he is," clarifies Maria a few lines later (2.3.124). Similar to Parton shifting from a dead bear to an out-of-gas bear, Shakespeare—now that he knows the audience has been thinking fast—delivers the punchline. The long punchline revealing that Malvolio is anything *but* a Puritan begins as Maria tells Malvolio that Olivia fancies him.

After hearing that Olivia fancies him, Malvolio falls into a reverie: "Besides," he says to himself, "she uses me with a more exalted respect than any one else that follows her. What should I think on't?" (2.5.22–24). He is beginning to convince himself. His fantasy rapidly expands: "To be Count Malvolio!" he says while recalling a precedent where "the Lady of the Strachy married the yeoman of the wardrobe" (2.5.30, 34–35). By revealing Malvolio's "interest in salacious gossip," Shakespeare starts undermining his Puritan credentials (Warren 2.5.36–37). By the time the steward fantasizes about "Calling my officers about me, in my branched velvet gown, having come from a day-bed, where I have left Olivia sleeping," the audience realizes they have been caught swimming without their swimsuits, and the tide is going out.

His Puritan credentials continue crumbling when he finds the fake letter. "By my life, this is my lady's hand," he says; "these be her very c's, her u's, and her t's, and thus makes she her great P's." (2.5.72–73). Neither does the "c" nor the capital "P" appears on the outside of the letter. "'Cut' was slang for the female genitals," writes Warren, "and 'makes her great P's' suggests 'urinates copiously'" (2.5.83–84). His mind is anything but pure. When he reads "Some are born great, some achieve greatness, and some have greatness thrust upon 'em," his heart is touched: his lady is calling him to fulfil his secret destiny. But his coy mistress, caught in sixteenth-century mores, expects him to win her with smiles and cross-gartered yellow stockings. Because he is not who he appears to be, he does it.

The dramatic punchline follows. "Where's Malvolio?" says Olivia, "He is sad and civil, / And suits well for a servant with my fortunes" (3.4.5–6). When Malvolio appears wearing cross-gartered yellow stockings, incongruity piles on incongruity like Ossa on Pelion. There is an incongruity of expectation: "Smil'st thou?" says an incredulous Olivia, "I sent for thee upon a sad occasion" (3.4.18). He has come to woo; she has come to mourn. There is an incongruity in decorum when steward addresses master with the familiar form "thee":

> OLIVIA. Wilt thou go to bed, Malvolio?
> MALVOLIO. To bed? Ay, sweetheart, and I'll come to thee.
> (3.4.27–28)

There is an incongruity in how she uses "bed," and how he interprets it. There is the incongruity of expectation when a steward hopes to succeed where dukes and knights fail. There is an incongruity between the wooer and the wooed: yellow is a color Olivia abhors and crossed garters a fashion she detests. There are many incongruities, and, for that reason, the scene makes the play. But the coup de théâtre is the incongruity between the two Malvolios, the one who is serious, sombre, dependable, discreet, puritanical, wise, chaste, businesslike, and efficient, and the other, who is smiling, hedonistic, megalomaniac, hypocritical, foolish, tactless, daring, and reckless. Like the little girl and the old lady, the white part of the egg, and the bear who fell, laughter erupts when all is not what it seems to be. That errors generated by fast thinking provoke laughter is the basis of incongruity theories of humor and it is through incongruity theory that the question of why Malvolio's cross-gartered yellow stockings are funny may be answered.

Incongruity Theory—Incoherent Coherence—False Alarms

Incongruity theories of humor go back to Aristotle, who found that jokes entertain through the element of surprise (*Rhetoric* 3.2). In the eighteenth and nineteenth centuries, writers began associating surprise with incongruity: "In every case," writes Arthur Schopenhauer, "*laughter* results from nothing but the suddenly perceived incongruity between a concept and the real objects" (1.1.13). From the 1960s, modern researchers such as Arthur Koestler speculated that the incongruity must be self-consistent with the joke's narrative. In other words, for a joke to be funny, it must be surprising yet coherent, an "unexpected and perfectly logical" event that "is made to vibrate simultaneously on two different wavelengths" (35). Consider the joke about the neighborhood borrower that researchers asked right-hemisphere-damaged patients as well as a neurologically sound control group to complete:

> The neighborhood borrower approached Mr. Smith on Sunday afternoon and inquired:
> "Say Smith, are you using your lawnmower this afternoon?"
> "Yes, I am," Smith replied warily.
> The neighborhood borrower then answered: "_____."

Respondents selected between three punchlines:

1) "Fine, then you won't be wanting your golf clubs. I'll just borrow them." [correct punchline that is both incongruent and coherent]
2) "You know the grass is greener on the other side." [incorrect punchline that, while incongruent, lacks coherence]
3) "Do you think I could use it when you're done?" [incorrect punchline that, while coherent, lacks incongruity]

(Brownell et al. 22–23)

The control group grasped the role of both incongruity and coherence. Although the right-side lesion group understood the role of incongruity, they failed to understand the role of coherence, frequently choosing the incoherent "You know the grass is greener on the other side." A subsequent study found that left hemisphere-damaged patients were the opposite: while they understood the role of coherence, they failed to understand the role of incongruity (Bihrle et al. 399–411). Together, the experiments support a two-element model of humor based on the cognitive dissonance of incongruent yet coherent events.

The next advance occurred in the 1970s with the advent of incongruity-resolution theories. In the incongruity-resolution model, jokes become an exercise in problem solving: we laugh not at the incongruity, but at the faulty heuristics of fast thinking. When listeners hear a joke, they predict the outcome. When the outcome is unexpected, they attempt to understand why. Once they resolve the incongruity, laughter results (Shultz 456–77; Suls 81–100).

The various incongruity theories describe how comedy provokes laughter through surprise, incongruity, coherence, and resolution. Sir Toby, Sir Andrew, and Fabian perform surprise by falling over one another when Maria's device works: Sir Toby is in such disbelief that he marries Maria and Fabian would "not give my part of this sport for a pension of thousands" (2.5.148). When an astonished Olivia says to the cross-gartered Malvolio "Why, this is very midsummer madness," she performs surprise (3.4.50). The atmosphere of surprise primes the audience for laughter. Surprise is around every corner: "I am not what I am," says Viola (3.1.126); "Nothing that is so is so," says Feste (4.1.6–7); "I swear," says Viola, "I am not that I play" (1.5.153); "I am mad" says Sebastian (4.3.15); "Most wonderful!" exclaims a starstruck Olivia (5.1.209).

Surprise is built into the setting: they are in Illyria, a dangerous and unpredictable town where Sebastian adopts an alias to stay safe (2.1.12). Characters talk about "natural perspectives" and "perspective glasses," natural and manufactured devices that baffle the senses (5.1.201, 5.1.249). Characters highlight the atmosphere of surprise through metatheatre: "If this were played upon a stage now," says Fabian, "I could condemn it as an improbable fiction" (3.4.108–09). "[T]his accident and flood of fortune," says Sebastian, "So far exceed all instance, all discourse, / That I am ready to distrust mine eyes" (4.3.11–13). Puns and riddles add to the atmosphere of comic instability ("Better a witty fool than a foolish wit," 1.5.30; "I am all the daughters of my father's house," 2.4.116). To set the stage for comic brouhaha, Shakespeare takes a shotgun approach to humor by planting surprises everywhere. Surprise is in the air because comedy dramatizes low-probability, high-consequence risk events: identical twins, shipwrecks, love at first sight, the dead coming back to life, a safe disguise that backfires, a trickster caught in the webs of his own ruse (Wong "Leverage" xxvii–xxxii; "Love and Chance" 62–85). Comedy is in order when it is most out of order.

Characters also perform incongruity. Olivia performs incongruity by mourning her brother seven years. Viola performs incongruity by dressing as a page. On the original stage, it is even more incongruous as Viola is acted by boy actor playing a girl disguised as a boy. Feste, the wisest person, plays the fool. The only thing constant about Orsino is his inconstancy. Aguecheek speaks "three or four languages word for word" yet asks "What is '*pourquoi*'?" (1.3.22, 1.3.77). Of all the incongruities, however, the incongruity between the two Malvolios is most memorable. The first Malvolio is stern and strict; the second Malvolio fantasizes about lounging around in a branched velvet gown while lording over "my people" (2.5.49). By putting on the cross-gartered yellow stockings,

Malvolio performs incongruity by throwing the two Malvolios into an incompatible relief.

Although Malvolio's stockings are surprising, they are, in the end, consistent with his state of being "sick of self-love" (1.5.73). Because he is full of himself to the point that he believes that "all that look on him love him," his decision to wear yellow stockings is consistent with his character as an egocentric maniac willing to do anything (2.3.128). In fact, not only are his stockings coherent, but every dissonant element about him turns out to be coherent. His haughtiness could be because he is a Puritan; it could also be because he is a megalomaniac. Likewise, "sheep-biter," an insult used against him, can mean "a censorious fellow" or "a hypocritical Puritan" (Lothian and Craik 2.5.5). His dislike of cakes and ale could be because he is a Puritan; it could also be because it is beneath his dignity to serve cakes and ale to drunken louts. As Shakespeare remarks in another play, the trick of comedy is to make "our jarring notes agree" (*Taming* 5.1.1). In other words, incoherent coherence, a state where "each circumstance, / Of place, time, fortune, do cohere and jump" with the result that Cesario becomes Viola and Malvolio one becomes Malvolio two (*Twelfth* 5.1.235–36).

Finally, the fulness of laughter results when spectators resolve the incongruity. Collapsing the incongruity proceeds along these lines: Malvolio possesses greatness and knows it. In the madhouse scene, he is truly great, noble, and beautiful, full of learning, pathos, and humanity. He is so much more than those who have done him wrong. In nature's bias, he is as noble as Orsino, as strong as Aguecheek, as witty as Belch, and in everything a worthy match for the noble Olivia. In another play, he could have been great. But, like a nightingale singing a song to jackdaws, in *this* play, he stares at the others with the eyes of one who rages for being born. When the letter offers him a chance to fulfill his greatness, he is compelled to follow because it calls him to become Malvolio. The stars revolve; new constellations blaze; fortune is at hand; destiny calls.

Spectators finally understand how years of servitude have embittered Malvolio with the result that his "secret wish is to violate decorum himself, then relish to the full its power over others" (Barber

255). Malvolio is repressive because he has been repressed. With power, he will make them feel how he has been made to feel; he will discharge his steward's rage. Just as there were no rednecks in the joke about the bear, there are no Puritans in *Twelfth Night*. It was all a ruse, and the whole house, from the galleries to the groundlings, fell for it, hook, line, and sinker. The Puritan stereotype is a bogey concealing all the men and women trapped by the great chain of being: here, the queen of Los Angeles who could have been Queen of England, there a Michelangelo painting the Walmart display. Malvolio, in the final examination, is funny because he represents all the great ones to whom greatness was denied. The only thing crueler than tragedy is comedy.

Inside Jokes—The Funny Bone—Animal Laughter

Despite the penetrating insights of incongruity theory, it fell short. It fell short because it described rather than explained humor. It fell short in the same way as the theory of evolution, in the early days, only described the process of evolution. It took Charles Darwin, by explaining how evolution works *through the mechanism of natural selection*, to make the theory of evolution whole. In the same way, incongruity theory was made whole in 2011 when cognitive scientist Matthew M. Hurley, philosopher Daniel C. Dennett, and psychologist Reginald B. Adams speculated that laughter is an adaptive trait encouraging erring organisms to correct false beliefs. By grounding incongruity theory in evolutionary biology, Hurley, Dennett, and Adams transformed the descriptive model of humor into an explanatory one.

In their landmark 2011 book, *Inside Jokes*, Hurley and his colleagues speculated that the funny bone, like the sweet tooth, is the product of natural selection. Just as the sweet tooth aids survival by rewarding organisms for consuming calories, the funny bone confers Darwinian fitness on animals by rewarding them for resolving incongruities. Because fast thinking is error-prone, laughter developed as a reward for expending mental energy to revise erroneous beliefs.

Their theory is based on laughter being an adaptive trait. There is abundant evidence to suggest that laughter developed through evolution. To express surprise, dolphins release a balloon-sized air bubble, and this is a dolphin's initial reaction to seeing a girl perform cartwheels in the YouTube video "Girl Makes Dolphin Laugh" (0.08). Watch the video and ask yourself whether the dolphin is laughing at the incongruity of seeing a human walking on her hands. Rats break out in ultrasonic (50 kHz) chirps of laughter when tickled and during play (Panksepp and Burgdorf 533). Primates make a panting sound reminiscent of laughter when tickled and during play (Provine 76). The rhythm of chimpanzee laughter, moreover, mirrors that of human laughter (79). As an adaptive trait, laughter may have descended from a false alarm signal. Many animals employ distinct alarm signals. Monkeys, for example, employ distinct alarms for eagles, snakes, and leopards (Hurley et al. 262). Birds also employ distinct and identifiable predator alarms. "Some species," writes Hurley, "also have a 'never mind, the coast is clear' signal that cancels a *false* alarm" (262). The false alarm signal, by communicating a resolution to an incongruity (the rustling sound is the wind rather than a predator) may be, through the long span of evolution, the antecedent to modern day laughter.

The idea of laughter as a false alarm signal can be illustrated through the action of tickling. When a person feels something on them, the subconscious mind makes a heuristic leap that creepy-crawlies are attacking. When the conscious mind resolves the error ("I am being tickled"), the false alarm signal of laughter results. Because the conscious mind cannot override the subconscious neurological detection mechanism, the alarm-resolution-laughter cycle may continue indefinitely (221–29). In the evolutionary version of the incongruity theory, the dramatic art of comedy is simply the commercialization of the funny bone. Just as makers of Mars bars, perfumers, the beauty industry, and pornographers have co-opted adaptive traits for commercial purposes by presenting consumers with supernormal stimuli, comic playwrights have co-opted biology's error-detection mechanisms to entertain.

The evolutionary-incongruity theory of laughter combines two promising strands. Of the approaches to humor, incongruity theory has the most fact-based support (Martin 110). Because evidence suggests animals laugh, to understand human laughter, it makes sense to look at its origins because it is far simpler to analyze animal behaviors: "If we finally take the emotions of the other animals seriously," says neuroscientist Jaak Panksepp, "we will finally understand how we have these feelings of joy and sorrow, anger and sadness" (15:55–16:07). In time, however, some—and perhaps many—elements of the evolutionary-incongruity theory will be debunked. But for now, although some disagree and others scoff, it is the best thing going because it is consilient.

Consilience—An Iron Curtain—Only the Social Survive

Consilience is the idea that unlimited human progress results from "a 'jumping together' [from Latin *con-* 'together' and *siliens* 'jumping'] of knowledge by the linking of facts and fact-based theory across disciplines to create a common groundwork of explanation" (Wilson 8). Consilience is the logical culmination of the Enlightenment, an eighteenth-century philosophical movement championing reason over tradition. Consilience posits that each of the great branches of learning holds a fragment of knowledge and that, by putting together the fragments, we may unify knowledge. The evolutionary theory of humor, by linking facts and fact-based theory from psychology, cognitive science, neuroscience, neurobiology, sociobiology, and philosophy, approaches consilience. The final piece of the puzzle is to see if it explains why we laugh at *Twelfth Night* and other works of art. *Inside Jokes* ends, accordingly, with an invitation to the new constructionists to unify knowledge in a grand synthesis:

> There is a huge body of scholarly work on comedy in literature already, and it would be very interesting to show how our theory applies to this wealth of material [. . .] Rather than try our hands at such a task, we prefer to offer a few words of guidance, and a few caveats to those who are more qualified for it.

> If, as we expect, science begins to bear out our theoretical claims, we invite literary analysts and rhetoricians to apply our theory in their analyses. (Hurley et al. 278–79)

In the new constructionism, literary analysts engage science to interpret literature. They ask, for example, whether Feste's joke provokes laughter by correcting false beliefs:

> FESTE. Good madonna, why mourn'st thou?
> OLIVIA. Good fool, for my brother's death.
> FESTE. I think his soul is in hell, madonna.
> OLIVIA. I know his soul is in heaven, fool.
> FESTE. The more fool, madonna, to mourn for your brother's
> soul being in heaven. (1.5.54–59)

They ask whether Malvolio's cross-gartered yellow stockings provoke laughter by uncovering the false belief he is a Puritan. If they answer yes, they continue pushing the limits of interpretation. Seeing that theatre holds up a mirror to life, they ask whether theatrical laughter also corrects false beliefs *outside the world of the play*. Inside the world of the play, the audiences laughed at Malvolio, but outside the world of the play, were the audiences laughing at the real life Malvolios who were taking up the sham front of Puritanism to oppress their oppressors? Perhaps Malvolio's cross-gartered yellow stockings were funny because they expose how real-life Puritans were putting on ridiculous pretenses to have greatness thrust upon them. Could it be that, like Malvolio, they are not who they appear to be? By unifying science with art, new critical insights emerge, insights into how laughter, "a rust that corrodes everything," functions as a social corrective by exposing error (Kundera 226). A door opens to writing a new and consilient poetics.

In the consilient future, scientists and literary critics work with facts and fact-based theory to advance knowledge. In the consilient model of progress, when a theory—no matter how influential—no longer corresponds with the facts, researchers move on:

> Apart from the inconsistency of the research evidence, the 'hydraulic model' of psychic energy on which Freudian theory is built, viewing laughter as a way of 'burning off' excess tension, is not consistent with our modern understanding of the nervous system. Consequently, the psychoanalytic theory of humor (like Freudian theory in general) has been largely abandoned by empirical researchers since the 1980s. (Martin 42)

To work on the borderlands of science and art, however, is terrifying. With our human bias, we humanists sounded the alarm as the animal encroached upon the human. In her 2014 book on laughter, classicist Mary Beard raises red flags: "The chirping of rats [...] remains even more controversial, with many scientists resisting any connection to human laughter at all" (47). Continuing, she writes:

> But even if we were to concede that similar neural pathways are involved in all these phenomena, and that there are at least some evolutionary links between the rats' chirping and the humans' chortling, there is a much more pressing question that is almost always sidestepped: What would we mean if we were to say that dogs or apes or rats "laugh"? (47)

To Beard, animal laughter heralds the beginning of the end as zoology digests the humanities in its savage maw. If, however, animals do not laugh, we may continue to disregard science.

A core anthropocentric bias is built into our humanist worldview. Whereas the sciences have evolution, in the humanities we have the great chain of being, immutable, unchanging, eternal. Although in public we said the right things, in our secret hearts, we denied evolution. We were with the 40 percent of Americans who, in a 2019 Gallup pole, rejected evolution (Brenan). We saw the six million geological years between the sapiens and the great apes as an unbridgeable chasm. Instead of understanding human behaviors and emotions as products of evolution, we came up with "free will," "the immortal soul," "culture," "knowledge of good and evil," "consciousness," "human rights," "rational choice," and other bulwarks to cleave the human from the animal. When they cited Darwin, we cited Aristotle. As the last stewards of humanity, we drew a line in the sand between the human and the beast by saying "man is the only animal that laughs," "man alone of the animals possesses speech," and "man is a political animal" (Aristotle *Animals* 673a; *Politics* 1253a). As science flung the earth and then the sun and then the solar system from their rightful place at the center, we created postmodernism to restore the human center. As science rooted out tradition and began encroaching upon and assimilating whole branches of the humanities, we made postmodernism the hill upon which we will die defending human decorum and propriety.

Instead of an unknown future, we retrenched into a traditional, familiar past. In 2016, anthropologist Elliott Oring, having concluded Hurley's theory has been "overly influenced by its evolutionary perspective," advocates a return to psychoanalytic theory: "Freud's is a book that the authors seem not to have read, however, and from which they might have benefited" (98, 227). Likewise, in his 2019 survey of incongruity theories, literary critic Terry Eagleton bypasses Hurley entirely and suggests the way forward is to return to psychoanalytic approaches by "splic[ing] the incongruity thesis with release theory" (89). Psychoanalytic theory *was* consilient and advanced knowledge by highlighting the aggressive and sexual aspects of humor. But although it is no longer consilient today, we, the defenders of the faith, will never move on.

Today, an iron curtain of postmodernism is descending between the liberal arts and the sciences. Because, in postmodernism, nothing can be known and everything is allowed, instead of talking *with* scientists, we talk *past* scientists (Wong "Truth" 69–87). Although scientists have long debunked the hydraulic model of the brain where emotions require periodic purging, we continue, in our post-truth kingdom, talking about the catharsis of pent-up comic and tragic emotions. Instead of engaging evolutionary biology, we continue talking about humor as a defence mechanism, a way of bypassing mental censors, an intrapsychic function mediating repressed libidinal desires. By drawing the iron curtain, we saved the human from being assimilated into God knows what. But the cost was consilience. As we continued talking about catharsis, psychic reservoirs, and magic lanterns, fewer and fewer listened until, at last, only Sir Topas remained.

The way forward is not to fear, but to embrace consilience. To tackle the complexity of the human mind without going through the archaeologies of evolution is too great a task. Only by excavating the fossils of laughter can we understand the descent of humor first, as a reward to detect error, second, as a joke to laugh over, and third, as a long joke exposing errors both inside and outside the world of the play. To retrodict human behavior by inference and deduction alone is impossible but, by considering the archaeology of laughter, the impossible becomes possible. In the analysis of humor, we accomplish the impossible when we take animal laughter seriously. To turn Beard's question on its head: how much evidence do we lose if we deny that animals laugh?

For all our nuanced interpretations of *Twelfth Night*, we have yet to grasp its core message that, when our counterparts are celebrating their discoveries with cakes and ale deep into the night, it is better to join them: whether in Olivia's kitchen or in the great branches of learning, only the social survive. To dissect why Malvolio's cross-gartered yellow stockings are funny is to show the sun with a lamp. But showing the sun with a lamp is better than to show the dark by turning out the light.

Notes

1. The first attested performance of *Twelfth Night* dates to Candlemas on 2 February 1602 at Middle Temple Hall. It was likely written in 1601. Thank you to Caroline Russell-King, Sarah Milne, and Elaine Tan for laughing at—and sometimes groaning over—the jokes in this essay.
2. Stage Puritans include, for example, Florilla in George Chapman's *A Humorous Day's Mirth* (1597), Lady Plus' family in Thomas Middleton's *The Puritan Widow* (1606), and Tribulation Wholesome, Ananias, and Zeal-of-the-land Busy in Ben Jonson's *The Alchemist* (1610) and *Bartholomew Fair* (1614).

Works Cited

Aristotle. *Art of Rhetoric*. Translated by J. H. Freese, Loeb-Harvard UP, 2020.

_____. *On the Part of Animals*. Translated by James G. Lennox, Oxford UP, 2004.

_____. *Politics*. Translated by H. Rackham, Loeb-Harvard UP, 1932.

Barber, C. L. *Shakespeare's Festive Comedy: A Study of Dramatic Form and Its Relation to Social Custom*. Princeton UP, 1959.

Beard, Mary. *Laughter in Ancient Rome: On Joking, Tickling, and Cracking Up*. U of California P, 2014.

Bihrle, Amy M., et al. "Comprehension of Humorous and Nonhumorous Materials by Left and Right Brain-Damaged Patients." *Brain and Cognition*, vol. 5, iss. 4, 1986, pp. 399–411.

Bloom, Harold. *The Invention of the Human*. Riverhead Books, 1998.

Brenan, Megan. "40% of Americans Believe in Creationism," Gallup. news.gallup.com/poll/261680/americans-believe-creationism.aspx.

Brownell, Hiram H., et al. "Surprise but Not Coherence: Sensitivity to Verbal Humor in Right-Hemisphere Patients." *Brain and Language*, vol. 18, iss. 1, 1983, pp. 20–27.

Davies, Stevie. *Shakespeare: Twelfth Night*, by William Shakespeare. Penguin, 1993.

Donno, Elizabeth Story. Commentary. *Twelfth Night*, by William Shakespeare, Cambridge UP, 2017.

Eagleton, Terry. *Humour*. Yale UP, 2019.

"Girl Makes Dolphin Laugh (Extended) Original Video." YouTube, uploaded by FunDippedProductions, 20 June 2014, www.youtube.com/watch?v=Bsp_JTtE3-w.

Hurley, Matthew M., et al. *Inside Jokes: Using Humor to Reverse-Engineer the Mind*. MIT P, 2013.

Kahneman, Daniel. *Thinking, Fast and Thinking Slow*. Anchor, 2013.

Koestler, Arthur. *The Act of Creation*. Hutchinson, 1964.

Kundera, Milan. *The Joke*. Translated by David Hamblyn and Oliver Stallybrass, Coward-McCann, 1969.

Linthicum, M. Channing "Malvolio's Cross-Gartered Yellow Stockings." *Modern Philology*, vol. 25, no. 1, 1927, pp. 87–93.

Lothian, J. M., and T. W. Craik. Commentary. *Twelfth Night*, by William Shakespeare. *The Arden Shakespeare*, 1988.

Mahood, M. M. Commentary. *Twelfth Night*, by William Shakespeare. *The New Penguin Shakespeare*, 1968.

Martin, Rod. A. *The Psychology of Humor: An Integrative Approach*. Elsevier, 2007.

Oring, Elliott. *Joking Asides: The Theory, Analysis, and Aesthetics of Humor*. Utah State UP, 2016.

Panksepp, Jaak. "The Science of Emotions: Jaak Panksepp at TEDxRainier." YouTube, uploaded by TEDx Talks, 13 Jan. 2014, www.youtube.com/watch?v=65e2qScV_K8.

Panksepp, Jaak, and Jeff Burgdorf. "'Laughing' Rats and the Evolutionary Antecedents of Human Joy?" *Physiology and Behavior*, vol. 79, iss. 3, 2003, pp. 533–47.

Parton, Dolly. "Dolly Parton Accidentally Star-Struck Jimmy's Uber Driver [Extended]," uploaded by *The Tonight Show* Starring Jimmy Fallon, 30 Nov. 2022, www.youtube.com/watch?v=z7f8fMIBAMg&t=449s.

Provine, Robert R. *Laughter: A Scientific Investigation*. Penguin, 2000.

Schopenhauer, Arthur. *The World as Will and Representation*. Translated by E. F. J. Payne, vol. 1, Dover, 1969.

Shakespeare, William. *The Taming of the Shrew*. Edited by Jonathan Bate and Eric Rasmussen, The Royal Shakespeare Company Shakespeare, 2010.

_____. *Twelfth Night, or What You Will*. Edited by Elizabeth Story Donno, 3rd ed., The New Cambridge Shakespeare, 2017.

Shultz, Thomas R. "The Role of Incongruity and Resolution in Children's Appreciation of Cartoon Humor." *Journal of Experimental Child Psychology*, vol. 13, iss. 3, 1972, pp. 456–77.

Suls, J. M. "A Two-Stage Model for the Appreciation of Jokes and Cartoons: An Information-Processing Analysis." *The Psychology of Humor: Theoretical Perspectives and Empirical Issues*. Edited by J. H. Goldstein and P. E. McGhee, Academic Press, 1972, pp. 81–100.

Warren, Roger. Commentary. *Twelfth Night, or What You Will*, by William Shakespeare, The Oxford Shakespeare, 1998.

_____. Introduction. *Twelfth Night, or What You Will*, by William Shakespeare, The Oxford Shakespeare, 1998, pp. 1–76.

Wilson, Edward O. *Consilience: The Unity of Knowledge*. Vintage, 1999.

Wong, Edwin. "Leverage, Risk, and Fragility in Shakespeare's *The Merchant of Venice*." *Critical Insights: The Merchant of Venice*. Edited by Robert C. Evans, Salem Press, 2023, pp. xxii–xxxiv.

_____. "Love and Chance in Comedy and Tragedy: Shakespeare's *Romeo and Juliet* and Plautus's *The Rope*." *Critical Insights: Love*. Edited by Robert C. Evans, Salem Press, 2022, pp. 62–86.

_____. "Truth and Lies in Life, Literature, and Literary Theory." *Critical Insights: Truth and Lies*. Edited by Robert C. Evans, Salem Press, 2022, pp. 69–90.

"It...makes him stand to and not stand to": Tragicomic Juxtaposition in *Macbeth, Twelfth Night*, and *Much Ado About Nothing*

Matthew M. Thiele

In her 1979 book *The Comic Matrix of Shakespeare's Tragedy*, Susan Snyder laments that the notion of comic relief is "much attacked of late but apparently indestructible" (5). The intervening decades have done little to change that assessment. The attacks and the futility of those attacks persist. "Comic relief" survives, the zombie literary theory that we have tried to kill but that annoyingly refuses to die.

Obviously, the idea of comic relief survives because people find it useful, but its usefulness is hard to explain. In my experience, people are likely to identify anything they find humorous as comic relief, which would seem to complicate unnecessarily an idea that is relatively simple and straightforward. The term itself is somewhat to blame. There is something deeply, gnostically true about pairing those two words. Comedy relieves. It is a relief to laugh. It is a relief to be amused by something clever. It is a relief to see conflicts resolved happily instead of tragically.

It is no help that what has passed as comic relief has almost always been mislabeled. A humorous scene in a play that is supposed to be deadly serious and extraordinarily passionate can seem out of place. It may seem to call attention to itself. But referring to such a scene as comic relief can betray a misunderstanding of both notions, of the notion of comedy and the notion of relief.

My main objection to the way people tend to use "comic relief" is the issue of what counts as "relief." Aside from this general notion of comedy as relief, what is relieving about the presence of a comedic scene or a comedic moment in a scene? Must a comedic scene in a tragic play always be chalked up to relief, or does another explanation for its purpose make more sense? I can show that far from offering relief, some comedic scenes actually create tension and suspense.

Another vexing problem I have encountered, particularly in my role as a professor of literature, is whether "comic relief" is an appropriate term to apply to a comedy. I have come to believe that it is appropriate, and perhaps only appropriate for comedy. Even when the effect is in dispute, however, the cause is fairly obvious. Whether tragic or comic, tension or relief, the source is tragicomic juxtaposition, and it is employed in drama in several ways, as Shakespeare demonstrates in many of his plays, including *Macbeth*, *Twelfth Night*, and *Much Ado About Nothing*.

Comedic Tension in *Macbeth*

The porter's lines in *Macbeth* (2.3), for example, in which there appears to be tragicomic juxtaposition, have been held up as a textbook case of comic relief (see, for example, Tromly 151). They are supposed to provide some kind of comedic buffer between the murder of Duncan in 2.2 and its discovery later in 2.3. There are two problems with this theory. One is that the comic nature of the porter seems to be misunderstood and misrepresented. Whenever I teach *Macbeth*, I ask students to explain what is humorous about the porter, (whom some of them have read online is supposed to be comedic). I innocently ask: "Did you laugh as you read his lines?" "No," it turns out; some brave souls usually admit that they did not even really understand much of it. "Humor is culturally specific," I explain, "and what is supposed to be comedic is not necessarily supposed to be humorous." What identifies material as comedic is less about what is humorous and more about the formal function of a character's words and actions. For example, what makes Polonius comedic in *Hamlet*, according to Robert Cardullo, has less to do with his putative humorousness and more to do with "his need to please or impress Claudius...as well as...his need to assert his parental prerogatives before Laertes. Polonius's delay is thus formally comic, because it is designed to accommodate or reconcile him to his society" (29). What makes the porter comic is his low social status and his apparent disregard for upper-class squeamishness concerning the body and its products: sweat (2.3.6), urine (2.3.27), erections (2.3.33–40), and so on.

The other problem with identifying the porter as a source of comic relief is the question of how his words produce relief. That his lines probably do not offer any relief might be evident in their predominant theme, impotence. Some may perceive this as humorous, and it seems as if Shakespeare's audience was expected to find it hilarious, but as with those other odd subjects that early modern audiences apparently found hilarious, rape and cuckoldry, it had the potential to induce some anxiety as well. So, we have a subject likely to produce uneasy laughter, or perhaps schadenfreude, but the porter's philosophizing is interspersed with knocking within at least six times within the first twenty lines. Macduff and Lennox have arrived, and their arrival immediately precedes the discovery of Duncan's murder.

The audience knows from act 2, scene 2 that Macbeth and his wife have succeeded in murdering Duncan and setting up his chamberlains to take the blame. What follows should be the discovery of the murder, but instead, the play delays the discovery of Duncan's murder with the porter. As the porter opines on the effect of alcohol on human physiology, the audience is essentially invited to forget that the murder occurred. But the knocking within makes sure the audience cannot forget. When we take the porter's lines as part of a continuum in the play and not a discreet element within the play, the effect seems to be a certain kind of suspense. When is Duncan's murder going to be discovered? When are Macbeth and his wife going to be exposed as Duncan's murderers? The porter's presence changes the rules of discovery in the play; it creates dread that would not be perceived otherwise by causing delay.

The ambivalence that the porter generates is also suggested by his words, which can be shown to formally reinforce the effect of the structural juxtaposition: "Lechery, sir, it provokes and unprovokes: it provokes the desire but it takes away the performance. Therefore much drink may be said to be an equivocator with lechery: it makes him and it mars him; it sets him on and it takes him off; it persuades him and disheartens him, makes him stand to and not stand to"

(2.3.28–33). These binary opposites, these contradictions that the audience is asked to try to make sense of, offer no relief. They intimate a deep uncertainty about what is true and real. The raw exercise of wit itself might be comic, but the wit calls attention to its own inappropriateness.

Tension, rather than relief, seems to be the likely effect generated by the juxtaposition of tragic and comic elements in this part of *Macbeth*. Tension is generated by the tragicomic juxtaposition within the scene between the knocking and the porter's commentary and between the porter's lines and the contiguous elements of the main plot. I have always found the ambivalence between comedy and tragedy at this point in the play to be unsettling.

An even starker example of this phenomenon appears in act 1 of *Richard III*, when the time between the audience's knowledge of Clarence's death sentence and his actual death at the hands of the two murderers is absurdly drawn out and comedic in tone. Act 1, scene 4 begins with an invitation to the audience to sympathize with Clarence, who describes a dream to his jailer. He says, "Oh, Lord, methought what a pain it was to drown! / What dreadful noise of waters in my ears! / What sights of ugly death within my eyes!" (1.4.21–23). The audience is invited through direct appeals to the senses to put themselves in Clarence's place and imagine what it must be like to experience what he describes in his dream. But instead of getting on with Clarence's murder, which would probably magnify the sympathy the play had generated for Clarence, he falls asleep, and what follows is over 200 lines of comedic banter, first between the murders and then between the murderers and Clarence. First, the second murderer objects to killing Clarence while he sleeps, and he argues about it with the first murderer. The second murderer is convinced by the first to commit to the deed, and he says, absurdly, "I hope this passionate humor of mine will change" (1.4.118–19). Then Clarence wakes up, and the murderers engage in irreverent witty banter with him:

> CLARENCE. In God's name, what art thou?
> FIRST MURDERER. A man, as you are.

CLARENCE. But not, as I am, royal.
FIRST MURDERER. Nor you, as we are, loyal. (1.4.166–69)

This ambivalent tone, established through the use of tragicomic juxtaposition, creates suspense and dread in at least two ways, by suggesting that the murderers are too incompetent or capricious to complete their task, which would give the audience some hope that Clarence might live (if they do not know their history very well), and by drawing out longer than anticipated the moment of Clarence's death.

Comic and Tragic Relief in *Twelfth Night*

The tragic elements of *Twelfth Night* have been acknowledged for a while now. For example, the subplot involving Maria, Toby, Feste, and Fabian's pursuit of revenge against Malvolio has tragic elements. Richard Madelaine notes Maria's "transformation" (77) from a comic character to a revenger, suggesting that she changes into a tragic character during the play. Although revenge plots are not unheard of in comedies, the one in *Twelfth Night* is notable for the lack of proportion between Malvolio's supposed offense and the lengths to which the revengers go to exact their revenge. Malvolio is so abused that swears revenge against his tormentors in his final lines (5.1.378), ending the play on a sour note.

The most interesting use of tragicomic juxtaposition in *Twelfth Night* is to provide relief when a potentially tragic situation is resolved peacefully. A few years ago, a student of mine stated that he particularly liked the scenes with Feste. When I pressed him for a reason, he claimed that it was because they provided comic relief. This is fairly typical. Students often believe that any humorous scene in a play represents "comic relief" in some way, and my standard reply used to be to state categorically that there can be no comic relief in a comedy for a few reasons. First of all, humorous scenes in a comedy would more appropriately be described as comic. Adding the term "relief" implies that there is need for relief from more serious or tragic material, and that is just less likely to occur in a comedy. In addition, the term "comic relief" may postdate Shakespeare.

A.P. Rossiter credits Dryden (274–75). Early Modern playwrights may not have recognized the concept or employed it as a dramatic technique.

Secondly, the characteristics of genre differ from time to time and from place to place. Today we are more inclined to think of comedy as humorous and tragedy as serious and sad. Judging by Shakespeare's plays, his audience tolerated a great deal more mixing of humorous, serious, passionate, and sad. What seems to have been the *sine qua non* was the way the play ended. Comedies ended happily, or at least without a death, and tragedies ended with a death. Lastly, humorous scenes that are more likely to be labeled as comic relief may not offer any actual relief.

As I gained more experience as a teacher, I began to reexamine my position about comic relief in comedy. Contrary to what I have compulsively told students for the last decade, I have come to believe that comic relief may *only* exist in comedy, and it is precisely because Shakespeare's comedies juxtapose tragic and comedic elements. What is at stake in *Twelfth Night* in the confrontation between Andrew Aguecheek and Viola, for example? What will happen if Viola's disguise is uncovered only after her complete inability to use a rapier is uncovered? The play asks us to consider just that when Viola says, "I am no fighter," (3.4.244), and then, "Pray God defend me! A little thing would make me tell them how much I lack of a man" (3.4.302–03). The first statement is more true than Sir Toby realizes, and the second shows how desperate Viola is not to fight Sir Andrew. Is the audience invited to sympathize with Viola here? Her desperation is apparent. Is it funny? Is our knowledge of Sir Andrew's own anxieties enough to dispel our concern for Viola's safety? Is the audience with Sir Toby and Fabian, reveling in the showcase of cowardice they have orchestrated? Perhaps, but the stakes seem real and serious. Antonio enters in the middle of all of this, and, believing Viola to be Sebastian, he rushes to defend her. Sir Toby draws, and for a moment it seems as if a fight might actually occur.

Much time is spent developing the tragic potential of the scene, and relatively little is spent developing the comedic potential. It has its humorous moments (I laugh every time when Sir Andrew offers his horse if Viola will "let the matter slip" (3.4.286–87)), and the comedy stems from Viola's need to be integrated, as she cannot stay disguised as Cesario indefinitely, but that integration will be deferred until everyone else's integration can be secured. Those humorous moments might lighten the tragic potential of the conflict and appear to offer some kind of relief from being concerned about Viola's safety, and in that sense, it might be appropriate to identify the effect as comic relief.

There is another important moment that introduces tragic elements near the end of the play. It appears that Orsino seriously contemplates murdering Olivia for refusing him before he settles on sacrificing Viola because he thinks that she is competing with him for Olivia's attention:

> Why should I not, had I the heart to do it,
> Like to th'Egyptian thief at point of death
> Kill what I love?—a savage jealousy
> That sometime savors nobly. But hear me this:
> Since you to nonregardance cast my faith,
> And that I partly know the instrument
> That screws me from my true place in your favor,
> Live you the marble-breasted tyrant still.
> But this, your minion, whom I know you love,
> And whom, by heaven I swear, I tender dearly,
> Him I will tear out of that cruel eye
> Where he sits crownèd in his master's spite.—
> Come, boy, with me. My thoughts are ripe in mischief.
> I'll sacrifice the lamb that I do love,
> To spite a raven's heart within a dove. (5.1.115–29)

The jealous lover murdering, or at least wanting to murder, the guiltless beloved is undeniably a tragic element, and although Orsino has confessed earlier in the play to being, along with all men, "giddy and unfirm" (2.4.33), this moment surprises as much for how childish and spiteful Orsino seems as for the conviction with which he announces his intention to sacrifice Viola. Perhaps more surprisingly, Viola agrees to go with him! In the words of Porter Williams, Jr., "Comedy touches here for a fleeting moment the pathos of tragedy" (198). This moment is sandwiched between lighter material, with the marriage of Sebastian and Olivia before and the long-anticipated public revelation of Viola's identity and her reunion with her brother after. All would seem ready for the recognition scene between Sebastian and Viola without this strange murder interlude. Could we call it tragic relief? Does the play resolve itself too smoothly without it? The moment seems to be designed to remind the audience of the stakes for everyone involved one last time before all of that tension is dispelled, and the happy ending that the audience expects is delivered.

Lisa Marciano recognizes this phenomenon in several of Shakespeare's comedies. In what she identifies as their "dark dimension," she suggests that a comedy's outcome is more satisfying if the characters experience trials and suffering: "Shakespeare's comic characters repeatedly come face to face with mortality, learn that one must, therefore, live well, and teach others wisdom accordingly" (3). Marciano does not directly identify the confrontations with mortality in comedies as tragic elements, but that is one way to understand this phenomenon. At least in Shakespeare, some degree of interplay between comedy and tragedy enhances the resolution of the comedy. It is a relief in *Twelfth Night* when it becomes clear that Viola and Aguecheek will not have to fight one another. It is a relief that *Twelfth Night* ends peacefully without Viola's execution.

Comedic Delay in Much Ado About Nothing

The structure of the plot in *Much Ado About Nothing* is unusual. The tragicomic subplot involving Benedick and Beatrice eclipses the rote and dopey tragicomic main plot involving Claudio and Hero, and the comic and tragic elements alternate fairly regularly. For example, 4.1, the scene in which Claudio and Don Pedro humiliate Hero, is bracketed by Dogberry scenes before and after. There is also tragicomic juxtaposition within act 4, scene 1. Beatrice and Benedick's lovely confessions of love for each other are placed between Hero's humiliation and Beatrice's sudden request that Benedick kill Claudio, which ends with Benedick agreeing to challenge Claudio.

Early Modern English humor has no problem ridiculing people for who they are, but I do not appreciate that kind of humor, and our culture is moving away from it. Dogberry's stupidity may be so far out of the norm that people feel safe laughing at it, but it still makes me uneasy. In production, it is usually the scenes with Dogberry and the watch that fail to entertain. I am thinking especially of Michael Keaton's over-the-top performance in Kenneth Branagh's otherwise delightful 1993 film. Even if the scenes with Dogberry and the watch are intended to be functionally, formally comic (as opposed to humorous), their presence and their essential silliness and meanness seem gratuitous. They clash with the comic elements of the Beatrice/Benedick subplot in a way that demands some kind of explanation.

One useful purpose might be delay. As Robert Cardullo points out with Polonius in *Hamlet*, the presence of the comic within the tragic may serve to delay. He writes,

"Polonius's delay, then, is intricately wound up with Hamlet's in the play. Polonius may provide us with 'comic relief' in Hamlet, but it is not of the gratuitous kind. Rather it is structurally necessary: his delay places Hamlet's own tragic delay or hesitation in perspective; and it leads, in the turning point in the drama—the closet scene—to the stunning, fateful meeting of both 'delaying' forces. Polonius can delay no more, for he is dead; or rather he delays, even in death, by remaining onstage as a corpse." (31)

Delay seems to be the whole point of act 3, scene 5 in *Much Ado About Nothing*, which occurs just before 4.1. The literal message of the scene reinforces the figurative message as Leonato tries to draw out of Dogberry the reason for his presence:

LEONATO. What would you with me, honest neighbor?
DOGBERRY. Marry, sir, I would have some confidence with
you that decerns you nearly.
LEONATO. Brief, I pray you, for you see it is a busy time with
me.

DOGBERRY. Marry, this it is, sir.
VERGES. Yes, in truth it is, sir.
LEONATO. What is it, my good friends?
DOGBERRY. Goodman Verges, sir, speaks a little off the matter —an old man, sir, and his wits are not so blunt as, God help, I would desire they were, but, in faith, honest as the skin between his brows.
VERGES. Yes, I thank God I am as honest as any man living that is an old man and no honester than I.
DOGBERRY. Comparisons are odorous. *Palabras*, neighbor Verges.
LEONATO. Neighbors, you are tedious. (3.5.1–16)

All of this bumbling by Dogberry and Verges serves a formal function within the play that is mirrored by the content of their lines. They are tedious. They create space between the culmination of Don John's plans against Hero, described by Borachio (3.3.142–60), and Hero's public humiliation at her wedding (4.1.30–154). They delay, and by delaying, they generate tension and suspense.

Much Ado About Nothing operates on two different scales of tragedy when it offers relief from potentially tragic outcomes. It is a relief in *Much Ado About Nothing* when Benedick and Beatrice submit to loving one another instead of continuing to act like petulant children, but the stakes are absurdly low from a certain point of view. They seem more real for it, and as a result, more important. Their union is not a matter of life and death, but it is tremendously gratifying to see both of them get to a point in their lives where they can maturely express and accept love for another. It is a relief when Hero gets what she wants, even if it is not what we would want for her, and the stakes are absurdly high and fantastical, with her honor and her life in the balance.

Conclusion

In the preceding ways, certain comic elements in some of Shakespeare's plays, both tragedies and comedies, can be shown to do the opposite of providing relief. That should unsettle anyone who unadvisedly uses that term. Another important function of tragicomic juxtaposition is to keep audiences off balance. Taken as a body of work, they often defy genre conventions and establish expectations that they then violate. Two comedic characters, Mercutio and Polonius, die relatively early in their respective plays. The sad madness and death of Ophelia is unexpected. The ending of King Lear was apparently so traumatic for early audiences that the original text was supplanted by Nahum Tate's adaptation for centuries partly because audiences could not tolerate Cordelia's death (Wells 63). These plays by Shakespeare take audiences for a ride, and sometimes the destination is not certain.

It is difficult for those of us who are so familiar with Shakespeare's plays to remember or imagine what it is like to experience them for the first time. Some may have stopped believing that it would be useful to do so, but doing so can help to get a grasp on these formal matters. The plays are designed to take the audience from no knowledge and understanding to total knowledge and understanding, and from knowing what to expect to wondering what will happen next. Shakespeare's plays employ tragicomic juxtaposition consistently to achieve those effects.

It is also difficult for those of us who primarily experience Shakespeare as a text, as opposed to a performance, to appreciate why genre matters to audiences. Market forces must play a role, and I imagine they are far more important than anyone has yet acknowledged. What would compel someone to decide they wanted to spend money to see one play or another? How could they know what they were buying? Advertisements and word of mouth would certainly have been important, but mostly, I think, it would have been a label. *The Comedy of This* or *The Tragedy of That*. In Shakespeare's plays, the words "comedy" and "tragedy" seem to be more or less marketing tools. When they labeled a play *The Comedy of This* or *The Tragedy of That*, the play's producers were developing expectations that they then managed in various interesting ways as the plays work themselves out. The point seems to be to surprise. Shakespeare's plays are written with the courageous attitude that the customer is not always right, and that they only think that they know what they want. What most of them want is to be surprised. Shakespeare's plays give that gift constantly. What is a label? It is a thing to subvert. Lawrence Danson reports that in Samuel Johnson's opinion, "genres exist precisely as the history of their own subversions and revisions" (5). It would be very surprising if Shakespeare's plays did not have a heavy influence on that opinion.

To return to the idea of comic relief, I know of no credible attempt to make it a useful concept. Given the fact that it has stubbornly refused to die so far, let us at least try to create some reasonable discourse around it. I offer the alternative of tragicomic juxtaposition, which can have various effects depending on situational and formal objectives.

Works Cited

Cardullo, Robert. "The Delay of Polonius in Shakespeare's *Hamlet*." *Studia Neophilologica*, vol. 84, no. 1, 2012, pp. 26–32.

Danson, Lawrence. *Shakespeare's Dramatic Genres*. Oxford UP, 2000.

Madelaine, Richard. "The Apprentice, the Clown, and the Puritan: Comic Revenge as Theatrical Drawing-out in *Twelfth Night*." *Parergon*, vol. 29, no. 1, 2012, pp. 71–82.

Marciano, Lisa. "The Serious Comedy of *Twelfth Night*: Dark Didacticism in Illyria." *Renascence*, vol. 56, no. 1, Spring 2003, pp. 3–19.

Rossiter, A.P. *Angel with Horns and Other Shakespeare Lectures*. Theatre Arts Books, 1961.

Shakespeare, William. *The Complete Works of William Shakespeare*. Edited by David Bevington, Pearson, 2014.

Snyder, Susan. *The Comic Matrix of Shakespeare's Tragedies:* Romeo and Juliet, Hamlet, Othello, *and* King Lear. Princeton UP, 1979.

Tromly, Frederic B. "Macbeth and His Porter." *Shakespeare Quarterly*, vol. 26, no. 2, Spring 1975, pp. 151–56.

Wells, Stanley. Introduction. *The History of King Lear*, by William Shakespeare, Oxford UP, 2000, pp. 1–80.

Williams, Porter, Jr. "Mistakes in *Twelfth Night* and Their Resolution: A Study in Some Relationships of Plot and Theme." *PMLA*, vol. 76, no. 3, June 1961, pp. 193–99.

CRITICAL READINGS

Important Editions of Shakespeare's *Twelfth Night*

Robert C. Evans

Some of the most important work done on any Shakespeare play is the work done by specific editors. The people chosen to edit Shakespeare's works, or to comment on them in "complete" collections, are usually top scholars, and when their work involves editing a single play, such as *Twelfth Night, or What You Will*, they are usually experts on that play in particular. Reading the introductions devoted to a play, either in collected editions or in editions focusing on a specific drama, is usually a good way to get a solid sense of "the best that has been thought and said" about that drama. Moreover, by reading *numerous* introductions, one soon becomes familiar with the main issues and controversies associated with a given play. One hears an ongoing conversation in which different editors and scholars express their sometimes similar, sometimes varied opinions about the topics at hand and present a wide range of relevant evidence to support their views and conclusions.

Editions from the 1950s and 1960s

Bernard Lott, in his introduction (v–xxii) to an edition devoted to *Twelfth Night* and published by Longman in 1959, discusses the play's plot, language, imagery, construction, characters, and effectiveness as drama. He notes the kinds of metaphors, similes, and imagery (especially the imagery found in verse) the play offers; observes that the upper-class characters seldom speak in prose; says that Sir Toby almost never speaks in verse; and suggests that the lower-class characters are most likely to use similes (vi–x). He accepts Leslie Hotson's controversial idea that the play was probably first staged before Queen Elizabeth in the middle of a great hall (x–xi); observes that it has two main plots and deals with the theme of "normal life turned upside down"; investigates its use of dramatic irony; and relates it to the tradition of appointing a "Lord of Misrule" during the holiday season. He finds Malvolio a touching, sympathetic character when he is imprisoned; calls even Sir Andrew pitiable; finds a general "air of sadness" in the play; and suggests that it was probably written immediately before the "great tragedies," such as *Hamlet* (xi–xv). Lott calls Orsino and Olivia "clever and sensible" until love entraps them (xv); says Viola resembles a "fairy-tale princess" (xvii); terms Sebastian a man of action, unlike Orsino (xvii); finds Malvolio's downfall "no laughing matter" (xvii); but thinks that we can ultimately forgive the mistreatment he suffers since we know he will "never improve" (xviii). Lott considers Toby rarely witty; says he seems the "most heartless and cruel" of the characters (xix); finds Sir Andrew more sympathetic because he seems "lonely and helpless" (xx); contends that Feste (probably an older man with a boyish streak) "knows himself as he knows his fellow men" (xx), and perceives Maria as young but level-headed (xx–xxii).

An anonymous 1965 introduction (876–79) to *Twelfth Night* included in a 1972 Signet Classics collected edition edited by Sylvan Barnett calls the play "saturnalian"; emphasizes the theme of misrule; and notes that this comedy both starts and ends with music (876). The play is termed neither escapist nor meaningless but instead relevant to human nature because it examines different kinds of folly and explores either "our native bent for self-deception" or our "difficulty in achieving self-awareness" (877). Shakespeare is said to use drama to "show our growth in self-awareness"; to craft a movement toward a comic conclusion delayed not by standard external impediments (as in his earlier plays) but by the characters' own "deceits and self-deceptions"; and to emphasize the "intellectual and emotional bewilderment" that almost every character exhibits (877). Orsino is called a "sentimentalist who prefers the comfort of his own illusions"; Olivia is said to exhibit a sentimentality "so unreal" that one encounter with Cesario quickly undercuts it and provides a "new obsession"; Toby is said to see others' faults but not his own; and even Viola is termed somewhat self-deceptive. Feste is said to challenge the folly of both Orsino and Olivia (although neither is finally really changed), and Sir Andrew is said to remain a fool while Malvolio remains a narcissist (878). This introduction notes that plots involving twins were used in Western literature long before Shakespeare; that *Twelfth Night* was influenced by various Italian sources (themselves influenced by Plautus); that Shakespeare's play is most indebted to a work by Barnaby Riche that was itself indebted to various sources; that Shakespeare himself invented the Malvolio subplot; and that the First Folio text (the only one) is "clean and tidy" (878–79).

The 1969 *Complete Pelican Shakespeare*, edited by Alfred Harbage, presents an introduction (305–07) to *Twelfth Night* composed by Charles T. Prouty, who suggests that the play was written "about 1600," around the same time as *As You Like It* and *Much Ado about Nothing*, saying that all three works can be called "Joyous Comedies." Prouty notes that two characters in one Italian source were named "Fabio and Malevolti," that an English source features characters named "Olivia and Violetta," and that Shakespeare, in *The Two Gentlemen of Verona*, had already featured "a girl disguised as a page wooing in her master's behalf." Although Prouty thinks Shakespeare's comedies often illustrate the foolishness of irrational love, he notes that Barnaby Riche, Shakespeare's main source, took a much more moralistic view of this issue (305), with Prouty asserting that Riche and another source considered such love "a disease which deprives man or woman of reason." But Shakespeare, according to Prouty, "is not interested in moral judgments; he accepts the [Petrarchan] conventions of love as they existed in the courtly world," presenting Orsino as one who "knows the game" and likening him (in contrast to Olivia and Viola) to Malvolio as a character who cannot see himself objectively. Prouty suggests that whereas some of Shakespeare's sources moralized, Shakespeare himself adopted a comic tone, as when depicting Orsino as a man "more in love with love than with Olivia" (306), and when presenting the love theme in both the main and subplots as anything but serious (307).

Editions from the 1970s

Irving Ribner and George Lyman Kittredge, introducing *Twelfth Night* (393–96) in a collected edition of Shakespeare's works published in 1971 by John Wiley, suggest that it may have been performed even before John Manningham reported seeing it in February 1602 and call it Shakespeare's "culminating achievement in the field of joyous romantic comedy" (393). They note its various Italian sources (some of which had been translated into French and Spanish) and well as various English sources (393–94) and say Olivia lives in "a typical English great house" whereas Orsino inhabits "a never-never land setting." They think Sir Andrew resembles "the gull" commonly found in ancient Roman comedy; note that the mock duel in *Twelfth Night* recalls a similar duel found in Sir Philip Sidney's *Arcadia*; and contend that the harsh treatment of Malvolio resembles the kind of treatment often accorded the "insane" in Elizabethan England (394). They suggest that although Riche treats love as folly to be ridiculed, Shakespeare does not; that Riche's "tone of harsh moralizing is utterly absent from Shakespeare's play"; that *Twelfth Night* illustrates the limitations of Petrarchan love; and that Viola exemplifies "what Plato conceived of as love in its highest and most noble form"—a "love of complete self-sacrifice. By Viola's standard of true devotion," they think, "all of the other varieties of love...are measured and found wanting." Ribner and Kittredge believe that the lovers in the underplot represent different kinds of *false* love; that Sir Andrew's love parodies Orsino's; and that Malvolio embodies self-love. Modern audiences are said to sometimes take the treatment of Malvolio "too seriously," especially because Malvolio is definitely not a "tragic figure" but instead a "comic butt" who is "never treated very harshly in Elizabethan terms" and who is "never more than ridiculous" (395). Sir Toby and Maria are called "wholesome English characters" who "embrace life fully and realistically" (395–96), and the play is said to be full of improbabilities that are part of romance traditions and that should not bother us if they seem improbable (396).

In a 1973 edition of Shakespeare's works, edited by Hardin Craig and David Bevington and often revised by Bevington in subsequent decades, the introduction to *Twelfth Night* (615–18)—ascribed to Alexander Leggatt in later printings—suggests that this play was possibly the last of the so-called "festive comedies" (such as *Much Ado about Nothing* and *As You Like It*). Leggatt thinks it was written possibly as early as 1599; that its "keynote is Saturnalian release and the carnival pursuit of love and mirth" (615); and that the carnival atmosphere is appropriate to the Twelfth Night season of Christmas festivity, when the "stern rigors of a rule-bound society gave way temporarily to playful inversions of authority." Leggatt contends that in this play "Shakespeare lovingly evokes a tradition of festivals and ceremonies that incorporates self-mockery into its celebration of renewal at Christmas time." He discusses the play's sources; notes that Riche moralizes whereas Shakespeare does not; and suggests that the "added subplot, with its rebuking of Malvolio's censoriousness, may have been conceived as a further answer to Riche" and other members of his "sober school" (326). Feste is called a "professional fool, an original stage type for Shakespeare in *Twelfth Night* and in *As You Like It*," who "reinforces the theme of seizing the moment of youth" and of "savoring life's pleasures while still young." Leggatt terms Orsino a "conventional wooer trapped in the courtly love artifice of love's rules" (616) and remarks that although Olivia and Viola both have lost brothers, each responds differently to such loss. He notes that the idea of "fools as naturally wise" was common in the Renaissance (327); and suggests that Olivia is attracted by Viola's "sincerity" in a way that prompts "her to reenter life and accept maturely both the risks and rewards of romantic involvement" (328). The play's same-sex situations are said to be present in Shakespeare's sources and to "reflect a convention quite different from a modern psychological understanding of homosexuality," while Antonio in this play is said to resemble Antonio in *The Merchant of Venice* just as Toby is said to resemble Shakespeare's beloved character named Falstaff (617). Leggatt thinks that Malvolio *does* resemble a Puritan in the way he over-ingeniously interprets Maria's letter and assumes God favors him, while the play's final emphasis on "vengeance and counter-vengeance" is said to suggest "that the triumph of festival will not last long" (618).

Anne Barton's introduction to the play (403–07) in a 1974 edition edited by G. Blakemore Evans et al. notes that King Charles I, like other early readers, took a strong interest in Malvolio. She considers Hotson's theory about an initial court performance hard to believe (403); observes that the play's action "seems to occupy about three months"; says that Shakespeare could easily have made the play obviously relevant to the Twelfth Night holiday but did not; and thinks the title alludes to misrule and "holiday abandon" in general, not to any specific holiday. She discusses the play's various sources; contends that we are not meant to question the idea of "love at first sight" or various other improbabilities; and argues that although Toby rules "as a kind of carnival, or temporary, king," there "is nothing lovely, or even honest, about [his] riotous little court." Barton thinks audiences enjoy the persecution of Malvolio at least until his imprisonment (404) and that Malvolio is victimized by the very holiday traditions he disdains. Although Barton considers many of the characters a bit mad, she thinks Orsino is not a mere "figure of fun," asserting that his early speeches are often beautiful and "intense, metaphoric, and imaginative" even if his obsession with Olivia depends on her "very absence and lack of response." Barton finds "something forced and abnormal" about Olivia's grieving but also "something noble" and believes that Olivia's "ignominious collapse" into passion for Viola is both "necessary" and "sad."

Barton thinks *Twelfth Night* simultaneously looks back to Shakespeare's early comedies and forward to his late "romances"; notes that Viola refuses to try to impose her own will on events; says she waits "to see what Time will bring"; and argues that her disguise allows her to do this, so that by remaining "aware but passive," Viola ultimately achieves all she could hope to achieve. According to Barton, Feste seems at home in neither household he visits and is not involved in the gulling of Malvolio until the imprisonment scene. She finds the play's final tone dark, especially concerning Andrew, Toby, and Antonio (406), and notes that we never hear how Maria feels about marrying Toby, while Malvolio remains alienated. Barton writes that "Olivia and Sebastian, Viola and Orsino confront us at the end less as representatives of a new society than as people who, by the special dispensation of Comedy, have been allowed to escape from death and time." Andrew, Toby, Maria, and Malvolio are all absent as the play concludes, while Feste is also absent except at the very end. His final song, Barton suggests, recalls the "ages of man" theme also dealt with in *As You Like It*, although this theme's "basic pessimism is informed and sweetened...not only by the music to which it is set, but by the tolerance and acceptance of Feste himself," who can "be trusted to speak for all mankind" (407).

One of the most important editions of *Twelfth Night* published in the 1970s (and indeed in the twentieth century) was the one edited by J. M. Lothian and T. W. Craik as part of the highly esteemed Arden Shakespeare series. Lothian and Craik devoted sections of their introduction (xvii–xcviii) to the play's text, date, title, sources, and critical tradition, while also offering their own detailed critical analysis by acts and scenes and discussing the ways the play has been staged. They also offered two appendices: one dealing with an important source (Riche's *Riche his Farewell to Militarie Profession*) and another dealing with the play's songs. Among their most interesting contentions were their claim that the very early performance at London's Middle Temple may not have been the first (xxvii), their reasons for rejecting Leslie Hotson's theories about the play (xxviii–xxx), their doubt that the play was composed specifically to commemorate the Twelfth Night Christmas-season holiday (xxxiv), and their reasons for thinking that the play was first performed sometime in the late fall of 1601 (xxxiv). Their discussion of the play's sources is extensive (xxxv–l) and includes the play's relations with Shakespeare's own earlier works. When surveying previous criticism (l–lxi), they note the popularity of scenes involving Malvolio, disagreements about how "moral" the play has been considered to be, the widespread nineteenth-century assumption that the play was generally "sunny" in mood, the later emphasis on both its "gaiety" and its "pathos," and the even later stress on its melancholy aspects, with some critics seeing it as Shakespeare's "farewell to comedy" (lii–liii). Twentieth-century critics often sought to explain the play's balance of moods (light and dark), its thematic unity (lv), and its complex treatment of Malvolio and other characters. Lothian and Craik warn against finding the work's conclusion too dark (lx).

Some main points of their own critical analysis involve their suggestions that the opening scene with Orsino should not be perceived as mainly satirical (as it often is); that Orsino is a generally admirable character (lxiii–lxiv); that Viola's soliloquy in 3.2 is "the pivot of the play" (lxvii); that the alternations between Orsino's court and Olivia's home often involve thematic juxtapositions (lxviii); and that the scene involving Malvolio's imprisonment focuses less on Malvolio than on Feste (lxxv). In general, Lothian and Craik find Malvolio, even at the end, a less sympathetic and pitiable character than other critics have found him (lxxix). Their overview of various theatrical productions (lxxix–xcviii) is detailed and substantive and emphasizes that Malvolio has often been seen as the central character and that he has been variously interpreted as either an object of ridicule or an object of sympathy (xc–xcii). They think audiences have always liked Viola (xciii), that she must never seem *too* male (xciv), that Feste has been increasingly treated as a major character (xcv), that the "kitchen scene" (2.3) is sometimes overdone (xcvi), that the duel scene is comical but need not be farcical (xcvii), and that the "prison scene" should focus less on Malvolio than on Feste (xcvii), who, they stress, should not end the play as an "outcast" (xcviii). As all these comments suggest, the "introduction" by Lothian and Craik is impressively thorough and exemplifies why the Arden Shakespeare editions are so much admired.

Editions from the 1980s and 1990s

Elizabeth Story Donno's 1985 New Cambridge edition includes an introduction (1–44) that discusses the play's date and title (1–5); disputes Leslie Hotson's thesis of an initial performance at court in winter (1–3); notes the play's setting in spring or summer; observes that John Marston also wrote a play called *What You Will* (a proverbial phrase); and mentions that a similar phrase ("that's all one") appears often in *Twelfth Night* (4–5). After noting the play's various source materials (5–8), Donno suggests that Shakespeare not only toned some of them down but also juxtaposed the fantastical main plot with the more realistic subplot (which he invented) and drew on his earlier comic writings while also skillfully blending the two main storylines (7–8). Offering her own critical commentary (8–23), she notes that early audiences focused on Malvolio (8), that Toby is given the most lines (8), and that most of the characters (except for Feste and perhaps Toby) seem young but have not always been played as such (8–9). Donno finds Feste "irresistible," thinks he distances himself mentally from both households (10), suggests that he was played by comedian Robert Armin (11), and comments that Feste presents "through his nonsense a no-nonsense point of view" (12). Commenting on Malvolio (12–16), she offers four artists' conceptions of this character (14–15; see also 21–22) and notes that he, like the play's structure, characterization, and plot, has provoked critical disagreements, with some critics suggesting inconsistencies in all these aspects of the play and with others (including Donno) commending Shakespeare's subtlety, especially in creating similarities between characters, such as Olivia and Viola (16–17), and even Olivia and Malvolio (17–23). Donno sees both "sad and merry madness" as a main trait of many characters (20) and comments on the sometimes positive, sometimes negative responses the final song has elicited, with Donno herself seeing it as signaling a return from fantasy to reality (23).

Briefly discussing "Critical Fashions" in the reception of the play, she notes that critics have often disagreed about its final tone and that it has been less studied than some of Shakespeare's earlier comedies (23–24). Then, turning to its theatrical history (24–40), she notes some plays it inspired (24–26), the ways it was adapted, the fact that it was not played for several decades after the 1660 Restoration (26–27), the nineteenth-century tendency to encumber it with stage spectacle (27–28), and the frequent return to "simplified staging" in the twentieth century (28; see also 33–34). In the nineteenth century, Malvolio was often presented as a pompous Spaniard (28–29) and the music and songs were sometimes dropped (29). Different actors' depictions of Malvolio are discussed (29–33): sometimes he was played "straight," sometimes given a "tragic aura," and sometimes "burlesqued" (33). Donno ends by discussing productions directed by Peter Hall, Clifford Williams, John Barton, Peter Gill, Terry Hands, and John Caird (33–40).

One of the most important editions from the 1990s was edited by Roger Warren and Stanley Wells in 1994 for Oxford University

Press. In their "Introduction" (1–80), Warren and Wells argue that *Twelfth Night* "was probably written in 1601, either immediately before or straight after *Hamlet*" (1). They note that it has not "always been as popular in the theatre as it is today" (1), that it was largely ignored in the later seventeenth century (2), that it became increasingly popular in the nineteenth century (3), but that the elaborate Victorian productions eventually gave way, in the twentieth century, to productions closer to the simpler ones of Shakespeare's own time (3–4). They caution against seeing the play as strictly relevant to the Christmas holiday of Twelfth Night, instead stressing its "autumnal" and even summery moods (4–8), and they then discuss the setting in Illyria, the ease with which the play can be staged and the ways it *has* been staged by such recent directors as Bill Alexander, Peter Hall, John Barton, Peter Gill, and others (8–14). They compare and contrast Shakespeare's work with its various English (and often Italian) sources; note the potential importance of Emanuel [sic] Forde's *Parismus* (14–19); and discuss this comedy's similarities to and differences from such earlier Shakespeare works as *The Comedy of Errors* and *Love's Labour's Lost* (19–24). Seeing "Kinds of Love" as a key theme in *Twelfth Night*, they then move carefully through discussions of various characters and scenes, calling Viola and Olivia equally poised and witty; stressing the importance of different perspectives in Shakespeare's comedy; and contending that in presenting Olivia on stage, a "careful balance" should be struck between "youth and maturity, between innocence and experience" (34). They consider 2.4 the play's "emotional heart" (34); suggest that both Orsino and the entire play are full of "shifting moods" (36); and regard the relationship between Antonio and Sebastian as yet another example of the larger "kinds of love" motif (39). Regarding Malvolio (another kind of "lover"), they note that he first became an object of some sympathy in the nineteenth century (43); that actors have often tried to present him as "human" and "complex" (44); that his very name, however, suggests that he is ill-intentioned (45); and that the very extremity of his passions makes the passions of Orsino and Olivia less ridiculous (51). Warren and Wells find various "problems" in the "intrigue actions" (52), especially in setting up the mock duel (53) and in the ways various productions have tried to handle such problems (55). They think Fabian's presence is problematic because he appears in scenes that would work best by emphasizing Feste (55), whose wisdom, they suggest, derives from his age and experience (57) and whose character has been the source of some disagreement among critics, with some finding him comic and others finding him callous (58). Commenting at length on the long final scene, Warren and Wells suggest that it presents Orsino in an often positive light (61); that it brings out a theme of violence implied earlier in the work (62); that it fails to present (as in other comedies) an "all-inclusive harmony" (63); that it juxtaposes the cruel dismissal of Aguecheek with the wondrous reunion of Viola and Sebastian (63); and that this reunion is the play's "emotional climax" (64). They see Malvolio's famous final outburst as perhaps implying "outraged bluster rather than heartbreak" (69); argue that Feste seems isolated at the end (70); and find his final song not entirely (if mostly) sad. They then comment extensively on textual issues (73–76).

In the 1997 Norton complete works, Stephen Greenblatt (1761–67) discusses *Twelfth Night*'s emphasis on costumes and suggests that even at the very end Orsino cannot "bring himself to call his bride-to-be by her rightful name or to address her as a woman" (1761). Greenblatt thinks that Shakespeare could have solved this problem but chose not to; that the "transforming power of costume unsettles fixed categories of gender and social class"; and that Shakespeare's culture was hostile to the "same-sex desire and cross-class marriage" this play presents (1762). According to Greenblatt, *Twelfth Night* shares with *Hamlet* an emphasis on "mourning, betrayal, antic humor, and tragic isolation" and links desire "repeatedly" with "frustration and loss" (1762). He thinks the play's title implies a "festivity" that offers "release from tensions that might otherwise prove dangerous" (1762) and that the play itself, unlike one of its main sources, mingles "melancholy and delight" and shows Viola trusting to fate (1763). Greenblatt argues that Malvolio desires less "erotic bliss" than "social domination"; that he is treated like "mad" people were often treated in Early Modern England; and that ultimately he suffers something worse than humiliation (being forgotten) while Viola and Sebastian both seem to achieve what Malvolio only desired: having an upper-class woman fall in love with them (1764). Greenblatt regards Orsino's love as self-centered —unlike Antonio's devoted, self-sacrificing affection for Sebastian (1765)—and asserts that the only real bond Orsino forges is with his page (Viola), in whom he expresses a sincere (and therefore unusual) interest. Viola herself, according to Greenblatt, is "extraordinarily resilient," resourceful, and adaptive: she exhibits an "improvisational boldness, an eloquent tongue, and a keen wit" that all "keep her afloat" in confusing situations, thus in some ways resembling Feste (1766).

Editions from the 2000s

Jonathan Crewe, introducing *Twelfth Night* (438–45) first in 2000 in a single-volume edition and then in 2002 for a comprehensive Penguin compilation of Shakespeare's works, notes that

> the common testimony of readers and theatergoers would suggest that the play is singularly accessible and unthreatening; that its characters are generally engaging and its situations amusing; that its language is eloquent and sometimes magical; that its romantic intensity is rendered all the more appealing by Shakespeare's delicate irony; that its humor is "dry" (the play's own term) rather than harsh; that many of its characters, with the touchingly sorry exception of Sir Andrew Aguecheek, show a dazzling capacity for repartee; that the entertainment provided, by turns poignant and witty, sensitive and robust, verbal and musical, never palls; that its comic plots and motifs are skillfully integrated; that it is, generally speaking, a reader-and actor-friendly play.

Yet Crewe also finds it "difficult to overlook the darker, more disillusioning moments in *Twelfth Night*—among them, its ending with the melancholic clown, soaked to the skin, alone onstage—as well as the persistence in the play of cruel spectacle, such as the tormenting of Malvolio, for which bearbaiting is one of the play's own recurrent metaphors." This mixed tone, he thinks, is appropriate to the holiday named in the title: "Twelfth Night, falling on January 6, was both a festive occasion and the date, twelve days after Christmas, on which the festive season traditionally ended" (438).

Commenting on the adjective "Saturnalian"—often used to describe the play—Crewe observes that in "ancient Rome, the term 'Saturnalia' referred to forms of unrestrained merrymaking that marked the festival of Saturn, held in the middle of December, yet the term became more broadly synonymous with festivities in which public order, authority, and restraint were grossly flouted." He reports that "the Latin term *Saturnalia* also recalled the Age of Saturn as the legendary golden age of humankind before the advent of social inequality, war, poverty, labor, and oppression. To participate in the Saturnalia, as even slaves were licensed to do, was thus to commemorate a legendary better world and a common humanity; paradoxically, then, the most disorderly festivities partook of the sacred." Crewe comments that "Saturnalian language and consciousness persisted strongly throughout the European Middle Ages, manifesting themselves in revelry, travesties and masquerades, aggressive verbal play, and celebrations of folly. The fool in *Twelfth Night*," he remarks, "is appropriately named Feste, festivity incarnate." According to Crewe, "*Twelfth Night* reveals an underlying concern on Shakespeare's part with forms of historical untimeliness, upsetting grossness, incivility, excess, boredom, ill humor, cruelty, manipulation, irresponsibility, cynicism, and outright madness that had rendered festive culture questionable." Yet the "denial of folly and its pleasures, attempted by Malvolio in the play, can thus only seem like the greatest folly of all, whatever its reasons, and like the one intolerable form of foolishness." Crewe suggests that what "contributes as well as festivity to the relaxed atmosphere of *Twelfth Night* is the marked absence in the play of powerful authority figures, whether familial, political, or religious." He thinks "Olivia's unusual independence as mistress of a household following the deaths of her father and brother (a situation no doubt modeled in part on that of the young Queen Elizabeth I) precludes Orsino from dominating her" (439) and that although "Olivia's uncle/kinsman, Sir Toby seeks to occupy the place of a father in her household,...his unruly behavior makes him more like a wayward child or brother than a parent to her, and his calculating introduction of Sir Andrew into her household as a suitor hardly fits him to be her guardian. It is into the empty space of masculine authority, dignity, and control that Malvolio...tries to insert himself" (439–40).

In a particularly interesting section of his generally interesting introduction, Crewe discusses the play's treatment of twins. "Normally," he suggests, "those who are not twins tend to take their identity for granted. The situation of identical twins, whose identities are forever at risk of being mistaken, seems anomalous. The peculiarity of an identical twin is that he or she is not unique (self-identical) but identical to someone else, thus apparently possessing only a shared, divided, or mirror identity." According to Crewe, "twins represent a threat to an assumed norm of human identity" although such anxiety is "less present" in this play than in, say, *The Comedy of Errors*. Through "our identification with stage twins," Crewe argues, "we are called on to recognize that the identity we carry around, as if it were a kind of inalienable property, exists only under particular conditions of place and time" (440), so that "the comedy of mistaken identity is a lesson in the complex, social, and always compromised nature of human identity" (441). In *Twelfth Night*, Crewe suggests, "the question of who has identity is posed in the context of gender as well as property. Does full identity belong to men only, while such identity and dignity as women can enjoy must always be derived from men (fathers, brothers, lovers, husbands)?" Is it only when "Viola goes into male disguise," he asks, "that women can temporarily borrow 'real' identity from men?"

Crewe also suggests that *Twelfth Night* asks us how we should "come to terms with selves that are not only internally divided but internally questing, fluid, and even promiscuous, their wishes not necessarily capable of being played out in any single identity, role, or gender." Both Orsino and Olivia, he thinks, "dangerously deviate from social norms when responding to the disguised Viola," so that the play may imply that "socially mandated heterosexual marriage cannot resolve all issues of desire and identity" and so that in "a manner consistent with the play's alternative title, *What You Will*, identities and roles can be doubled, improvised, or transgressively played, both despite and because of coercive, homogenizing social norms" (442). Those social norms also restrict Malvolio, especially his ambition to marry above his social rank; thus, his eventual humiliation, among other things, "could hardly have failed to operate as a public warning as well: know your place; do not presume too far; do not take the promises of romance too seriously; do not take fiction literally" (443–44). "Malvolio's fate," according to Crewe, "serves as a warning," and "Maria's play-within-the-play is performing one of the main traditional functions of comedy—namely, to impose discipline and inflict punishment on social transgressors. Contrary to first impressions, it is the repressive, controlling, yet desiring Malvolio—not the riotous Sir Toby—who is potentially the most disruptive figure in *Twelfth Night*." Thus, paradoxically, "it is Malvolio's excess of desire rather than any lack of it that makes him seem dangerous," so that, as "much as Malvolio is an agent of repression in the play, he is ultimately the object of its repression." Crewe arguably offers an unusually thought-provoking brief introduction to *Twelfth Night*.

Jonathan Bate and Eric Rasmussen, in an edition published in 2007 for the Modern Library, introduce *Twelfth Night* (645–49) by emphasizing the relevance of Plato's idea that we are all seeking the soul mates with whom we were originally joined but from whom we are now split (645). Noting the traditional literature of twins falling in love but observing that Shakespeare avoids that tradition's incestual overtones, they mention the recent death of his own twin son Hamnet, the brother of his daughter Judith (646). Bate and Rasmussen contend that by pretending to be male, Viola can "break the shackles of [female] passivity" and that she plays a male well because of her familiarity with her brother Sebastian (646–47) but that she ultimately seems to revert to female "silence and passivity." Arguing that *Twelfth Night* quickly followed *Hamlet* and that complex relations exist between the two works (647), they also think *Twelfth Night* reflects Shakespeare's "friendly rivalry" with fellow playwright Ben Jonson, who had recently begun penning satirical comedies, so that Shakespeare's double-titled comedy may mock the similar double title of Jonson's *Cynthia's Revels* (which also deals with self-love), just as it may mock that play's emphasis on the word "element." They write that "Jonsonian comedy is peopled with narcissists" and that "*Twelfth Night* responds with an astonishing exploration of the relationship between knowledge of self and sympathy for others" (648). In a brief but useful list of facts, they note such matters as the percentage of lines assigned to each character (Toby-13 percent, Viola-13 percent, Olivia-12 percent, Feste-12 percent, Malvolio-11 percent, Orsino-9 percent, Sir Andrew-6 percent, Maria-6 percent, Sebastian-5 percent, Fabian-4 percent, Antonio-4 percent) and report that 40 percent of the play is written in verse and 60 percent in prose (649).

In a new and quite substantial Arden Shakespeare edition published in 2008, Keir Elam's lengthy introduction (1–153) calls *Twelfth Night* one of Shakespeare's "most popular and admired" plays; says it "demonstrably works on stage" (1); comments that it gives "many actors the chance to shine"; observes that it has long been approved by audiences and critics; and says that it is often considered its author's best and most mature comedy (2). Surveying the history of audience responses, he observes that Malvolio, right from the start, was often emphasized in those reactions (4–6); that after the Restoration Samuel Pepys and others influenced by neo-classical ideas often disliked the play (6–7); but notes that it was, in fact, admired by such important later critics as Samuel Johnson and William Hazlitt, among others (7). Elam reports that audiences often become sympathetic to Malvolio either in the cross-gartering scene or in the imprisonment scene (8); comments that *Twelfth Night* is in "many ways one of Shakespeare's most enigmatic" works; suggests that it plays on our "yearning to know and to understand" (11); and thinks that the decipherment of texts, bodies, hearts, and events is a main theme (15). He notes, for instance, many (often strained) critical attempts to decipher the "M.O.A.I." riddle (16) and the "c.u.t. joke," which has sometimes been seen as sexual and sometimes as alluding to cutpurses (17).

Like many previous commentators, Elam associates the work with carnival. He wonders who (Feste? Toby? Maria?) is in charge of the misrule presented (18–19); notes that religious Puritans opposed holiday misrule; and observes that the play is now commonly associated with social renewal (20–21). He reports that one critic (Barbara Lewalski) has seen Viola and Sebastian as comically resembling the incarnate Christ (in line with the Christian Twelfth Night holiday [21]) and that R. Chris Hassell has related it to the tradition of religious epiphany plays (21–22), which often involve enlightenment (22). Elam himself suggests that perhaps *Twelfth Night*, through its title, promises an epiphany but "strategically withholds it" (24).

He sees Feste as the play's "most astute commentator" (24); notes that the work presents many anagrammatically named characters (such as Viola and Olivia); and discusses the similarities between Viola and Olivia, including the fact that both have recently suffered the losses of their fathers and brothers. Elam thinks Malvolio's name suggests that he is the women's "negative image" (25) and that the name of Sir Topas echoes Sir Toby's. He comments that *Twelfth Night* is Shakespeare's second play (along with *The Comedy of Errors*) featuring twins and suggests that Viola becomes her own twin and thus undermines sexual difference (27) and "binarity" (28). He thinks the play's many references to eyes imply the importance of different perspectives (28); finds Orsino's opening speech almost auto-erotic (30); and argues that Malvolio, Orsino, and Olivia all fail to perceive the "illusory nature of their supposed desire," which is "only nominally directed outside themselves" (32). Elam's lengthy discussion of "pictures, paintings, and other iconographic images" (33–50) mentions various kinds of material objects, such as architecture, furniture, clothing, and fabrics. Later come discussions of such matters as whether transvestism in Shakespeare's day was erotically arousing (49); the paradoxes of Viola's cross-dressing (49–50); and the issue of Antonio's homoeroticism, which has been variously suppressed (on some nineteenth-century stages) and acknowledged (in many modern productions; 50). Viola, according to Elam, arouses homoerotic desire both in Olivia and

Orsino, while Sebastian arouses it in Antonio (50). Discussions soon follow of "reading the body" and of "the body as text" (50–55); of "disease, contagion, and death" (55–57); of "castration, civility, and intertextuality" (including Andrew's emasculation; 57–68); of "space and place" (including the two locations; 77); of "levels of temporality" (77–78); and of "language and discourse" (including rhetorical doubling; 78–87).

Elam calls *Twelfth Night* "perhaps Shakespeare's most class-conscious play" (86), while the section on the play in performance says it is "replete with the language of performance" (88); is full of detailed scripting of costume and behavior (88); involves frequent use of doors (89); requires a "dark-room" space (a problem that has been variously solved; 90–91); but is otherwise minimalist in specified staging and props (91). According to Elam, the work juxtaposes Andrew's thinness with Toby's corpulence (91); has been seen as divided either into two halves or as full of scenes juxtaposed with one another (92); and has frequently succeeded on stage, from its first known staging down to the present day (92–93). Elam is more open than many critics to Hotson's theory about an initial performance before the queen (94) and skeptically discusses recent claims that it was first performed for lawyers (95–96). He surveys four different possible first performances: at court, at the Middle Temple (where lawyers studied), at the Globe, and at a private venue before the play then transferred first to the Middle Temple and then to the public stage. He finds the last possibility most convincing but admits that the evidence for any of these claims is scanty (96).

Elam next surveys later productions, including the post-Restoration performances Pepys saw and disliked in the 1660s; a 1703 adaptation; and many performances (often with various textual revisions) in the nineteenth century, which are reflected both in various acting editions from that period as well as in various musical adaptations (96–100). He discusses "Victorian special effects and modernist experiments" (100–06); the tendency of productions in the last fifty years to emphasize either particular seasons or specific (especially "exotic") locations (106–17); and the tendency to offer particular approaches, such as a famous version from the early 2000s featuring an all-male cast (113–17). Commenting about "*Twelfth Night* on film" (117–21), Elam discusses how films from 1910, 1955, 1972, 1996, and 1998 have dealt with the play and how it was televised in 1937, 1949, 1950, 1957, 1970, 1980, 1987, and 2003. He then briefly deals with various roles and how actors have approached them (122–23) before focusing especially on Malvolio (123–30), whom actors have played by variously emphasizing his pomposity, dignity, grotesqueness, psychological problems, class consciousness, ambition, eccentricity, comic behavior, and odd movements. Toby has been played as large, farcical, and alcoholic (131–32); Sir Andrew as either slow-witted, fearful, effeminate, or pathetic (132–34); while Feste (probably first played by Robert Armin) has sometimes seen his role cut or pruned. When it has been retained, he has been variously played as older, sardonic, angry, and/or speaking a variety of accents (134–37). Orsino has been played as "sincerely passionate," as decadent, as effetely sensual, and/or as violent, angry, or macho (137–38), while Olivia has appeared either as "gracefully mature," skittishly impulsive, frivolously youthful, or openly erotic (138–42). Actors playing Viola have presented her as variously grave, graceful, feminine, exaggeratedly male, convincingly male, deliberately androgynous, and/or vocally musical (142–45).

Finally, one more edition seems worth mentioning: the revised Cambridge edition updated in 2017 with a new introduction (1–60) by Penny Gay. In her introduction's initial pages, Gay covers much familiar ground. She comments on the play's date and early performances (1–3) and concludes that it "is safest to assume that the play had its first performance at the Globe in 1600 or 1601" (3). Commenting on the work's sources (4–6), she finds in one Italian source "at least four scenes that are strikingly close to scenes in Shakespeare" (4) while also stressing that the main source was Barnaby Riche (4–5) and additionally mentioning another Italian source (5–6). In a section on "Imaginary Geography and Stage Space" (6–8), Gay discusses the setting in Illyria (which she suggests "may evoke *illusion* and *lyrical* to modern ears"; 6) while also noting how the text often alludes to places in London and how often the two doors used in early (and many later) productions provide many chances for "near misses" as Viola and Sebastian enter and exits scenes (7). Commenting on "Puritans and Clowns" (9–15), she observes that the subplot echoes the main plot; that the play alludes to the seasons of carnival and Lent; that Malvolio is associated both with Lenten attitudes (9) and the controversial rise of Elizabethan Puritanism (9–10); and that in the nineteenth century he was often portrayed as a pompous Spaniard (10–11). Stewards, Gay reports, were expected to supervise their underlings, but she also suggests that Malvolio, in his relations with Olivia, symbolizes the powerful male father and brother figures now absent from her life (11). She says that in his yellow stockings he resembles the kind of clown he disdains; that clowns and madmen often resembled each other in Shakespeare's day; and that clowns "in Shakespearean comedy are liminal figures—wanderers, observers, commentators, with a sceptical, even cynical perspective on the world of romance and myth" (13). Noting that many recent productions therefore keep Feste onstage throughout the play, she also observes that Viola and Feste sometimes act like a comic stand-up duo; that both rely on their "intelligence and wit"; and that there "is no place for either the clown or the puritan in the world of romance" (15).

Next discussing "Time, Chance and the Poetry of Romance" (15–19), Gay contrasts Orsino's passivity with Sebastian's active nature; suggests that Viola's trust in "'time' is one of the keynotes" of her character (16); notes the explicit reference to clock time in 3.1 (17); and suggests that in his very final comments Orsino may be as complacent as he has been through most of the play (19). In a section on "Myths and Metamorphosis" (19–23), Gay discusses the Ovidian myth of Narcissus (whom Orsino resembles; 20–21); the related myth of Echo (21–23); and mythic treatments of twins (23–25). She next explores issues of "Gender, Sexuality and the Stage" (25–27), suggesting that the play "flirts with the possibility of same-sex love, only, apparently, to eschew it in the 'real' social world of Orsino and Olivia"; that while the play seems to endorse heterosexuality it also alludes to the Platonic ideal of close friendship between males (25); and that male-male affection would probably not have shocked Shakespeare's audience because there was so much precedent for it, especially in classical literature (26). Concerning the play's "Language" (27–29), Gay suggests that much of "Viola's attraction as a heroine lies in her eloquence"; that Viola often speaks in soliloquy (27); that she sometimes speaks pathetically and sometimes as a "self-delighting performer" (especially when addressing the audience); and that she inhabits a play full of puns, riddles, and "near-anagrams" (28), such as "Viola, Olivia, and Malvolio"—names not in Shakespeare's sources (29). The play's focus on "Riddles" (29–31), according to Gay, involves even its title and subtitle (29); is apparent especially when Malvolio tries to interpret the letter; and that Viola, unlike Malvolio, "is a *maker* of riddles" (30). Commenting on the topic of "Music" (31–33), Gay notes that six of the play's eighteen scenes "contain specific directions for music" (31); that Feste's final song (which Gay finds somewhat depressingly repetitive) echoes such key themes of the play as "love, death, and time"; and that the play's stress on music may reflect the likelihood that Robert Armin, who probably first played Feste, was a talented singer (33). Briefly discussing "Critical Fashions" in interpreting *Twelfth Night*, Gay contends that "reading the play as a simple instance of carnival festivity has been found inadequate" (35) and that feminism is in many ways "the strongest and most influential strand of contemporary criticism" (35–36).

In a survey of *Twelfth Night*'s "Stage History" (36–41), Gay comments briefly on various early, post-Restoration, and eighteenth-century productions; notes the rise of women actors playing the women's roles (38–39); comments on Victorian preferences for using the whole original play (rather than pruned versions or adaptations) and for "realistic" settings; and discusses the frequent modernist preference for minimalism and symbolism. In the early twentieth century the play was often set in the period from 1600–1630 and melancholy was often stressed. According to Gay, often "Feste was an ageing clown, Viola tended to be petite and somewhat timid, [and] Olivia a rather grand dignified lady in her thirties (or more)" (39). Things began to change, however, after World War II, when women became more assertive and the play's characters were sometimes presented as members of minority groups, such as Jews an homosexuals, with Viola becoming "a much stronger and more competent figure" (40–41). Discussing "'Autumnal'" stagings of the play, with a sometimes-Chekhovian flavor (41–48), Gay surveyed productions directed by Peter Hall, Terry Hands, John Caird, Sam Mendes, Adrian Noble, Declan Donnellan, Timothy Sheader, Neil Bartlett, David Farr, and others, while her comments about "Carnival *Twelfth Night*s" (49) featured references to productions directed by Sean Holmes, Des McAnuff, Aaron Posner, John Basill, and others. A section on "Local Shakespeares" (53–57) dealt especially with Australian productions; a section on "'Original Practices'" (57–58) preferred an American Shakespeare Center production over the one directed by Tim Carroll for the London Globe theater; while a concluding section of "Adaptations" (58–60) mentioned various continental European stagings, several films, and a one-man show based on Malvolio.

Conclusion

As the foregoing survey suggests, scholars have found no dearth of issues to discuss when introducing the play, whether confining themselves to just a few pages or when writing introductions of much greater length. Each author of a new introduction has probably examined the introductions that came before, if only to avoid merely repeating what has already been said. This means that each new introduction has usually had, at least to some degree, something new to say—some fresh evidence to discuss or some novel insights to offer. The result is a critical "conversation" that has lasted for decades if not centuries—a conversation in which each new voice profits from having listened carefully to prior voices before trying to add something useful to the discussion.

Works Cited

Anonymous. "Introduction." *Twelfth Night*, by William Shakespeare. *Complete Signet Shakespeare*. Edited by Sylvan Barnett. Harcourt, Brace, Jovanovich, 1972, pp. 876–79.

Barton, Anne. [Introduction]. *Twelfth Night*, by William Shakespeare. *The Riverside Shakespeare*. Edited by G. Blakemore Evans, et al. Houghton Mifflin, 1974, pp. 403–07.

Bate, Jonathan, and Eric Rasmussen. [Introduction]. *Complete Works*, by William Shakespeare. Edited by Bate and Rasmussen. Modern Library, 2007, pp. 645–49.

Crewe, Jonathan. "Introduction." *Twelfth Night*, by William Shakespeare. *William Shakespeare: The Complete Works*. Edited by Stephen Orgel and A. R. Braunmuller. Penguin, 2002, pp. 436–45.

Donno, Elizabeth Story. "Introduction." *Twelfth Night*, by William Shakespeare. Cambridge UP, 1985, pp. 1–40.

Elam, Keir. "Introduction." *Twelfth Night*, by William Shakespeare. The Arden Shakespeare series. Arden, 2008, pp. 1–153.

Gay, Penny. "Introduction." *Twelfth Night*, by William Shakespeare. Cambridge UP, 2017, pp. 1–60.

Greenblatt, Stephen. [Introduction]. *Twelfth Night*, by William Shakespeare. *The Norton Shakespeare*. Edited by Stephen Greenblatt, et al. Norton, 1997, pp. 1761–67.

Leggatt, Alexander. "Introduction." *Twelfth Night*, by William Shakespeare. *Complete Works of William* Shakespeare. Edited by Hardin Craig and David Bevington. Addison-Wesley, 1973, pp. 615–18.

Lott, Bernard. "Introduction." *Twelfth Night*, by William Shakespeare. Longman, 1959, pp. v–xxii.

Lothian, J. M., and T. W. Craik. "Introduction." *Twelfth Night*, by William Shakespeare. Edited by Lothian and Craik. Methuen, 1975, pp. xvii–xcviii.

Prouty, Charles T. "Introduction." *Twelfth Night*, by William Shakespeare. *William Shakespeare: The Complete Works*. Edited by Alfred Harbage. Penguin Books, 1969, pp. 305–07.

Ribner, Irving, and Hardin Craig. "Introduction." *Twelfth Night*, by William Shakespeare. *Complete Works of Shakespeare*. Edited by Ribner and Craig. John Wiley, 1971, pp. 393–96.

Warren, Roger, and Stanley Wells. "Introduction." *Twelfth Night*, by William Shakespeare. Oxford UP, 1994, pp. 1–80.

Religion in *Twelfth Night*: A Critical Overview

Brandon Schneeberger

One of the most discussed aspects of Shakespeare's popular play *Twelfth Night* concerns the subject of religion. Critics have primarily commented on the Christian allusions in the play. This includes discussion of the relevance of the feast of Epiphany from Shakespeare's title, the importance of Puritanism, theological topics such as the Trinity, and possible allusions to Catholicism and post-Reformation theological debates. This essay will chronologically survey ten articles or book chapters, covering over forty years of criticism. While topics have certainly overlapped throughout the years, earlier discussion of the play in the 1970s and 1980s tended to focus on the importance of *Twelfth Night*'s title and the relevance of Twelfth Night festivities in the comedy as well as commentary on Malvolio's supposed Puritanism. Essays following the 1990s invite discussion on other religious themes within the play, including the Trinity, the possible influence of Catholicism, and the religious implications of mourning and grief.

1970s–1990s: The Feast of Epiphany and Anti-Puritanism

Chris Hassel discusses the importance of Christian feast days, specifically Epiphany and Candlemas, in his book *Renaissance Drama and the English Church Year* (1979). Hassel argues that the theme of "the humility of Christ and the humiliation of man...lies close to the systematic humiliations that Olivia and Orsino must undergo to escape the bondage of their excessive self-love" (79). Olivia must give up her prideful, self-indulgent grief, and falls in love with a page who not only rejects her love for Orsino but is in fact a woman (81). Indeed, her "ultimate humiliation is public and painful" and she must "wonder what on earth she has chosen to wed...through much of the final act" (81). Orsino's cure, however, takes more time as his self-love is greater and he "thus makes an absolute fool of himself in public" when he banishes Viola in act 5 (82). Both nevertheless end up in gratuitous, unmerited love relationships, which Hassel describes as "joy [that is] a romantic experience of the first order" and "an experience not irrelevant to the festival of Epiphany" (82). Moreover, Feste's character also serves as a light-hearted call to humility and self-knowledge and Hassel traces the religious background of the wise fool to provide context for Feste's important role. Feste functions as "fool and curate" who "repeatedly leads his victims to the acknowledgement of their folly that will ultimately free them to rejoice in the festivity of a greater wisdom" (83). Feste's most difficult, and unsuccessful, "ministry" in *Twelfth Night* is Malvolio, who "will never laugh at himself as [Olivia] did" and will "never enact this comic equivalent of wisdom and salvation" (84). In a following chapter of his book, Hassel touches on the importance of Candlemas, the feast day on which *Twelfth Night* was at least twice performed. Hassel points to "Marian characteristics of the festival" as well as its relationship to Epiphany (95). Just as Epiphany is a festival of lights and a call for spiritual purification, so, too, is Candlemas, a feast that celebrates the purification of the Virgin Mary and the grace received from her (95–97). Hassel finishes his discussion of *Twelfth Night* by drawing parallels between Robert Nelson's commentary on Candlemas, Donne's Candlemas sermons, and the play (97–100).

In his book chapter titled "Malvolio: Comic Puritan Automaton" (1980), Paul N. Siegel argues that the self-disciplined, mechanical nature of Puritanism makes it suitable for comedy, and "Such a comic character is Shakespeare's Malvolio" who is the "Puritan spoilsport in the midst of gaiety" (217). Siegel disagrees with the general reading that Malvolio is only a type of Puritanical character and, therefore, does not represent actual Puritans. On the contrary, Maria "is merely making the charge that was made against Puritans generally: they are concerned with their religion only insofar as it serves their profit" (218). Siegel then draws attention to various anti-Puritan epithets in the play. Sir Toby's abuses, for instance, "express...antagonism...toward the social classes among whom Puritanism was strong" (219). Because Puritans were associated with trade and a bourgeois ethic that stressed labor and money-making,

Malvolio is "opposed to the very spirit of the twelve days of Christmas culminating in Twelfth Night, with its extended merrymaking" (220). Another common epithet directed at Malvolio and the Puritans is the sin of pride, and Malvolio manifests this sin most notably in his delusional belief that Olivia loves him (220–21). Siegel next points to the nonconformist nature of Puritans and shows how details in Maria's letter emphasize Malvolio's "singularity" (221–22). Moreover, Maria's advice for Malvolio to don his usual sober face and yet, uncharacteristically, smile in Olivia's presence forces Malvolio to "seem the more automaton" as he can only smile in a forced, mechanical way (224). Siegel next examines Malvolio's madness. Just as his reading made him "a contemplative idiot," according to Maria, so the "Puritans were often regarded as religious maniacs in the fantasizing prompted by their zealous reading of the Bible" (225). Likewise, the darkness of Malvolio's cell alludes to hell, and Puritans "were spoken of as incarnations of the devil, the chief occupant of hell" (225). Siegel ends his chapter focusing on Puritan responses to holiday festivities. Puritans, he points out, objected to the "Christmas season festivities, with their lords of misrule presiding over the indoor hearty eating, drinking, and reveling" as it clashed with the usual rhythm of the year (226). At the end of the play, Malvolio gets what he deserves: "the laughter roused by his automatism, the essence of the comic character" (228).

In her essay "Viola, Antonio, and Epiphany in *Twelfth Night*" (1986), Cynthia Lewis argues that Epiphany, the revelation of truth, is the major theme of the play, but "before any such revelation can occur in *Twelfth Night,* most of the characters must be transformed by the Christian folly which Saint Paul discusses and which Erasmus further develops" (187). Lewis adds that the moral center of the play is not Viola but Antonio, whose "behavior, language, and history mirror Christ's in ways suggesting Christian folly" (187). Indeed, Antonio "embodies and acts out the play's highest standard of Christian love, morally eclipsing Viola at first and yet finally linking Viola to the play's central moral" (187). Lewis further asserts that the title *Twelfth Night*—Christ's manifestation to the magi—and the secular idea of epiphany, or revealed truth, provide helpful contextualization for understanding events in the play, especially in act 5. For Viola must grow into a deeper knowledge of herself and "has much to learn about love, both romantic and Christian" (189). Lewis points to Shakespeare's departure from his source, a tale by Barnabe Riche, whose captain forces himself on Silla, as a clear example that Shakespeare intended Antonio as an example of Christian charity (190). Lewis argues that "While Antonio reveals to the characters and the audience an ideal behavior that is difficult for most of us to practice, Feste shows us the next best thing: a worldly, practical honesty" (192). Feste "aims to make everyone a fool of [a] higher quality" and because of this, "it is a freeing kind of foolery" (192). Nevertheless, in the case of Malvolio, Feste's attempts to draw him out of himself, into salvation, ultimately fail because "Malvolio insistently suffers from the very pride in himself and attachment to his own opinions that work against tolerant Christian love" (193). Lewis ends her essay by discussing the growth of Viola in the play. Although Viola is a good character, she exhibits traits of self-indulgence at times, and "a great deal of the potential and actual destructiveness in *Twelfth Night* arises from Viola's refusal to expose herself openly to others—to give herself away" (195). Viola's disguise is indeed a barrier to her opening herself up to love and mimics the barriers other characters put up to guard against love. Ultimately, Viola's conversion at the end of the play and her "altruistic attitude toward love...alludes to a Christian ideal [and] permits spiritual love and romantic love to be linked in *Twelfth Night*" (197).

In his essay "The Religion of *Twelfth Night*" (1990), Maurice Hunt argues that, despite the arguments that support a Christian reading of the play, *Twelfth Night* "is not as consistently Christian as might be supposed" (189). The play satirizes aspects of Puritanism, Brownism, and Catholicism and "approximates an Anglican perspective on Providence, but only in an ambiguous manner" (190). Hunt traces several of the Christian allusions to God in the play before examining the Christian reading of Feste's character offered by critics like Chris Hassel. For Hunt, Feste's disguise as Sir Topas, and his apparent acceptance of reincarnation, "leads auditors away from the play's focus upon the epiphany of spiritual incarnation"

(192). In addition, the fact that characters repeatedly invoke non-Christian ruling deities and that they appeal to chance rather than providence complicates the idea that *Twelfth Night* is an orthodox play (192). Hunt points to the episode involving the Captain and Viola in act 1, scene 2 and argues that "the Captain has comforted her with a portrait of a hopeful, brave brother who enacts his own providence in a world of accident" (193). Likewise does Viola appeal not to God for help but to Time, a clue that "may convince playgoers that Shakespeare was either careless or unconcerned with dramatizing a single ruling deity in *Twelfth Night*" (194). Nevertheless, the sustained satire of Puritanism suggests that "in its broader strokes" the play conforms to Anglicanism (195). Hunt points to the ruse created by Maria, whose name has Catholic undertones, to trick Malvolio as an instance of her "'out-policying' and punishing the politician who delights in secret codes and love-games." This satirizes "the narrow, self-serving idea of Providence as the economic reward of the religious elect" (196). Specifically, because Malvolio appeals to Jove instead of God as determining his fate with Olivia, "he is a heathen, a renegade to the true English church" (198). Dressed in yellow, cross-gartered stockings, he represents both Puritan and Catholic extremes, as only old, male Puritans dressed in cross-gartered stockings, and yellow represented the color from the flag of Spain, a color Queen Elizabeth disliked (198). Hunt finishes his essay by drawing parallels between Viola and Richard Hooker's ideas of providence. Just as Hooker believes that God "works generally (that is remotely) through natural agents" (202), so Viola accepts the tempests as works of God's design. Thus, *Twelfth Night* "celebrates in delightful secular form key events in God's design such as the Epiphany and the Purification of the Virgin Mary" (202).

2000–2023: The Trinity, Catholicism and Mourning, Assurance and Charity

In his essay "'Comfortable Doctrine': 'Twelfth Night' and the Trinity" (2001), Paul Dean argues that the play makes allusions to Plato, the Bible, Ovid, and St. Augustine's *On the Trinity*. Dean suggests that Shakespeare likely read Plato in Latin and that he "was also well acquainted with Augustinian theology, if not specifically with the treatise on the Trinity" (504). *Twelfth Night* is a "characteristic fusion...of these ideas" and "Shakespeare uses the device of the twins, two individuals with, as it were, one flesh in Cesario, to explore the mystery of human love whereby twain become one, understood Neoplatonically as an analogy of the doctrine of the Trinity" (504). Dean traces the Platonic conception of gender from the *Symposium* and its relevance to *Twelfth Night* (504–07). In addition, he examines two myths from Ovid, Narcissus and Echo and Salmacis and Hermaphroditus, both of which were "lodged in the minds of Shakespeare and his contemporaries" (507). Both myths speak to the fusion of Viola and Sebastian in act 5 (508). In the third section of his essay, Dean discusses the relevance of Augustine's *On the Trinity* (509–11). He summarizes Augustine's arguments from mathematics, applying the number three to the Feast of Epiphany in which three wise men traveled to "adore a baby who was both a single child with two human parents, and a Person of the Trinity" (509). Augustine himself allegorizes the story of the Magi and their journey, which Dean argues parallels Viola and Sebastian's journey "to their reconciliation by an indirect and apparently circuitous path" (510). Dean then analyzes Augustine's analogies of self-love and their application to Trinitarian theology, suggesting, "in Christian terms Viola, Sebastian, and their relationship, which is so strong that it has its own separate existence as Cesario, are the Trinity of this play of love" (511). In his final section, Dean considers contemporary insights concerning the Trinity (511–15). He laments that some contemporary critics have dismissed the relevance to Shakespeare's play of Andrei Rublev's 1411 icon "The Hospitality of Abraham," which depicts the visit of three angels to Abraham, meant as a figure of the Trinity (512). For Dean, the tradition of Rublev's icon was known by Shakespeare and should be taken "seriously as an explanation of the picture of 'we three'" from act 2, scene 3 in *Twelfth Night* (512).

In her book chapter "Country House, Catholicity, and the Crypt(ic) in *Twelfth Night*" (2003), Anne Lecercle argues that Olivia's choice to cloister herself in her estate suggests possible allusions to Elizabethan and Jacobean recusant estates in the years before the Gunpowder Plot (86). Lecercle posits that "the 'other scene' of *Twelfth Night*'s opening is the cloister," which retains "notable vestiges of the recent Catholic past" (87). But if Olivia begins in the cloister of her estate, she ultimately ends in the chantry with Sebastian (89–90). Lecercle explains the importance of Shakespeare's choice of a chantry, as chantries were reserved for prayers for the dead, something that would clearly have offended Protestants (90). She further connects the chantry scene both with the ritual of rosemary branches in *Hamlet* (act 4, scene 5) and also with the parallels between rosemary and chastity in *Pericles* (act 4, scene 6). The rose, Lecercle explains, was one of the foremost Renaissance images of iconography for the Virgin Mary (89), and *Twelfth Night*'s chantry scene (like the scenes from *Hamlet* and *Pericles*) "involves on the one hand remembrance and on the other an insistently Catholic set of signs, symbols, and sense-systems imbued with nostalgia" (91). Lecercle then focuses on the importance of the Feast of Epiphany, which Eamon Duffy describes as one of the ten most important feasts honoring Christ and Mary (92–94). In the final section of her article, Lecercle discusses how the walled garden scenes in *Twelfth Night* evoke allusions to the Annunciation, one of the premier images iconoclasts whitewashed over in churches after the split with Rome (94). She points to Orsino's use of the word "nuncio" in act 1, scene 4, as a word that had Catholic associations and referred to "a permanent representative of the Roman See at a foreign court" (94). "Nuncio," moreover, would have been familiarized in England by "the prayers to the Virgin Mary that found their way into the Books of Hours or *Horae*, mostly in Latin" (94). Lecercle concludes her article with a brief discussion of the setting of Trevor Nunn's 1996 version of *Twelfth Night* and its connections to the Catholic martyr Cuthbert Mayne during the reign of Elizabeth (97–99).

Suzanne Penuel examines the post-Reformation context of mourning in her article "Missing Fathers: *Twelfth Night* and the Reformation of Mourning" (2010). She argues that the presence of doubling in the play "takes its force from changes in mourning rituals that accompanied the decline of English Catholicism" (75). Penuel first discusses the importance of doubling and its relation to death in the play. She argues that Sebastian's longing that both he and Viola had died together is a wish to "trump death, his father's real death, and Viola's supposed one, by dying" (77). She contends that Sebastian must "*double* the dying—adding his own death to Viola's"—and that this "suicidal duplication makes death less powerful" (77). Similarly, Viola's decision to take on a male disguise and look like her brother is an attempt to replace both father and brother (78–79). Likewise does Olivia's mourning for her dead brother double her mourning for a missing father. Penuel suggests that both Viola and Olivia thus "generate a *socially* potent parent" and treat fatherhood as a "flexible concept" rather than as a "live bodily representation" (81, 83). She connects this view to post-Reformation changes to mourning for the dead and argues that "a rigorist neo-Stoic hostility to grief" not only characterizes the play but also suggests "Protestant hostility to traditional Catholic forms of mourning" (84). Olivia and Sebastian's marriage in a chantry, however, insinuates that "*Twelfth Night*'s mourning is also a hearkening back to a denied form of expression deeply intertwined with family life" (86–87). Penuel then turns to the theme of doubling in the play and how it "registers as a wistful vision of escape from the constraints of the early modern family" (90). Suggesting that the "sexual confusions" of the play speak to this, Penuel discusses the play's apparent homoeroticism and argues that "*Twelfth Night*'s ambivalence about heterosexuality may serve as both cause and effect of an ambivalence about biological kinship" (92). In this, *Twelfth Night* complicates the notion that social stability requires marriage (93). She concludes that "[t]his comedy re-verses that dynamic: both men and women deny birth in denying death. Refashioning bonds broken by mortality, they formulate a symbolic mimetic world where the production of humans is independent of ordinary genital processes" (96).

In his article "'Thy speech serves for authority': From Personal Fantasy to Personal Encounter in Shakespeare's *Twelfth Night*" (2018), Kevin Ashenbach argues that "Malvolio and Viola's contrasting approaches to the world dramatize a struggle between internal and external modes of interpretive authority as that conflict was represented in the anti-Puritan discourse of Shakespeare's day" (47–48). Whereas Malvolio represents an internalized, egocentric reading of events, Viola's selfless encounter with others represents a more communal hermeneutic. Thus does Malvolio's "interpretation of other persons' behavior and of the letter [written by Maria]" lead to his persecution in the play because the "hermeneutical paradigm he applies is radically different from the one operative in Olivia's household" (49). One instance in the play that suggests this contrast is Malvolio's anti-festive nature and his tension with Feste (50–51). Other examples include Malvolio's interpretation of the supposed "signs" that Olivia is in love with him and his anti-social nature with the revelers Toby, Andrew, and Feste (51–53). It is principally because of his social isolation, rather than his exegetical skills, that Malvolio misinterprets Maria's letter as truly coming from Olivia. Indeed, Malvolio's "alienation from the revelers deprives him of the festive, oral context through which the written text was devised and continues to be enjoyed by that same community" (53–54). By contrast, Viola "practices a form of reading consonant" with her "view of providence and which was promoted by anti-Puritan clergy in their campaign to extinguish religious dissent" (55). Ashenbach then traces connections between the play and both Richard Bancroft's 1589 sermon "Sermon Preached at Paul's Cross" and Richard Hooker's *Laws of Ecclesiastical Polity* (54–60). Bancroft and Hooker's arguments for an episcopal, communal interpretation of the scriptures, rooted in an oral tradition, contrasts with the methods taken by Malvolio to interpret Maria's letter, as well as with Orsino and Olivia's own specific brands of self-centeredness (60–62). On the other hand, "Viola's self-denying nature grants her an adaptability that allows her to excel in interpersonal communication and move freely between the Illyrian households" (62). Specifically, both her service to Orsino, and her willingness to woo for him despite her hidden love, recall "the radical commitment to communal assimilation to which anti-Puritan writers summoned dissidents" (64). Ashenbach concludes that by following the selfless hermeneutic put forward by Bancroft and Hooker, "Viola empowers others to realize their desires, and in the process, attains her own" (64).

In his book chapter, "Double Predestination and Assurance in Shakespeare: *Macbeth* and *Twelfth Night*" (2022), Jason Gleckman argues that a particular Protestant desire for assurance resides in characters like Macbeth and Malvolio. On the one hand, Protestants agreed with Catholics that having complete assurance of one's salvation could lead to pride, arrogance, or idleness (92). But Protestants such as Luther, Calvin, and the Englishman William Perkins detested the medieval Catholic teaching against assurance (92–95). Gleckman argues that Macbeth "demonstrates throughout [the play] the mentality of a man desperately seeking a truly authentic assurance" (98). Macbeth may be brutal and vile, but, like the English Puritans, "He does not seek assurance so he can dominate others or perfect his villainy" but "to feel safe in an ordinary life" (98). For this reason, Macbeth must eschew "traditional Christian approaches of remorse, repentance, and contrition" as well as "a *pactum* theology that would meet God 'half-way' through renewed spiritual efforts" (98). By the end of the play, Macbeth attains what looks like assurance of his position, and "His words evoke the Roman stoic, the medieval Scottish warrior, and also the Protestant who is assured of his election and consequent righteousness in the sight of God" (100). Gleckman concludes that despite Macbeth's brutality and sinfulness, his certainty of his salvation "seems to be one [Shakespeare's] culture entertained" (100). In *Twelfth Night*, Malvolio likewise demonstrates an anxious concern for certainty. Gleckman writes that as Malvolio "reads Maria's forged letter expressing Olivia's love, he not only seeks signs of his election, but tries quite hard, as Protestants did, to distinguish this sense of election from its evil *doppelgänger*, namely a misguided belief that he is saved" (101–02). This quest for his election also mimics Protestants in their "'close-reading' of a sacred text" (102). Gleckman argues that "It is indeed through his reading practices and his response to them that Malvolio most fully dramatizes the situation of the Protestant seeker of assurance, finding himself, through the encounter with a sacred text, on the cusp of a long-sought enlightenment" (103). Malvolio further mimics extreme Protestantism in that he "anticipates a future in which he will be guided, in mysterious ways, toward conditions (such as smiling) that may at the moment be antithetical to his nature" (103). Gleckman concludes with a brief analysis of Sebastian, who, unlike Malvolio, is not assured of his salvation but of his damnation (105). Paradoxically, despite Sebastian's pessimistic outlook, it is he who ends up with Olivia, suggesting that assurance of one's damnation may be a better alternative than assurance of one's election (105).

Mark Bayer, in his article "*Twelfth Night* and the Economics of Christian Charity" (2023), writes that "Twelfth Night reaffirms the importance of charity for a London community that was largely dependent on it, at the time of year when it was most visible— and most expected" (35). Bayer traces the Christian tradition of charitable almsgiving during Christmastide, with a special emphasis on the Protestant tradition in England (35–37), before examining charitable practices in early modern England (37–39). In England, "Actors were significant players in greater London's philanthropy," and their actions were especially prominent during Christmastide (40). Bayer points out that specific players, including Shakespeare, participated in philanthropic efforts whose money "was spent locally, either in parish efforts to assist the less fortunate or to fund hospitals and other institutions in the community" (40). Regarding *Twelfth Night*, Bayer asserts that it progresses from "a world of atomized and disconnected individuals" to that of a "reconciled and interdependent society based in mutual respect and understanding" (40). This newfound sense of community, however, "depends upon the harmonious and efficient exchange of money and other valuable goods among previously unfamiliar characters" (41). Bayer notes the copious amount of gift-giving in the play, whether literally or by allusions, and he examines several characters as examples. Antonio, for instance, pledges to be Sebastian's servant, gives him his purse, and follows him into Illyria despite its danger to him (41–42). Nevertheless, following early modern conventions, Antonio "expects and eventually demands 'recompense,' the word most frequently used in the play to describe the exchange or gift of goods and services" (42). By contrast, Malvolio functions as a character whose "fantasy is one of social control rather than one of reconciliation and equitable redistribution" (42). Feste, on the other hand, best exemplifies the "multifaceted economics of charity" and "demonstrates the generalized principle of reciprocity that characterizes the play and highlights the mutual benefits conferred on all participants in a charitable economy" (43). Sir Toby Belch, Andrew Aguecheek, and their companions meanwhile institute "an economics of mirth in Olivia's household and inhabit a mise-en-scène dominated almost exclusively by charity" (45). Bayer concludes by discussing Orsino and Olivia, both of whom have to grow into a less romantic, more charitable understanding of empathetic love for others (46–47). He then touches on the important symbolism of water in the play, which he sees as clearly alluding to Christian practices such as baptism (47–48).

Conclusion

Although other topics have certainly been discussed regarding the play, religious commentary continues to shape much of the criticism, suggesting that a robust understanding of *Twelfth Night* should include a thorough understanding of the religious conversation both within the play and in Shakespeare's England. The above review provides an overview of criticism over the past forty years on the religion in *Twelfth Night*, but much more has been written on the subject, too much to be succinctly summarized in a single essay.[1] Although critics may not agree on certain religious aspects of Shakespeare's play, we can be certain that critics, teachers, and directors will continue to consider how religion shapes one of Shakespeare's most enduring comedies.

Note

1. The following articles also speak to religious themes in *Twelfth Night*: John Hollander, "Twelfth Night and the Morality of Indulgence" (1959); Barbara K. Lewalski, "Thematic Patterns in Twelfth Night" (1965); J. L. Simmons, "A Source for Shakespeare's Malvolio: The Elizabethan Controversy with the Puritans" (1973); James F. Forest, "Malvolio and Puritan 'Singularity'" (1974), Chris Hassel, *Faith and Folly in Shakespeare's Romantic Comedies* (1980), pages 149–75; Maurice Hunt "'Twelfth Night' and the Annunciation"

(1989); Hunt, "Malvolio, Viola, and the Question of Instrumentality: Defining Providence in 'Twelfth Night'" (1993); Dean Paul, "The Harrowing of Malvolio: The Theological Background of *Twelfth Night*, Act 2, Scene 2" (1997–98); Paul, "'Nothing that is so is so': Twelfth Night and Transubstantiation" (2003); Hunt, "Shakespeare's *Twelfth Night* and the 'Pregnant Enemy': The Devil in What You Will" (2011); and Velma Bourgeois Richmond, Shakespeare, Catholicism, and Romance (2015), pages 139–44.

Works Cited

Ashenbach, Kevin. "'Thy speech serves for authority': From Personal Fantasy to Personal Encounter in Shakespeare's *Twelfth Night*." *Religion and Literature*, vol. 50, no. 3, 2018, pp. 47–70.

Bayer, Mark. "*Twelfth Night* and the Economics of Christian Charity." *Reformation*, vol. 28, no. 1, 2023, pp. 34–49.

Dean, Paul. "'Comfortable Doctrine': 'Twelfth Night' and the Trinity." *Review of English Studies*, vol. 52, no. 208, 2001, pp. 500–15.

_____. "'Nothing that is so is so': 'Twelfth Night' and Transubstantiation." *Literature and Theology*, vol. 17, no. 3, 2003, pp. 281–97.

_____. "The Harrowing of Malvolio: The Theological Background of *Twelfth Night*, Act 4, Scene 2." *Connotations*, vol. 7, no. 2, 1997–98, pp. 203–14.

Forest, James F. "Malvolio and Puritan 'Singularity.'" *English Language Notes*, vol. 11, no. 4, 1974, pp. 259–64.

Gleckman, Jason. *Shakespeare and Protestant Poetics*. Palgrave Macmillan, 2019.

Hassel, Jr., Chris. *Faith and Folly in Shakespeare's Romantic Comedies*. U of Georgia P, 1980.

_____. *Renaissance Drama and the English Church Year*. U of Nebraska P, 1979.

Hollander, John. "*Twelfth Night* and the Morality of Indulgence." *The Sewanee Review*, vol. 67, no. 2, 1959, 220–38.

Hunt, Maurice. "Malvolio, Viola, and the Question of Instrumentality: Defining Providence in 'Twelfth Night.'" *Studies in Philology*, vol. 90, no. 3, 1993, pp. 277–97.

_____. "Shakespeare's *Twelfth Night* and the 'Pregnant Enemy': The Devil in What You Will." *The Upstart Crow*, vol. 30, 2011, pp. 5–17.

_____. "The Religion of *Twelfth Night*." *College Language Association*, vol. 37, no. 2, 1993, 189–203.

_____. "'Twelfth Night' and the Annunciation." *Papers on Language and Literature*, vol. 25, no. 3, 1989, pp. 264–71.

Lecercle, Anne. "Country House, Catholicity, and the Crypt(ic) in *Twelfth Night*." *Region, Religion, and Patronage: Lancaster Shakespeare*. Edited by Richard Dutton, et al., Manchester UP, 2003, pp. 84–100.

Lewalski, Barbara K. "Thematic Patterns in *Twelfth Night*." *Shakespeare Studies: An Annual Gathering of Research, Criticism, and Reviews*. Edited by J. Leeds Barroll. The U of Cincinnati P, 1965, pp. 168–81.

Lewis, Cynthia. "Viola, Antonio, and Epiphany in *Twelfth Night*." *Essays in Literature*, vol 13, 1986, pp. 187–99.

Penuel, Suzanne. "Missing Fathers: *Twelfth Night* and the Reformation of Mourning." *Studies in Philology*, vol. 107, no. 1, 2010, pp. 74–96.

Richmond, Velma Bourgeois. *Shakespeare, Catholicism, and Romance*. Bloomsbury, 2015.

Siegel, Paul N. "Malvolio: Comic Puritan Automaton," *Shakespearean Comedy*. Edited by Maurice Charney. New York Literary Forum, 1980, pp. 217–30.

Simmons, J. L. "A Source for Shakespeare's Malvolio: The Elizabethan Controversy with the Puritans," *Huntington Quarterly Library*, vol. 36, no. 3, 1973, pp. 181–201.

The Puzzling Title of *Twelfth Night, or What You Will*

James Hirsh

In crafting a number of his plays Shakespeare adopted a subtle technique that elicits from playgoers empathy in regard to a character as no other technique can. Instead of simply telling or showing playgoers something about a character's situation and inviting them to imagine what it *might* be like to be in such a situation, he constructed each of these plays in such a way that playgoers (merely by trying to respond appropriately to the play) are *in fact* placed in a situation that, however faintly, resembles the situation in which the character finds himself. This is one of Shakespeare's most original and inventive techniques. The present essay will explore a particularly intriguing example of Shakespeare's employment of this technique.[1]

Titles

Experienced playgoers and readers are predisposed to assume that there is some significant connection between the title of a play and its dramatized action. In the cases of some of Shakespeare's works, the connection between the title and the dramatized action is not obvious. This lack of obvious appropriateness of the title is an invitation to playgoers to exercise their reason and imagination to discover *implicit* connections. In some of these works, the title turns out, in retrospect, to have been misleading. Playgoers are invited to consider the implications of the discrepancy between the title and action. In some cases, a title turns out to be appropriate but in an unexpected or ironic way. If the title of a play is in simple, obvious accord with the dramatized action, the relationship between the title and the dramatized action is in that respect undramatic, lacking in conflict. If the title of a play is somehow at odds with the action, the relationship is dramatic. The latter relationship is far more likely to be thought-provoking. It calls for an explanation.

One example of a play with a misleading, ironic title is *Julius Caesar*. In Renaissance England, the assassination of Julius Caesar was possibly the most famous event of ancient times other than those recorded in the Bible. Even illiterate people would have encountered references to it in sermons, plays, and other genres of oral literature. A playgoer who entered the theater to attend a play entitled *Julius Caesar* would expect that the play would depict the actions of this man of action as he rose to power and that the play would end with his assassination. The play defeats these expectations. For example, one of the most decisive and famous actions of Caesar in his rise to power was his (disingenuous) public refusal of the crown, but this crucial action occurs *offstage* and is merely *reported* to onstage characters. Instead of depicting the *behavior* of the title character, *Julius Caesar* focuses much more attention on the depiction of the *effect* of the title character on others. The play is less about Julius Caesar as an agent than about Julius Caesar as an object of the speculation, adulation, or trepidation of others. The title becomes even more conspicuously incongruous when the assassination of the title character occurs at what will turn out to be barely the midpoint of the play (in 3.1). It is a case of premature assassination. All told, the title character appears in only four of 19 scenes of the play (according to the conventional scene numbering). The superficially misleading title turns out to be appropriate in an unexpected and ironic way. Julius Caesar looms over the play not because of his dramatized actions but because of his association with the idea of autocracy (as opposed to republicanism). In this sense Caesar continues to dominate the thoughts and actions of other characters even after the assassination. As a corpse, Caesar is a crucial prop used by Antony to turn the populace against the republican assassins, and in 4.2 the Ghost of Caesar briefly appears to Brutus. The autocracy that Caesar represents haunts every scene of the play. Fewer than 130 lines from the end of the play Brutus declares in an apostrophe,

> O Julius Caesar, thou art mighty yet.
> Thy spirit walks abroad, and turns our swords
> In our own proper entrails. (5.3.94–96)

As it turns out, you can kill Caesar, but it is harder to kill Caesarism. Julius Caesar the personification of autocracy ironically steals the play from Julius Caesar the individual historical man of action.

The Cryptic Title

The relevance of the title of *Twelfth Night, or What You Will* to the dramatized action of the play is not explicit or immediately obvious.[2] The first part of the title refers to the Feast of the Epiphany in the Christian calendar, which falls on January 6, the twelfth night after Christmas. The play is not explicitly set in January, nor is the holiday explicitly mentioned in the dialogue. When Sir Toby sings a song that contains the words "the twelfth *day* of *December*" (2.3.73, italics added), playgoers are teasingly reminded that the holiday specified in the title is *not* mentioned in the dialogue. The holiday specified in the title is thus conspicuous by its absence from the dialogue of the play. Many editors of the play and other commentators have exercised great ingenuity in proposing solutions to the puzzle posed by the title.

In *The First Night of Twelfth Night*, Leslie Hotson argued that the play was specifically written to be performed at Queen Elizabeth's court on 6 January 1601. Some of the evidence is intriguing. The Lord Chamberlain's Men did perform at the court on that day, and the performance coincided with a visit by Virginio Orsino, the Duke of Bracciano. A major character of Shakespeare's play is Orsino, the Duke of Illyria. But some features of Hotson's argument are speculative. According to Andrew Gurr, "to stage a play featuring a lovesick lord whose namesake was the chief guest in the royal audience...seems far from likely" (333).

In the judgment of Paul Edmondson, "Hotson's theory seems as 'high fantastical' (I.i.15) as the play itself" (4). Edmondson supplies his own explanation for the title, which he suggests was partly inspired by an element in *Gl'Ingannati* ("The Deceived"), an anonymous Italian play (1537) that was one of several sources for Shakespeare's play:

> The Feast of the Epiphany ('la notte di Beffana') is mentioned explicitly in the prologue as well as being referred to in Act I, scene ii, and might have helped Shakespeare choose the first of his two titles. (16)

But Edmondson does not explain what would have been Shakespeare's artistic purpose in alluding in the title of his play to elements of an Italian play that few if any Elizabethan playgoers would have read.

Other commentators have suggested that the connection between the title and the play is metaphorical. There are numerous possibilities for such a connection. According to Barbara Everett, "the greatest 'party' of the Christian world of the Renaissance took place on Twelfth Night" (303). In Shakespeare's *Twelfth Night*, a boisterous revel is depicted in 2.3; the culmination of the play is a joyous occasion for most of the characters; and an important character is named Feste. Stephen Booth connects the title and the dramatized action by describing the play as "Shakespeare's festively named festive comedy" (121–22).

A more specific connection to this particular holiday has been detected by some scholars. During Twelfth Night festivities, normal social rules of decorum were relaxed or turned upside down, and the master of ceremonies was a Lord of Misrule. According to L. G. Salingar,

> As the main title implies, the idea of a time of misrule gives the underlying constructive principle of the whole play.... The sub-plot shows a prolonged season of misrule...with Sir Toby turning night into day; there are drinking, dancing, and singing, scenes of mock wooing, a mock sword fight,...gulling of an unpopular member of the household,...[and] a mock exorcism in the manner of the Feast of Fools. (118)

In his classic study of Shakespeare's allusions to social customs, C. L. Barber concurred with Salingar: "The title tells us that the play is like holiday misrule" (241). Roger Warren and Stanley Wells noted further examples of topsy-turviness in the play: Viola eventually becomes her "master's mistress" (5.1.306), and "in the subplot, Olivia's steward aspires to become his mistress's master" (5). Characters in the play behave foolishly and play practical jokes on one another. A woman pretends to be a man; and another woman falls in love with her under the misimpression that she is a he; a man forms an intense attachment to the same woman while under the impression that she is a he; a foolish but sane man is treated as if he were insane; and so on. And yet a great many comedies contain examples of misrule and topsy-turviness, and a great many have festively happy endings. According to the line of reasoning used by these scholars, any of those other comedies could also have been appropriately entitled *Twelfth Night*. In these respects, the title is generic rather than particular.

Occurring on the evening of the last of the twelve days of Christmas, Twelfth Night in Shakespeare's time marked the end of the Christmas holiday season. Beneath its superficial festivity, it carried an undertone of melancholy nostalgia. (In these respects, it more closely resembles New Year's Eve in our time. New Year's Eve in our time marks the final opportunity for night-time revelry of the Christmas season. The tone of "Auld Lang Syne," the quintessential New Year's Eve song, is not light-heartedness but melancholy nostalgia.) The action of the play entitled *Twelfth Night* contains a similar undertone. Interspersed among the hilarious and joyous moments in the play are melancholy and nostalgic moments.[3] The very first speech of the play, spoken by Orsino, expresses a melancholy longing. Orsino suffers from unrequited love for Olivia, who in turn is mourning the death of her brother. Viola mourns for her brother, whose survival after the shipwreck seems unlikely. Malvolio's punishment eventually seems excessive and should provoke uneasiness in playgoers rather than light-hearted amusement. Devoted to Sebastian, who marries Olivia at the end of the play, Antonio is also an odd man out. Despite his name, Feste is not a happy-go-lucky character. His songs and commentary often express a gloomy or cynical attitude.

According to Hugh McLean, the "title clearly invites association with the feast of Epiphany, i.e., the celebration of the revealing of

Jesus as the Christ to the Gentiles in the persons of the Magi at Bethlehem, and thereby with the larger concept of a movement from bondage to freedom, falsehood to truth, death to life" (31). But the "movement" McLean associates with both the religious holiday and the play is not very specific in the case of either. If in Christian belief Jesus represents freedom, truth, and life, then every reference to Jesus and every Christian holiday is associated with those things. A great many comedies dramatize a movement from an unfortunate state to a happy ending.

There is a more specific and compelling metaphoric connection between the religious associations of the holiday and the play. "Epiphany" in Greek means "revealing," and the holiday commemorates not one but three examples of revelations in the New Testament: (1) the arrival of the Magi in Bethlehem, which marked the first public showing of Jesus to Gentiles; (2) the baptism of Jesus by John the Baptist, during which the Holy Spirit descended in the form of a dove and a supernatural voice revealed Jesus's divinity; and (3) the feast of Canaan, during which Jesus first revealed that he had the ability to perform miracles. The play contains numerous mundane, secular epiphanies, moments in which characters reveal something significant about themselves. Some of these revelations seem almost miraculous and are occasions of joy. Viola spends most of the play in disguise as the male Cesario but is revealed to be a woman in the final scene. This revelation leads almost immediately to a proposal from the man she loves. Having presumed that her brother is dead, Viola is overjoyed at the revelation of his survival near the end of the play. Sebastian allows Olivia to believe he is Cesario until his true identity is revealed. In other cases, the association of the title with revelations of divinity is appropriate in an ironic way. Malvolio is tricked into revealing that he has delusions of grandeur, and several characters reveal their foolishness.

Tiffany Stern points out that Twelfth Night celebrations at court typically included the performance of masques. She then asks, "What does this say of Shakespeare's *Twelfth Night*?" Her answer is that "The piece is obviously a play, not a masque; it does, however, flirt with masque elements—music in particular" (167).

The Twelfth Night activities of feasting and music may be alluded to in the opening line of the play, which link music and food. Kathryn Roberts Parker argues that "the communal, participatory style of the music for Wassailing, a Saturnalian festival celebrated on Twelfth Night, is reflected in one lengthy scene in the middle of the play" (159). According to Parker,

> Significantly, the most musical scene (Act 2, Scene 3)...begins with Sir Toby, Sir Andrew, and Feste sharing a "stoop of wine" (2.3.12), which John Long has suggested to be a wassailing bowl. (162)

Some of the connections described by Parker seem tenuous at best.

> It is likely that when Sir Toby says 'welkin'..., he is referring to a loud, raucous sound that the three of them are going to produce together in singing the catch, enough to make the "welkin dance" [2.3.52] in response to them. This kind of natural imagery for arousing a loud sound in singing is evocative of the communal practices of wassailing festivals to encourage fruit-bearing trees into bloom. (175)

The second part of the title (or the subtitle or the alternative title) has also provoked ingenious commentary. Everett has argued that the seeming casualness of this part of the title is meant to exemplify "that specifically courtly style of throwaway lightness which the age itself called *sprezzatura*" (304), and she goes on to imply that some elements of the dramatized action exhibit this quality. Penny Gay argues that in Shakespeare's day the word "will" was sometimes used to mean "sexual desire"; that the subtitle may involve "sexual punning of a kind that Will Shakespeare particularly delighted in"; and that this pun alludes to "the multiple erotic entanglements of the play" (29).[4] Gay's use of a short form of Shakespeare's first name implies that Shakespeare also may have been slyly inserting his own name into the title. Shakespeare uses both forms of punning insistently in Sonnet 135. The invitation to playgoers to invent their own title for the play is facetious. It is unlikely that many playgoers accept the invitation to propose their own titles.[5]

As noted above, experienced playgoers and readers are predisposed to assume that there is some significant connection between the title of a play and its dramatized action. By not providing an overt connection, an author invites playgoers to consider possible implicit connections. According to Gay, "The very title *Twelfth Night, or What You Will* is a riddle set by the elusive author, and not yet satisfactorily solved" (29). The appropriate audience response to a riddle is to attempt to solve it. In this case there is no shortage of possible solutions. Once a reader or playgoer begins to exercise his or her imagination to solve the puzzle of the title, it is hard to know when to stop. As Keir Elam has argued,

> *Twelfth Night*...promises an epiphany—a secret or encoded transcendental signified waiting to be revealed—but strategically withholds it. Hence the search for a semantic key to open up the comedy's supposed mysteries. The danger is... over-interpretation.... But the risk...is one that the comedy itself challenges us to run, and it cannot and should not put an end to speculative hermeneutic readings. (24)

On the apparent assumption that the omission of an explicit connection between the body of the play and its title was simply an oversight that might annoy playgoers, some directors of post-Renaissance productions have interpolated an explicit connection. The 1969–72 Royal Shakespeare Company production of the play, directed by John Barton, reversed the effect produced by the words "the twelfth day of December." Instead of an ironic reminder that the dialogue of the play does *not* refer to the holiday of the title, this production interpolated at this point a conspicuous allusion to the title of the play. The reference to "the twelfth day of December" was immediately followed, incongruously, by a rendition of "The Twelve Days of Christmas" (Wells, 52). While Shakespeare chose to leave *unsatisfied* a playgoer's desire for an overt connection between the title and the play, this production provided satisfaction and thereby reduced the impulse of a playgoer to engage in the kind of speculation Shakespeare went out of his way to provoke by *not* supplying an overt connection.

In light of the above catalogue of critical commentary, Andrew Gurr's assertion that the play "has evoked maximum guesswork about its doubled name" (332) is not hyperbolic. In a different context, Gurr notes that "Each of its two titles is puzzling" (333). He does not make a connection between these two assertions, but the "maximum guesswork" is clearly the result of the fact that the two titles are puzzling. A puzzle arouses curiosity, a powerful appetite.

Not every playgoer accepts Shakespeare's invitation to speculate about the title. Samuel Pepys complained that *Twelfth Night* is "a silly play and not relating at all to the name or day" (vol. 4, entry for 6 January 1663). A few scholars have argued that the title or subtitle was chosen almost at random and does not imply a specific metaphorical or thematic connection to the dramatized action. Noting that John Marston's play *What You Will* was first performed at about the time that Shakespeare was writing *Twelfth Night*, some scholars have surmised that the eventual subtitle was Shakespeare's original choice for the main title until it was pre-empted by Marston. T. W. Craik proposed that "it is very possible that Shakespeare retained the original title in order to make it absolutely clear to his audiences that the new title *Twelfth Night* bore no more significance than had the casual titles of his two previous comedies, *Much Ado About Nothing* and *As You Like It* and that it was...irrelevant to the story" (xxxiii–xxxiv). Craik dismissed efforts to find specific connections between the title and dramatized action: "the whirligig of time has brought in its revenges, since Shakespeare's capriciousness has exposed both titles to attempts at explanation" that are "strained" and based on "super-subtlety" (xxxiv). According to Bill Alexander, who directed the 1987 Royal Shakespeare production, "the title was a kind of distraction" (3).

The Cryptic Letter

In 2.5, Malvolio is deceived into believing that Olivia loves him and will welcome his courtship. Maria devises a plan to forge a supposed love letter from Olivia to Malvolio that she "will drop in his way" (2.3.131), that is, that she will leave in a path that Malvolio is known to frequent. An interesting feature of this letter is that it does not overtly name Malvolio or identify the author as Olivia. Maria had at least two implicit motives for making these key features of the letter implicit rather than explicit. First, if the letter were explicit, Malvolio might have been more likely to smell a rat. By making the letter merely suggestive, Maria channels Malvolio's intellectual energy into the question *What does it mean?* and away from the question *Is it genuine?* A second purpose of Maria's use of implication rather than explication is to allow Toby (along with Andrew and Fabian) to witness how Malvolio will make a fool of himself by projecting onto the cryptic letter his fantasy that Olivia is in love with him. In the worlds depicted in Shakespearean drama, it went without saying that a person who believed he was alone would, as a matter of course, speak aloud to himself.[6]

Malvolio does not disappoint. In a series of self-addressed speeches, he strains his ingenuity to find in each element of the letter a confirmation of his wishful thinking that Olivia is in love with him.

> "I may command where I adore." Why, she may command me; I serve her, she is my lady. Why, this is evident to any formal capacity. There is no obstruction in this. (2.5.99–101)

Malvolio is at first puzzled by an abbreviation but after a strenuous intellectual effort eventually arrives at a satisfactory solution:

> And the end–what should that alphabetical position portend? If I could make that resemble something in me! Softly—"M. O. A. I." (2.5.101–03)
> "M"—Malvolio. M! Why that begins my name! (2.5.107)
> "M." But then there is no consonancy in the sequel. That suffers under probation.
> "A" should follow, but "O" does. (2.5.109–10)
> And then "I" comes behind. (2.5.113)

> "M. O. A. I." This simulation is not as the former; and yet to crush this a little, it would bow to me, for every one of these letters is in my name. (2.5.116–18)

Maria could have made the process of interpretation easier by writing the letters of the cryptogram in the same order as they appear in Malvolio's name. Shakespeare's implication is that Maria thought that the intellectual satisfaction of solving a more challenging puzzle will reinforce Malvolio's belief in his solution.[7]

Some critics have expressed utter contempt for Malvolio's hermeneutic procedures in responding to the bogus letter.

> Harold Bloom: "Malvolio is more the victim of his own psychic propensities than he is Maria's gull. His dream of socio- erotic greatness—'To be Count Malvolio!'—is one of Shakespeare's supreme inventions, permanently disturbing as a study of self-deception." (238)

> David Bevington: "Without Malvolio's infatuated predisposition to believe that Olivia could actually love him..., Maria's scheme would have no hope of success. He tortures the text to make it yield a suitable meaning, much in the style of Puritan theologizing." (336)

> Marjorie Garber: "In Malvolio's reading and interpretation of the letter, Shakespeare...provides a classic example of self-delusion." (530)

This utter contempt for Malvolio allies these critics with Sir Toby and Sir Andrew who express contempt for Malvolio within the scene. Toby and Andrew are at least as foolish as Malvolio. One might recognize the foolishness of others and be unaware of one's own susceptibility to foolishness.

A few critics have defended Malvolio from the charge that his response to the letter is foolish. According to Stephen Booth,

> The credentials of and in that letter are awfully convincing. The letter gives Malvolio plentiful and persuasive evidence

> that Olivia loves him.... Sherlock Holmes himself would accept Maria's letter as a love letter from Olivia to Malvolio. (147)

Sean Benson has argued that the scholarly "consensus on Malvolio's alleged misreading is in need of serious revision: his hermeneutic, far from being the mark of Puritan excess, is remarkably astute" (262). If Sherlock Holmes or any astute person came upon a cryptic letter left in a path that he is known to frequent, he would not immediately assume that it was authentic, that its implied author was its actual author. He would suspect some stratagem. Malvolio never considers the issue of the authenticity of the letter. If he had given that issue a moment's thought, he would have asked himself questions such as *Might this be a trick? Is there any member of the household who bears me a grudge?* If he had, he would have recalled that he quite recently admonished, reviled, humiliated, and ridiculed Toby, Andrew, Feste, and Maria for carousing:

> Have you no wit, manners, nor honesty, but to gabble like tinkers at this time of night? Do ye make an alehouse of my lady's house, that ye squeak out your coziers' [i.e., cobblers'] catches without any mitigation or remorse of voice? (2.3.75–79)

He threatened Toby with exile from Olivia's household: "If you can separate yourself and your misdemeanours you are welcome to the house; if not,...she is very willing to bid you farewell" (2.3.83–85). In the last words he spoke before the scene in which he finds the letter, he threatened to tattle on Maria: "Mistress Mary, if you prized my lady's favour at anything more than contempt you would not give means for this uncivil rule. She shall know of it, by this hand" (2.3.103–05).

Malvolio is foolish not to consider the possibility that those he has reviled and threatened might seek retribution. After he himself is humiliated and tormented, he responds, "I'll be revenged on the whole pack of you" (5.1.356). It is a failure of his imagination not to recognize the human propensity to seek revenge for ill-treatment.

Failing to question the authenticity of the document, Malvolio engages in confirmation bias. He searches only for explanations that support his wishful thinking. He denies that he is deceiving himself: "I do not now fool myself to let imagination jade me; for every reason excites to this, that my lady loves me" (2.5.133–35). Playgoers realize that he is fooling himself. His denial that he is fooling himself is part of the means by which he fools himself.[8] In his mind, his unequivocal denial of self-deception serves as a kind of talisman against self-deception. Shakespeare's point is not that Malvolio's interpretation of the letter is either uniquely foolish or astute, but that the interpretive strategies he employs, including flawed strategies, are common, even pervasive. Most of the other characters in the play at one time or another engage in similar strategies.

Playgoers and Malvolio

I hope that I have implicitly stimulated a reader of this essay to recognize that the effect of the title of the play on thoughtful playgoers has an odd and disturbing similarity to the effect of the forged letter on Malvolio. The section of this essay cataloguing speculations about the relevance of the title of *Twelfth Night, or What You Will* to the dramatized action might be summarized by paraphrasing Malvolio's MOAI soliloquies:

> "Twelfth Night." Why, that refers to a festive occasion, and this is a festive comedy. Why, this is evident to any formal capacity. There is no obstruction in this. And the other associations of that holiday—what should they portend? If I could make those resemble something in the play. Softly—"Twelfth Night."
>
> "Twelfth"–why that word occurs in the dialogue of the play!
>
> "Twelfth." But then there is no consonancy in the sequel. That suffers under probation. "Night" should follow, but "day" does.
>
> And then Twelfth Night is associated with melancholy and epiphanies. To crush this a little, it would bow to me, for the play also contains melancholy elements and epiphanies.

Just as Maria tempts Malvolio to make sense of cryptic elements of her ingeniously crafted letter, Shakespeare tempts playgoers to make sense of the cryptic title of his ingeniously crafted play. Just as Malvolio is led to interpret the letter in ways that conform to his pre-existing wishful thinking, playgoers are led to interpret the title in ways that conform to the conventional and quite reasonable assumption that the title of a dramatic work was chosen by the author because it has some specific relevance to the content of the work. In the case of a particularly ingenious play, there might be a multitude of connections between the title and the play, and this is a particularly ingenious play. When thoughtful playgoers or readers have seen or read the entire play without ever encountering any explicit reference to the Twelfth Night holiday, such playgoers are enticed to exercise their ingenuity in ways that resemble the ways in which Malvolio is enticed to decipher Maria's letter.[9]

Unlike the first part of the title, the second part is echoed in the dialogue of the play. Informed that "a young gentleman much desires to speak with" her (1.5.81–82), Olivia responds,

> Go you, Malvolio. If it be a suit from the Count, I am sick, or not at home—*what you will* to dismiss it.
>
> (1.5.88–89, italics added)

The "you" here is Malvolio. The "you" of the second part of the title is the theater audience. Very few playgoers will hear the echo, and fewer still will recognize the connection between Malvolio and themselves. Unlike writers who make everything obvious in fear that readers or playgoers will fail to notice something, Shakespeare included countless subtleties in his works in full knowledge that few if any playgoers would notice all of them or recognize all of their implications. The subtleties of Shakespeare's works entice playgoers and readers to draw inferences not unlike those made by Malvolio in responding to Maria's letter.

This analogy between Malvolio's situation when confronted with Maria's cryptic letter and a thoughtful playgoer's situation when confronted with the cryptic title of the play is not a trivial matter. It has profound thematic implications. By constructing this implicit analogy, Shakespeare encourages playgoers either (a) to recognize consciously that they themselves engage in intellectual activities that resemble those in which Malvolio engages or (b) to experience an uneasy subconscious sense of affinity with Malvolio. Each of these alternatives was designed to undermine a feeling of complacent superiority to the character. This feature of the play does not have a simple moral. It does not mean that speculating about the title of a play or engaging in other forms of inference is a mistake to be avoided at all costs. Nearly every day of our lives we have to make inferences of one sort or another based on incomplete or ambiguous evidence. The necessity of making inferences is inherent in the human condition. The present essay has drawn numerous inferences. But making inferences is a risky business. Inferences are both unavoidable and fallible.[10] As a result, even the smartest people are vulnerable to making fools of themselves. Indeed, ingenious, imaginative people are more likely to be lured into making ingenious, imaginative, and therefore risky inferences. In responding to *Twelfth Night*, the more experienced and imaginative a playgoer is—that is, the better playgoer a playgoer is—the more likely the playgoer will engage in speculation about the title. A dull-witted playgoer will not even notice that the title is left unexplained. An incurious playgoer will not care. The more imaginative and intellectually daring one is, the more one is susceptible to Malvolianism. The only way of avoiding the danger of making risky inferences is not to make inferences at all, not to exercise one's imagination at all.

Instead of merely telling playgoers about the rewards and the risks of exercising one's imagination or merely depicting characters who are rewarded or punished for exercising their imaginations, Shakespeare places playgoers in situations that tempt them to exercise their imaginations and thereby to run the risk of being foolish.

Notes

1. For analyses of other examples of Shakespeare's employment of this technique, see the following publications by the present author in the Works Cited: "Laughter at *Titus Andronicus*"; "*Othello* and Perception"; "Teaching Paradoxes"; and "Through Dramatic Structure."

2. The only authoritative text of the play is that in the First Folio (1623), where it is entitled *Twelfe Night, Or what you will*. The double title was not the creation of the Folio editors. John Manningham recorded in his diary that on 2 February 1602 he attended a performance of "Twelfth Night, or What You Will" at the Middle Temple Hall. See Gurr, p. 331.

3. According to Ralph Berry, "It is curious that [the title of *Twelfth Night*] has been so widely interpreted as an unequivocal call to revelry. In fact, most people understand perfectly well that the last day of the Christmas festivities finds one sated." (113–14) As quoted by Linda Anderson, p. 229, n. 64.

4. After noting the sexual connotation of the word "will" in the subtitle, Bruce R. Smith catalogues the numerous and various erotic entanglements in the play and concludes that "the love plots in *Twelfth Night* truly offer 'what you will'" (15).

5. A 1968 off-Broadway musical adaptation was entitled *Your Own Thing*, a rough paraphrase of *What You Will*.

6. See *Shakespeare and the History of Soliloquies* by the present author for numerous other examples.

7. In light of the attention paid to the letters of Malvolio's name, it does not seem to be a mere coincidence that all the letters of the names of Viola and Olivia are also contained in the name of Malvolio. This may imply that, beneath their obvious differences, the three characters have something significant in common.

8. In *As You Like It*, written about the same time as *Twelfth Night*, Touchstone quotes a "saying": "The fool doth think he is wise, but the wise man knows himself to be a fool" (5.1.26–27).

9. In *Precious Nonsense*, Stephen Booth has compared Malvolio and the audience on different grounds than those adduced here. First, Booth demonstrates that, meticulously analyzed, the language of the opening scene contains numerous illogicalities but that playgoers have no trouble understanding the meaning. He compares this to the fact that modern listeners have no trouble understanding that "I could care less" actually means "I couldn't care less." In response to the language of 1.1, playgoers disregard the evidence of their ears. They resemble Malvolio, "the preeminent example of a character who mistakes evidence" (147). Second, Booth argues that Sir Toby Belch seems to fit the character type of "a loveable swaggerer, a ne'er-do-well, a bluff hearty eccentric, who...commands our affection," but that he "fails to live up to the generic expectations he evokes: he...is not funny" (153–54). He is no Falstaff. As a result, "when Malvolio the spoilsport enters [in 2.3] to end the revelry, we the audience—firmly and forever allied with the forces of free-spirited good fellowship—feel something different from, but uncomfortably akin to, sympathy with Malvolio's point of view" (173). Alison

Findlay and Liz Oakley-Brown have noted a similarity between Malvolio's attempt to decipher the letter and the general search for meaning by playgoers to the play as a whole: "Uncertainty, then, characterizes *Twelfth Night* at the outset and, like Malvolio's scrutiny of the letter in 2.5, generations of actors, critics, readers and audiences have searched for meaning" (2).

10. Elam has argued that a major theme of the play is interpretation: "it warns us of the dangers of making fools of ourselves through interpretation, including the interpretation of *Twelfth Night* itself, even as...it irresistibly invites an interpretive response" (11).

Works Cited

Alexander, Bill. *Directors' Shakespeare: Approaches to* Twelfth Night. Edited by Michael Billington. Nick Hern, 1990.

Anderson, Linda. "Performance and Adaptation." Twelfth Night: *A Critical Reader*. Edited by Alison Findlay and Liz Oakley Brown. Bloomsbury Arden, 2014, pp. 52–70.

Barber, C. L. *Shakespeare's Festive Comedy: A Study of Dramatic Form and Its Relation to Social Custom*. 1959. Rpt. World, 1963.

Benson, Sean. "'Perverse Fantasies'? Rehabilitating Malvolio's Reading." *Papers on Language and Literature*, vol. 45, iss. 3, Summer 2009, pp. 261–86.

Berry, Ralph. *Changing Styles in Shakespeare*. Allen and Unwin, 1981.

Bevington, David. Headnote to *Twelfth Night. The Complete Works of Shakespeare*. Edited by Bevington. 5th ed., Pearson, 2004, pp. 333–36.

Bloom, Harold. *Shakespeare: The Invention of the Human*. Riverhead / Penguin, 1998.

Booth, Stephen. *Precious Nonsense: The Gettysburg Address, Ben Jonson's Epitaphs on His Children, and* Twelfth Night. U of California P, 1998.

Craik, T. W. "Introduction." *Twelfth Night*. Edited by J. M. Lothian and Craik. Methuen / Arden Shakespeare, 1975.

Edmondson, Paul. Twelfth Night: *A Guide to the Text and Its Theatrical Life*. Palgrave, 2005.

Elam, Keir. "Introduction." *Twelfth Night or What You Will*. Edited by Elam. Bloomsbury Arden, 2008, pp. 1–153.

Everett, Barbara. "Or What You Will." *Essays in Criticism*, vol. 35, 1985, pp. 294–314.

Findlay, Alison, and Liz Oakley-Brown, editors. Twelfth Night: *A Critical Reader*. Bloomsbury Arden, 2014.

Garber, Marjorie. *Shakespeare After All*. Pantheon, 2004.

Gay, Penny. "Introduction." *Twelfth Night*. Edited by Elizabeth Story Dunno. Updated edition. Cambridge UP, 2004, pp. 1–52.

Gurr, Andrew. "Double Play Titles." *Notes and Queries*, vol. 64, no. 2, June 2017, pp. 331–36.

Hirsh, James. "Laughter at *Titus Andronicus*." *Essays in Theatre*, vol. 7, 1988, pp. 59–74.

_____. "*Othello* and Perception." Othello: *New Perspectives*. Edited by Virginia Mason Vaughan and Kent Cartwright. Fairleigh Dickinson UP, 1991, pp. 135–59. Rpt. *Shakespearean Criticism Yearbook 1991: A Selection of the Year's Most Noteworthy Studies*. Edited by Ralph Berry, et al. Gale, 1993, pp. 276–86.

_____. *Shakespeare and the History of Soliloquies*. Fairleigh Dickinson UP, 2003.

_____. "Teaching Paradoxes." *Shakespeare Quarterly*, vol. 41, 1990, pp. 222–29.

_____. "Through Dramatic Structure." *Approaches to Teaching* King Lear. Edited by Robert H. Ray. Modern Language Association, 1986, pp. 86–90.

Hotson, Leslie. *The First Night of Twelfth Night*. Rupert Hart-Davis, 1954.

McLean, Hugh. "Shakespeare in the Classroom: Titles in the Text." *English Record*, vol. 23, 1972, pp. 27–33.

Parker, Kathryn Roberts. "Wassailing and Festive Music in Shakespeare's *Twelfth Night*." *Australian Drama Studies*, vol. 76, 2020, pp. 158–82.

Pepys, Samuel. *The Diary of Samuel Pepys*. 11 volumes. Edited by Robert Lanham and William Matthews. Vol. 4. U of California P, 1971.

Salingar, L. G. "The Design of *Twelfth Night*." *Shakespeare Quarterly*, vol. 9, 1958, pp. 117–39.

Shakespeare, William. *The New Oxford Shakespeare*. Edited by Gary Taylor, et al. Oxford UP, 2016.

Smith, Bruce R. "Introduction." Twelfth Night or What You Will: *Texts and Contexts*. Bedford / St Martin's Press, 2001, pp. 1–25.

Stern, Tiffany. "Inverted Commas around the 'Fun': Music in *Twelfth Night.*" Twelfth Night: *A Critical Reader*. Edited by Alison Findlay and Liz Oakley-Brown. Bloomsbury Arden, 2014, pp. 166–88.

Warren, Roger, and Stanley Wells. "Introduction." *Twelfth Night*. Edited by Warren and Wells. Oxford UP, 1995.

Wells, Stanley. *Royal Shakespeare*. Manchester UP, 1976.

"Who governs here?": Government, Sovereignty, and the Unruly Household in Shakespeare's *Twelfth Night*

Matthew M. Thiele

When she first sets foot in Illyria, Viola, a young shipwrecked lady, asks her rescuer, a Captain, "Who governs here?" (1.2.24). The Captain names Orsino, who is vested with the authority of a duke, but instead of showing him governing, the play shows him in various states of distraction. He sulks as he listens to music, moans about his lovesickness, and fruitlessly pursues a woman who cannot love him. Although there appear to be few real consequences for his neglect of his duties, his actions in the play raise serious doubts about his fitness to govern. If Illyria has to depend on Duke Orsino for governance, then people are going to suffer. As it happens, the people of Illyria are doing alright by themselves, and the play shows that one character, Countess Olivia, struggles but ultimately succeeds to manage her household affairs. By presenting Olivia's house and its environs as the main setting of the play, *Twelfth Night* suggests that it is really the household that is at the center of civil governance, and that a sovereign household is the foundation of civil order.

The Derelict Duke

Although Viola's question of who governs in Illyria functions mainly as an invitation to the Captain to deliver some important exposition, the answer is not trivial. The nominal governor, Orsino, is shown to be unsuitable in various ways in the play. Jackie Watson shows how Orsino's first lines reflect a kind of furor that is unproductive and unreasonable: "in the opening scene of *Twelfth Night* the uncontrolled sensuality of Orsino seems more likely to signify that the love he feels is in some sense not reasonable, even culpable" (231). Karin S. Coddon explains that Orsino's first lines may have alienated Elizabethan audiences because of their reference to extravagance: "Orsino's elaborate tropes of appetite and satiety might well have prompted a subversive laughter, given the mind-boggling extravagances of the Elizabethan aristocrat's table. On the other hand, certain factions were less likely to find such gluttony a laughing matter in the inflation- and famine-plagued 1590s" (313). Coddon suggests that the play may have been designed to alienate audiences from Orsino by calling attention to the excesses of the aristocracy.

Orsino is sullen and unsociable, and both of those qualities are causes and symptoms of illness for Early Modern audiences (Thiele 241–43). He tells Viola, "I myself am best / When least in company" (1.4.37–38). Although that statement might be ironically correct, Orsino's unsociability is an illness that reflects a sickness in governance, and that is a common metaphor in Medieval and Early Modern literature. His neglect of his official responsibilities is evident from the beginning of the play onward. The longer the audience goes without seeing Orsino doing anything related to governance, the clearer it becomes that Orsino's pursuit of Olivia has become a dangerous distraction. It is really only when Orsino has to confront the fugitive pirate Antonio in act 5, scene 1 that we see him perform an official duty. Even that encounter is compromised by self-interest. The First Officer reminds Orsino that Antonio was the one who participated in an attack that led to Orsino's nephew Titus losing a leg (5.1.57–59). The situation is thus presented as a matter of personal enmity in addition to being a matter of law enforcement and governance.

More importantly, Orsino contributes to disorder and instructs his employees to be disruptive. When he sends Viola for the first time to communicate his love to Olivia, he encourages her to "Be clamorous and leap all civil bounds / Rather than make unprofited return" (1.4.21–22). Although this might be unremarkable for a typical lover, it is surprising coming from the chief civil authority in Illyria. Orsino himself seems to take this approach later in the play when he calls on Olivia personally. He insults her by calling her "uncivil lady" (5.1.110), and then he goes beyond all limits of propriety by announcing that he has contemplated killing her and fully intends to get back at her by harming Viola as retribution for rejecting him:

> Why should I not, had I the heart to do it,
> Like to th'Egyptian thief at point of death
> Kill what I love?—a savage jealousy
> That sometime savors nobly. But hear me this:
> Since you to nonregardance cast my faith,
> And that I partly know the instrument
> That screws me from my true place in your favor,
> Live you the marble-breasted tyrant still.
> But this your minion, whom I know you love,
> And whom, by heaven I swear, I tender dearly,
> Him will I tear out of that cruel eye,
> Where he sits crownéd in his master's spite. (5.1.115–26)

That he lacks the heart to implement his wishes is hardly any comfort at all. At this moment in the play, Orsino abuses Olivia's hospitality and betrays his responsibilities as the leader of Illyria. By comparing himself to a thief who is desperately facing his own death, Orsino implicitly acknowledges the criminality of his intentions and suggests that Olivia's rejection of him is a matter of life and death, which is entirely out of proportion with the reality of the situation. By announcing his intention to harm Viola with the phrase "hear me this," Orsino borrows the rhetoric of governance for personal purposes, attempting to put an official stamp on illicit deeds, or perhaps forgetting the necessary boundary between his personal wishes and his official responsibilities.

The Unruly Household

"Who governs here" could also reasonably be asked at Countess Olivia's door. Although her seven-year mourning period serves as an important plot point, being the reason that Viola decides to disguise herself as a eunuch and seek to serve Orsino, she violates the terms of her mourning period early in the play, which suggests that she can be inconsistent and unreliable. Given her rank, Olivia should be expected to delegate responsibility for managing her household to her employees, but her nearly total removal from household matters makes it possible for her profligate uncle, Sir Toby Belch, to use her household as the stage for disruptive drunken revelry and cruel practical jokes.

The people Olivia employs to help her are unreliable and that reflects her own instability and capriciousness. Maria, Olivia's chambermaid, initially seems competent and stable, but even though she does her job by trying to encourage Toby and his friend Sir Andrew Aguecheek to moderate their reveling, Maria ultimately sides with Toby against the peace of the household when she decides to take revenge on Malvolio. Early in the play, she says, "By my troth, Sir Toby, you must come in earlier o'nights. Your cousin, my lady, takes great exceptions to your ill hours...you must confine yourself within the modest limits of order" (1.3.4–9). Right before Malvolio confronts Toby and Andrew on another occasion, Maria gives them a warning: "What a caterwauling do you keep here! If my lady have not called up her steward Malvolio and bid him turn you out of doors, never trust me" (2.3.72–74). She takes up Toby's grudge against Malvolio after he scolds them for disrupting the household, to the point that she forges Olivia's handwriting to help Toby pursue a childish scheme to humiliate him. That subplot eventually leads to Malvolio being cruelly imprisoned and tortured somewhere in Olivia's house.

Malvolio himself is haughty, vain, and rude at times, which makes him a poor representative of the household. When Olivia sends him to deliver a ring to Viola, he casts the ring on the ground and walks away instead of making a courteous and proper exchange: "If it be worth stooping for, there it lies, in your eye; if not, be it his that finds it" (2.2.15–16). Malvolio's rudeness might be excusable, but it creates a poor impression of his character and of Olivia's command over her household.

Although Malvolio disrupts the order of the house in various ways, he also tries to enforce order, and he fantasizes about having more authority in the house so that he can pursue orderliness. As Malvolio imagines what it might be like to be married to Olivia, he envisions bringing order to the household. Malvolio's fantasy is actually endearingly mundane; he wants to tell Toby to "amend" his drunkenness (2.5.72), and stop hanging out with that loser, Sir Andrew (2.5.75–79). His reforms are unlikely to succeed, and so they seem a little silly, but Malvolio's concern for the household shows that he cares about his job and his employer.

Most of what happens with Toby, Sir Andrew, Malvolio, Maria, and the rest is to be expected in a comedy. Bumbling or tricky servants and unruly houseguests have been stock characters in comedy since the beginning. The kind of misrule represented by the reveling that goes on in Olivia's household has been well explored by other critics. Malvolio describes the conduct of the revelers as "uncivil rule" (2.3.122), which, along with the title of *Twelfth Night*, serves as a direct reference to the kind of misrule that was a standard element of Early Modern English holiday celebrations (e.g., Barber 24–29, Coddon 314, Watson 225).

I will add that Olivia's household affairs are in such disarray that the drunk uncle appears to be the one answering the door. It is apparently Toby who receives Viola during her first visit. When Maria tells her that Toby has received Viola and is holding her in delay, Olivia reacts with frustration: "He speaks nothing / but madman. Fie on him!" (1.5.103–40). Olivia's frustration is directed at Toby, but competent household employees should be able to prevent this kind of situation. Having Toby as the outward-facing representative of the household communicates publically the disorder within the house. It is that reception, among other things that Viola criticizes when she complains about the rudeness she has received. When Olivia scolds Viola for her rudeness at their first meeting ("you began rudely" [1.5.207]), Viola justifies her conduct as a reaction to the way she was treated: "The rudeness that hath appeared in me have I learned from my entertainment" (1.5.209–10). This is a different perspective on misrule than one might expect. Viola fits her unruliness to the house's as a way of reprimanding Olivia about the state of her hospitality.

What is usually not pointed out in criticism about the reveling in *Twelfth Night* is its connection to serious violence and civil disorder. Fabian refers to organizing a bearbaiting, which is at its heart a public spectacle of violence. Fabian holds a grudge against Malvolio for bringing him "out of favor" with Olivia "about a bearbaiting here"

(2.5.8), and Toby proposes to upset Malvolio by bringing the bear back: "To anger him we'll have the bear again" (2.5.9). Toby and Fabian work together to stoke Andrew's jealousy of Viola, whom Olivia prefers over him, which incites an attempt at a duel. They may not anticipate that it would result in actual violence, but they are certainly not responsible enough to make sure that it does not. The original site of the duel is "at orchard end" (3.4.225) of Olivia's house; that is where Toby tells Viola that Andrew is waiting to fight her. The orchard is apparently open to the public, however, because Antonio, the pirate, stumbles through in search of Viola's brother Sebastian. The arrival of a group of officers, who are pursuing Antonio to arrest him, interrupts the duel. The appearance of Antonio, who is the main representative of civil disorder in Illyria, serves as a bridge between the domestic violence in Olivia's house and the official employment of state violence by law enforcement officers to maintain civil order.

The violence that Toby, Fabian, and Andrew instigate does not stay confined to the house; it spills out into the streets, and, in doing so, it becomes a problem for the community. After mistaking him for Viola, Andrew confronts Sebastian in the street before Olivia's house to pursue his grudge against Viola, and the result is that Sebastian bloodies him and Toby. Although it is satisfying and funny to see Toby and Andrew take a beating for exposing Viola to real violence, Toby for the sake of pursuing his own amusement and Andrew for his foolish jealous possessiveness of Olivia and his trust in Toby, the message the play sends about the consequences of violence is a serious one. Violence is rarely contained within the limits people set for it. As guests in Olivia's household, Toby and Andrew should confine their actions within the modest limits of order. Their failure to do so has real consequences beyond the household. Thus, the misrule in Olivia's household is not necessarily harmless and not necessarily fun.

The Lady of the House

There is a debate among critics over how to see Olivia's character. Some critics see Olivia as a victim who is at the mercy of the men around her. For example, Joan Pong Linton writes,

> These designs on Olivia's person by her male dependents [Toby, Malvolio, and Feste] as their means to wealth reveal her vulnerability as the unmarried head of an aristocratic household in disrepair—a household with no intact boundaries. In this sense the strangers are already in the house, these familiar faces whose mercenary motives and transactions have thoroughly infiltrated its social space, and redefined her as property up for grabs, turning any semblance of hospitality into a form of prostitution. (224)

Although this may seem valid nearer to the beginning of the play, by the end of the play it is clear that Olivia desires autonomy and pursues it. Her consistent refusal of Orsino's advances suggests that she can handle him perfectly well, and even though she struggles to handle Toby in particular, there are obvious reasons for her struggle that have nothing to do with the kind of abjection and helplessness that some critics attribute to her.

Other critics acknowledge Olivia's fundamental competence and autonomy, and they see a purpose to the disorder in the house. Ruth Nevo suggests that the play highlights Olivia's command over her household:

> Fatherless and brotherless, Olivia is the sole mistress of her household. She is its source of authority, and her unruly house guests are there to show that she is able to take command, though the turbulence below stairs under Sir Toby's aegis indicates that her control is not impregnable. She leans upon her steward in her lonely eminence, and not only to ward off a suit from the count (1.5.109). But her even-handed distribution of remonstrance and consolation to the former shows her not inconsiderable capacity for mastery. (Nevo 30–31)

It is exactly that command that Sebastian notices when he is trying to understand and justify Olivia's sudden offer to marry him. When Sebastian questions Olivia's sanity, he concludes that she is sane because she competently manages her household. He says,

> Or else the lady's mad. Yet if 'twere so,
> She could not sway her house, command her followers,
> Take and give back affairs and their dispatch
> With such a smooth, discreet, and stable bearing
> As I perceive she does. (4.3.16–20)

Sebastian reasons that Olivia is competent to run her household because her employees follow her commands. Given what the play has shown its audience about Olivia's shortcomings, Sebastian's observations may be humorously ironic, but these lines invite the audience to reflect on how well they correspond to the objective reality of the play.

Olivia commands respect from Malvolio even when he is suffering extremely, even though he seems to believe that Toby has imprisoned him under her authority. In the letter he writes during his imprisonment, Malvolio complains politely, "Though you have put me into darkness and given your drunken cousin rule over me, yet have I the benefit of my senses as well as Your Ladyship" (5.1.303–06). Malvolio, at least, continues to treat Olivia respectfully, addressing her properly as "Your Ladyship," even when he perceives her to be the cause of his trouble.

Who Governs Here?

Because so much of the play takes place in an around Olivia's house, the obvious answer to the question "Who governs here?" is Olivia. However, as we see, Olivia does not manage her affairs well, and she does not always do her best. For example, she admits to Viola that she abused Malvolio by sending him with a ring under false pretenses (3.1.111–14). In addition, Feste, Malvolio, and Maria cause problems of their own, and those problems represent challenges to Olivia's authority and ability to lead.

On the other hand, it is unreasonable to expect Olivia to be able to exercise absolute control over every person in and around her house. It is also important to note that Olivia appears to be trying to do the right thing in all situations, which is more than we can say for most of the other characters in the play.

Various abuses occur under Olivia's roof without her knowledge, and she bears some responsibility for that. The most severe abuse is the imprisonment and torture of Malvolio in a dark room by Feste and Sir Toby. This has to reflect poorly on Olivia, but it provides an opportunity for her to try to make it right, and the audience sees in her efforts to satisfy Malvolio at the end of the play that she is concerned with justice. She tells Malvolio after he has been freed from his imprisonment,

> This practice hath most shrewdly passed upon thee;
> But when we know the grounds and authors of it,
> Thou shalt be both the plaintiff and the judge
> Of thine own cause. (5.1.352–55).

Although she grants him more authority than perhaps she should, her commitment to helping him seek justice is clear.

It is noteworthy that the guarantee of justice for Malvolio comes from Olivia and not Orsino, because he is present at this moment, and it could reasonably be assumed that administering justice would be within his jurisdiction, particularly if Malvolio has been the victim of a crime. Fabian tries to minimize the wrong done to Malvolio by saying, "How with a sportful malice it was followed / May rather pluck on laughter than revenge, / If that the injuries be justly weighed / That have on both sides passed" (5.1.365–68), but false imprisonment is definitely a crime under English Common Law. Bramble mentions it in *Eastward Ho* by George Chapman, Ben Jonson, and John Marston, for example. Bramble, a lawyer, tells Sir Petronel Flash that he should sue Touchstone when he is released: "you shall haue an Action of *false Imprisonment* against him, when you come out" (5.3.76–78).

At least one real case involving wrongful imprisonment deals with wrongful confinement by someone who is not a law enforcement officer. In a 1593 text that addresses complications arising from jurisdictional conflicts between civil law, English Common Law, and Ecclesiastical Law, Richard Cosin writes,

> Aman reported that the Abbot of S. Albanes did detaine his wife in the said Abbots lodging against her will; to the intent to make her his harlot. the Abbot hereupon brought his action of Diffamation in the Court ecclesiasticall; and the husband his prohibition. nowe because the husband might haue his action of false imprisonment at the Common lawe agaynst the Abbot. (123)

What this means for the purposes of my argument is that the understanding of false imprisonment under the law would be broad enough to apply to Malvolio's imprisonment. He is the victim of a crime; as such, it should be Orsino's business, but he says nothing about it.

Although she could be accused of tolerating Sir Toby and Sir Andrew for too long, Olivia is constrained by the conventions of hospitality and family to be generous and tolerant, and she does so for a long time before finally scolding Sir Toby for his participation in a drunken brawl before her house:

> OLIVIA. Hold, Toby! On thy life I charge thee, hold!
> SIR TOBY. Madam—
> OLIVIA. Will it be ever thus? Ungracious wretch,
> Fit for the mountains and the barbarous caves,
> Where manners ne'er were preached! Out of my sight!—
> (4.1.44–48)

This shows Olivia to be capable of checking Sir Toby when she needs to, suggesting that her earlier tolerance of his misbehavior was not the product of any reluctance or inability to confront him.

Sovereignty and Individual Autonomy

In a play populated by characters who are almost unanimously demented in one way or another, where control and order seem to be abdicated or suspended, one of the ideas that remains consistent in the face of threats and challenges is Olivia's sovereignty in her home. It is one of the only stable elements in a play full of chaos. Sovereignty becomes an issue at various points in the play, and the play links individual autonomy and sovereignty through Olivia's actions and Orsino's words. Orsino refers to organs as "sovereign thrones" of the body when he fantasizes about how intense Olivia's love is likely to be:

> Oh, she that hath a heart of that fine frame
> To pay this debt of love but to a brother,
> How will she love, when the rich golden shaft
> Hath killed the flock of all affections else
> That live in her; when liver, brain and heart,
> These sovereign thrones, are all supplied, and filled
> Her sweet perfections, with one self king! (1.1.32–38)

In this arresting and somewhat troubling image, Orsino imagines Olivia's organs as thrones in which he will sit as king, suggesting that he wants to override Olivia's individual autonomy with his own sovereignty. In this context, it makes sense that Orsino would speak about Olivia's sovereignty with resentment. When Orsino prepares Viola for her second visit to Olivia, he says, "Get thee to yond same sovereign cruelty. / Tell her, my love, more noble than the world, / Prizes not quantity of dirty lands" (2.4.80–82). That term of disdain, "sovereign cruelty," reflects Orsino's resentment at having to submit to Olivia's wishes in her choice of partner. It shows a bitterness about having to respect something he would rather be able to disregard.

Although Orsino desperately wants Olivia to give him sovereignty over her, she insists on preserving her sovereignty, which is one of the most remarkable features of the play. And while falling in love with Viola and marrying Sebastian could be seen as a loss of control, her pursuit of both characters is straightforward and honest, aside from the business with the ring, and she does all of her own courting.

Conclusion

What we see in Olivia's household is a representative example of the kind of disorder bad leadership can cause. She appears to be unable to dislodge her unruly guests, and her household employees are actively disruptive. However, Olivia reacts to the disorders in her house with responsibility and care. Although Olivia cannot control everyone in her household, she admirably takes responsibility for their well-being. When she believes that Malvolio is suffering madness, she tells Maria, "Let some of my people have a special care of him. I would not have him miscarry for the half of my dowry" (3.4.63–65). Her concern for others is one of the qualities that sets her apart from Orsino, who never really stops being morose and dull.

The disorder in Olivia's house reflects the disorder of the state and Orsino's abandonment of his official duties, which is evident in his single-minded and futile pursuit of Olivia's consent in love. Just as an absolute system of governance that has no real ability to check a ruler usually produces incompetent leaders who abuse authority and neglect their duties, an unregulated household provides the venue for various abuses if not checked and corrected by a competent head.

In the world of *Twelfth Night*, Orsino needs Olivia more than Olivia needs Orsino, and that obviously has interesting and important political implications. For one, it suggests that Olivia should have the autonomy to choose a suitable partner, even if the one she chooses is a woman. It also suggests that government needs sovereign households more than sovereign households need government, and that rulers should tread lightly. The play reserves significant sovereignty over household affairs for the owner of the house, suggesting that a sovereign household is the foundation of civil order.

Works Cited

Barber, C.L. *Shakespeare's Festive Comedy: A Study of Dramatic Form and Its Relation to Social Custom*. Meridian Books, 1963.

Coddon, Karin S. "'Slander in an allowed fool': *Twelfth Night*'s Crisis of the Aristocracy." *SEL*, vol. 33, no. 2, Spring 1993, pp. 309–25.

Cosin, Richard. *An apologie for svndrie proceedings by iurisdiction ecclesiasticall, of late times by some chalenged, and also diuersly by them impugned*, 1593. ProQuest, www.proquest.com/books/apologie-svndrie-proceedings-iurisdiction/docview/2240927571/se-2.

Jonson, Ben. *Eastward Ho*, in *Ben Jonson*. Edited by C. H. Herford and Percy Simpson, vol. IV. Clarendon Press, 1954, pp. 487–619.

Linton, Joan Pong. "Hospitality in *Twelfth Night*: Playing at (the Limits of) Home." *Shakespeare and Hospitality: Ethics, Politics, and Exchange*. Edited by David B. Goldstein and Julia Reinhard Lupton. Routledge, 2016, pp. 222–41.

Nevo, Ruth. "Nature's Bias." *Modern Critical Interpretations: William Shakespeare's* Twelfth Night. Edited by Harold Bloom, Chelsea House, 1987, pp. 27–40.

Shakespeare, William. *The Complete Works of William Shakespeare*. Edited by David Bevington, Pearson, 2014.

Thiele, Matthew M. "The Sociability Cure: Expelling the Plague in Ben Jonson's *Epicoene*." *Ben Jonson Journal*, vol. 19, no. 2, November 2012, pp. 240–60.

Watson, Jackie. "Sense and Community: Twelfth Night and Early Modern Playgoing." *Shakespeare / SENSE: Contemporary Readings in Sensory Culture*. Edited by Simon Smith, The Arden Shakespeare, 2020, pp. 224–44.

Malvolio Annoyed: Early Illustrations of the Rowdy Party Scene in Shakespeare's *Twelfth Night*

Robert C. Evans

The nineteenth century was the hey-day of illustrated editions of Shakespeare, both in Britain and abroad. Lacking films, television, and even (for many persons) easy access to "serious" theater, people living in the 1800s and even into the early twentieth century often prized editions of Shakespeare that helped them visualize important characters and key scenes. Many of these illustrations featured actual photographs of famous actors, but most of them offered drawings by talented artists, some of them very prominent, others less so. Many of these illustrated editions are quite intriguing, and the ways different illustrators imagined the same scenes and characters is often illuminating in their own rights. Both the similarities and the differences between representative drawings suggest a good deal about how Shakespeare could be visualized in the Victorian era, both on the stage and on the printed page.

One especially popular scene among illustrators of *Twelfth Night* was the episode in act 2, scene 3 involving the rowdy, riotous partying of Feste (the play's fool), Sir Toby Belch (the Countess Olivia's uncle), and Sir Andrew Aguecheek (who is both Toby's friend and his gull). Illustrations of this episode also often include Maria (Countess Olivia's servant) and Malvolio (the countess's domineering steward). Maria tries at first to suppress the drunken, boisterous noise created by Toby and his friends (the party, after all, is taking place late at night). But it is not until the outraged Malvolio appears on the scene that the party runs out of steam. Malvolio manages to insult and demean the other characters, including Maria, so that when he leaves it is Maria who hatches a plot to make a fool of him in a most humiliating way. Maria's plotting is sometimes featured in illustrations dealing with the party's aftermath.[1]

The 1861 Chambers Edition

A black-and-white drawing featured in the 1861 W. R. Chambers edition highlights the work of Keeley Halswelle, a talented British artist who lived from 1831–1891, who was both a respected painter and an illustrator both for the popular press (such as the *Illustrated London News*) and for the book trade. Halswelle's illustration (see fig. 1) is specifically relevant to the moment in 3.2 when Sir Andrew urges Feste to begin singing. In this drawing, Sir Andrew is on the left, Toby is in the middle, and Feste is on the right. Neither Maria nor Malvolio has yet appeared. All three of the men Halswelle depicts seem to be in advanced middle age, a fact that makes their drunken revelry all the more blameworthy (at least as far as Maria and Malvolio will soon be concerned), since these men do not have youth as an excuse for their unruly midnight exuberance.

Sir Andrew's hair, in this depiction, does not look a bit stringy, as Shakespeare describes it (1.3.89), nor does he look, at this point, especially foolish. Later he becomes hilariously ridiculous, but here he seems relaxed and happy; he is simply one of the middle-aged boys and is still being treated with some regard and respect by Toby,

Figure 1. From the 1861 Chambers edition.

who later treats him as a figure of fun and even disdain before eventually dismissing him with contempt. Sir Andrew's costume, in this illustration, implies his status and wealth, although he is not foolishly overdressed, as Malvolio will be later in the play.

Alcohol is prominently and symbolically featured here. A pitcher of wine occupies the literal center of the drawing, and Sir Toby lifts a stein (almost as big as the pitcher) into the air. As in most drawings of Toby, here he is obviously a fat, Falstaffian-looking figure with a large smile and dimples in his fleshy face when he smiles, as he is doing right at this moment. His face is fat; his torso is fat; and even his legs seem fat—suggesting a lifetime of sensual self-indulgence involving food and alcohol. His waistline contrasts with Sir Andrew's much slimmer waist—slimness accentuated by the belt Sir Andrew is wearing. Similarly, Sir Andrew's legs seem much trimmer than Toby's.

Feste's legs and overall physique are also trimmer than Toby's, a fact especially evident as each has a leg raised, each is on the right side of the drawing, and each (like Sir Andrew) has his head thrown back and is laughing. Feste's costume, with its very large buttons, almost resembles the sort of uniform a fool might wear, and his left foot looks bare, which makes him seem the most relaxed of all three of these very relaxed figures. Feste's fool's cap suggests his role in the play, and, from one perspective, that cap can even look like a head-on view of a long-eared ass.

The positions of Andrew and Feste, on left and right, not only help emphasize the container of wine in the middle of the drawing but also helps "frame" Sir Toby, the most important, dominant, and domineering of the three and thus the one who deserves to take the central position. In the moment illustrated here (2.3.61–62), Sir Andrew has just asked Toby to sing a song titled "Hold thy peace," and Feste, in response, has just made a joke ("I shall never begin if I hold my peace"). All three men apparently find the joke, and the whole mutual song-singing, hilariously funny. Feste seems to be laughing at his own joke here, just as Toby urges him to begin singing. The eyes of all three men seem squeezed shut from laughing. Of course, their merriment is about to be abruptly interrupted by the appearance first of Maria and then of Malvolio. The doorway through which Maria and then Malvolio will enter looms in the background of this drawing, implying that the present merriment will soon be cut short.

The 1876 Davis Edition

In another black-and-white drawing—this one from an edition published by Charles H. Davis in 1876—Toby and Andrew are the only male characters present, but Maria has now been added into the mix (see fig. 2). The absence of Feste seems odd; he is definitely in the play when Maria enters, as she is shown doing here. His absence would decrease the sheer volume of noise being made by the revelers, and indeed neither Sir Toby nor Sir Andrew seems to be singing here. Both, in fact, have their mouths closed. If anything, they have been (or still are, in Toby's case) smoking, which again would result in less raucous noise.

Appropriately enough, Sir Andrew looks the most ridiculous of the three figures. His feathered cap seems to be on backwards; the feathers are flopping in front of his face; his hair looks both thin and long (below shoulder length); and his pipe is as upside-down as the feathers on his hat. He and Toby seem quite close physically (as they are quite close in other ways); have they been (or are they still here) dancing? Andrew's hair style, clothing, and the light color of his clothing make him look almost effeminate, while his downward look—as if he is staring at his pipe—make him seem mentally distant from Toby here even if they are physically close. As expected, Andrew looks thinner than Toby, but his feet look almost tiny in comparison to Toby's. It is clear that Toby is the dominant partner here; it almost looks as if he is grabbing Andrew's arm, as if they are dancing, with Toby the figure who is obviously in control.

Toby's paunch contrasts sharply with Andrew's slimmer figure, and his boots help accentuate the greater size of his feet. The fact that he wears a sword foreshadows his later love of fighting and the trick he uses (involving a sword) at Andrew's expense. Neither Toby nor Andrew is smiling. They do not look especially celebratory, and although they are physically close, neither is looking in the other's eyes. There is a lack of social engagement despite the fact that Toby seems to have grasped Andrew's arm. Toby's hair is darker and shorter than Andrew's and Toby's hat (unlike Andrew's) seems properly arranged. He is the least comical of the two, although neither seems as comical as the Tobys and Andrews who appear in other drawings of this scene. There does seem to be a small

Figure 2. From the 1876 Charles H. Davis edition.

bottle of wine on the table behind Toby, and next to that bottle are two tiny glasses. In some other drawings, the men have obviously been drinking from massive steins of wine, and in some of these drawings they *are* actually drinking at the present moment, with the wine right in front of them, not hidden in the background.

Meanwhile, Maria, who is even further in the background of this drawing, does not look particularly disturbed by the noise Toby and Andrew are making. Her features are hard to see, but she does not look angry or aggressive, as if she is in the process of moving toward the unruly pair. She looks attractive (contrast her tiny waistline with Toby's massive gut); it is hard to imagine why she would ever be *physically* attracted to Toby, however much she may be attracted by his status and wealth. Ironically, it is Maria, not Malvolio, who ultimately "marries up" in this play, and it is partly her witty and successful plot against Malvolio that makes Toby decide to marry her. Nothing in this drawing, however, suggests that she is presently witty or self-assertive. She is the third character in this illustration who seems to lack any real interaction with the others. Each character shown here seems physically and/or mentally distant from the other two.

An Undated London Printing and Publishing Company Edition

In a black-and-white illustration of the "party" episode for an undated edition issued by the London Printing and Publishing Company, the immensely talented artist Kenny Meadows (1790–1874) offered his own distinctive conception of a key moment in the play—the moment when Malvolio suddenly appears and kills all the fun, thereby unleashing the eventual wrath of everyone else in the drawing (see fig. 3).

In this drawing Malvolio is appropriately dressed in humorless black, in contrast to the other characters. We see him from behind, standing bolt upright, so that his body looks as inflexible as his disposition. But we glimpse enough of his face to notice that he is not smiling. His face, with its small moustache, looks smaller than the faces of the other men, and his lips appear to be pursed. He is looking disdainfully in the direction of Sir Toby (the ringleader of the

Figure 3. From the undated London Printing and Publishing Company edition.

chaos) and Maria. He seems to be dressed in grimly dark pajamas, although he also seems to be wearing a ring-topped (possibly red and white) sleeping cap at the apex of his very long head. He is relatively thin (unlike Sir Toby, his symbolic opposite), and his posture also contrasts with Sir Toby's. Even Malvolio's left hand looks dark, and he literally casts a shadow that is pointed toward Sir Toby—surely another bit of symbolism.

Unlike Malvolio, who is dressed almost entirely in black, Feste, on the extreme left, is dressed entirely in much lighter colors and his spotted leggings in particular make him resemble a clown. He is, in fact, in almost every way, Malvolio's symbolic opposite. Malvolio stands; Feste sprawls. Malvolio is grim; Feste is smiling. Malvolio stares in disgust at Sir Toby; Feste stares in wry amusement at Malvolio. Malvolio takes the chaos seriously; Feste refuses to take Malvolio seriously. Malvolio stands ramrod stiff; Feste has his left leg resting on the table top and his right leg suspended in mid-air. Malvolio's left arm is up near his throat; Feste's is hanging down toward the floor. Malvolio is rigid; Feste is totally relaxed.

Meanwhile, Sir Andrew, with a ridiculously elaborate, tall, broad-brimmed, and feathered hat on his head and a fancy outfit reaching the whole way up his neck, definitely seems the most overdressed of the characters here. Unlike Feste (who is looking directly at Malvolio) or Malvolio (who is looking directly at Toby), or Toby (who is looking directly at Maria), or Maria (who is looking directly at Toby), Sir Andrew is simply looking down at the table. He seems to be neither smiling nor singing nor even engaged with the other characters. Only his outfit might suggest that in this play he is far more of a genuine fool than Feste.

Toby resembles Feste in his posture but not in his physique or age. He looks older than the fool, and the way his left leg is splayed over the arm of his chair emphasizes just how fat his legs are (not to mention his stomach, which is on full display in this drawing). His thick boots contrast with Feste's slim slippers. Significantly, it is Toby who has his exceptionally long arm reached out toward the jug of wine. It is almost as if he is guarding it from Sir Andrew, who does not seem especially interested either in it or in anything else. The flask of wine here is large, and the glasses used for drinking from it are tall, unlike the flasks and glasses shown in some other depictions of this scene. Both of the only visible wine glasses are placed directly in front of Sir Toby; nothing visibly suggests that he has been sharing the wine with anyone else, although the behavior and appearance of both Andrew and Feste may suggest that they are already at least as drunk as Toby. Toby seems to be singing as he ignores Malvolio; he is instead staring directly up into the face of Maria.

Although Maria may be a participant in the festivities, she may instead, at this point, merely be holding her hands over her ears to stifle the noise of Toby's singing. She looks quite young in this depiction (her rich black hair contrasts with Toby's mostly bald pate). It is hard to imagine that she considers him an attractive potential husband because of his looks, suggesting that her main motive in later marrying him is because of his social status. With her small waist, prominent breasts, and wide hips, she could probably attract a more handsome husband than Sir Toby, but perhaps not a husband with the kind of money and social prominence he possesses.

Meadows, with his typical wit, manages to make each of his characters memorably distinctive and uses contrasting symbolism to real effect.

An Undated Sherwood Jones Edition

Another black-and-white drawing, included in an edition published in London by Sherwood Jones and Co. for the "Proprietors of the 'London Stage'" (title page), once again features all five of the main comic characters (see fig. 4). This illustration is especially interesting because the artist was Mary Byfield (1795–1871), a talented woman who was born into a family of wood engravers and who, under the tutelage of her father, was able to make a successful career as an illustrator of numerous important books.

As in other black -and-white drawings of the party scene, Malvolio here is dressed entirely in dark colors. He seems genuinely distressed here, rather than simply forbidding or arrogant. He does

Figure 4. From the undated Sherwood Jones edition.

not seem to be looking at anyone in particular (unless it is at Sir Andrew on the far right). Apparently he has just entered the scene and has not yet had a chance to say anything. His lips are pursed; his left hand is over his left ear to try to block the noise; and he seems to have just stepped down into the room from a raised platform. Everything about him—especially his hands and legs—suggests current and recent movement. He seems to be a more active figure than some other illustrated Malvolios. He also looks younger than some other illustrated versions of this character—young enough, perhaps, to make him a plausible husband for Olivia (at least in his own mind).

Feste, in this drawing as in others, is dressed almost entirely in white (or at least light-colored) clothing to help distinguish him symbolically from the dark-clad Malvolio. As in other drawings, he is seated (*sprawling* would be a better verb) while Malvolio stands, and if Malvolio seems truly distressed here, Feste seems quite happy (perhaps drunk) as he stares up worshipfully at a tall, large, half-full glass of dark wine. Like most of the others in the room, he seems to be ignoring Malvolio, at least for the moment; perhaps none of the other characters at this point are aware that Malvolio has even arrived. Feste looks as if he may be singing; in any case, he is definitely fixated on his drink.

Sir Toby, the only character shown in a full-frontal profile, may also be singing. He stares either at Feste or at the flask of wine he is holding, or at both. The flask seems smaller than the quite large glasses it fills, and although three glasses are visible, only Feste seems to be drinking at the moment. The glass closest to Toby (directly behind his right elbow) looks as if it is full. Here, as in other drawings, the raised flask is quite close to the very center of the drawing, symbolizing how important wine and self-indulgence are to these three men, and especially to Sir Toby in particular. As in most drawings, he is plump: a tightly fastened belt emphasizes his gut; his cheeks and neck are chubby; and the way his right leg is positioned emphasizes his thick, flabby calf. His elaborate clothing emphasizes his wealth and social status, and he seems better-dressed than either Malvolio or Feste. If he holds a flask in his right hand, he holds a small tobacco pipe in his right. Everything about him implies his love of sensual pleasures, whether it be singing, drinking, smoking or all three together.

Of all the characters in this illustration, Sir Andrew is the strangest of the three. He looks tiny compared to anyone else in the room, especially (of course) the gigantic Sir Toby, who is seated closest to him. This Sir Andrew almost looks like a doll or toy rather than a fully grown human being. (No wonder Olivia apparently has no interest in him!) Dressed entirely in white (or in some other light color), he visually balances Sir Toby in the same way that Feste visually balances Malvolio: anyone whose eyes move across the drawing from left to right will see black, then white, then black, then white again in the characters shown in the drawing's foreground. (The white tablecloth helps emphasize this series of contrasts.) Sir Andrew's cap looks far more foolish than the fool's cap worn by Feste, the actual professional fool. It looks too small even for *his* tiny head, and the tassel dangling from its top (a tassel that seems to be defying gravity), only adds to its bizarre appearance. Sir Andrew is smoking tobacco rather than drinking wine (no wine glass is within his easy reach), and he holds the pipe with his left hand while resting his right hand on his knee. He and Feste, dressed in light colors, "frame" the dark-colored depiction of Sir Toby, who sits between them, thus giving this drawing another element of visual symmetry. Feste and Sir Andrew sit on chairs, Feste facing right and Sir Andrew facing left, and while Feste uses his right hand to hold up a large, half-full glass of dark wine, Sir Andrew uses his left hand to hold up a small white pipe of tobacco. In this drawing, symmetry abounds.

Symmetrical in another way is the positioning of Maria. She and Malvolio, both in the background and both dressed in dark colors, "frame" Feste and Toby, who appear between them. If Malvolio wears striped puffed breeches below his waist, she wears striped puffed sleeves above her waist, and if his face is pointed right, hers is pointed left. Similarly, if he seems to have just entered the scene from the left, she seems to have just entered it from the right. Likewise, their short, dark, curly hairstyles also add balance to the drawing (and contrast with the long, blond, stringy hair worn by Sir Andrew), and both Malvolio and Maria wear concerned looks, indicating that both of them—at least at this point in the play—are bothered by the ruckus being made by Toby and his friends.

Mary Byfield, then, created an especially well-balanced drawing, even as she also created a particularly memorable (if somewhat bizarre) Sir Andrew.

A 1926 World Syndicate Edition

Another drawing of the episode in which Malvolio crashes the party appeared in a 1926 edition published by the World Syndicate company (see fig. 5). In this black-and-white illustration, Malvolio enters from the left, dressed in white bed clothes (including a white cap), wearing a whitish-gray beard and moustache, and holding a lit candle in a white candlestick. His long white flowing robe makes him look almost like a ghost, and the expression on his face implies (at least at this point) curiosity rather than great distress. He is much older than many other illustrated Malvolios and thus seems (except in his own mind) not an especially appealing husband for Olivia. His

Figure 5. From a 1926 World Syndicate edition (act II, scene III).

heftiness might also count against him as a prospective husband in the countess's eyes.

Sir Andrew, in this drawing, is closest to the approaching Malvolio. He looks more normally dressed than in some other drawings—less an obvious object of immediate ridicule. He lifts a dark wine glass high in his right hand and seems to be singing while looking off into empty space rather than staring directly at any of the other characters. He seems to be wearing boots, and his hair does not look especially long or thin. While Sir Andrew is on the left-hand side of the table, Sir Toby is on its right side, thereby adding some symmetry to the drawing in various ways. Toby also holds a dark wine glass in *his* right hand, and he, too (like Sir Andrew) seems to be leaning back and singing. He and Andrew help "frame" Feste and Maria, the characters who are drawn between the two knights, but Toby in this illustration looks remarkably short. His prominent gut is emphasized by the light blouse he wears, but his face looks smaller than that of any other character depicted, including Maria. His sword foreshadows his later aggressiveness, his willingness to duel with swords, and his involvement in tricking Sir Andrew and Viola into a fake sword fight. The way Toby and Andrew are used to frame Feste and Maria reminds us that the two knights seem (for the moment at least) close comrades. Despite some obvious differences between them, their gesturing arms, basically dark clothing, feathered hats, and stretched and booted legs make them seem to have much in common, both in appearance and in character.

In this drawing, Feste seems younger than usual; he almost looks like a teenager, with his beardless face and long hair. His face is mostly turned away from this edition's readers, and he seems to be looking at, gesturing toward, and perhaps also talking to Maria rather than focusing on anyone else. Like all the other men in this drawing, his head is covered, whereas Maria's blonde hair is mostly visible. But if Feste is looking at Maria, Maria is looking directly at Sir Toby. Her raised arms resemble his similarly raised arms, but the reasons their arms are raised seem to differ completely. He is making merry; she seems alarmed by his merrymaking. Interestingly, Maria, in this drawing, seems to tower over Sir Toby; if they were standing next to each other, she would still probably be the taller, even if he were wearing his hat. As with other illustrated Marias, it is hard to imagine this attractive woman being interested in Toby for his physique, although she might fancy marrying him for his money and social status.

If Andrew and Toby "frame" Feste and Maria, all four characters "frame" the large containers of wine that seem at the literal and symbolic center of this drawing. Four cups are visible—one for each of the four central characters here. No fifth cup is visible that might be extended to Malvolio when he finally enters the room where all the ruckus is taking place. Finally, the position of this drawing—immediately underneath the title of the entire work—suggests how popular this scene must have seemed to many early readers and playgoers. This was the scene the publishers and illustrator apparently saw as central to the whole work, the scene most readers might best remember and want to see drawn.

The 1890 Scribner and Welford Edition

One more little-known illustration of the "party scene" in *Twelfth Night* seems worth mentioning here—although this one depicts the immediate *aftermath* of Malvolio's intervention. In an 1890 edition published by Scribner and Welford, the illustrator depicts Maria sharing her ideas for achieving revenge on Malvolio while Toby, Andrew, and Feste simply listen (see fig. 6). The play's second-most-powerful woman has now seized the initiative, and her male co-conspirators are only too willing to let her take the lead. Indeed, it will be Maria's witty conniving here that will ultimately lead an admiring Sir Toby to marry her. Maria's words, shown beneath the illustration, are "If I do not gull him [i.e., Malvolio] into a nayword, and make him a common recreation do not think I have wit enough to lie straight in my bed."

Interestingly, although Maria's face and the faces of Sir Andrew and Feste are clearly visible here, Toby's is not, perhaps symbolizing that it is she rather than he who is now in command. She leans forward, apparently speaking directly either to Andrew or Feste (or both) but apparently ignoring Toby—another indication that she is

"If I do not gull him into a nayword, and make him a common recreation, do not think I have wit enough to lie straight in my bed." Figure 6. From the 1890 Scribner and Welford edition (act II, scene 3, pp. 145–48).

in charge at this point in the play. She is young, slim, and conventionally attractive, and all three older men seem to be listening intently to her plans as she gestures in Feste's direction. Indeed, her apparent focus on Feste symbolizes the fact that she, for the time being, will be the immediate source of merriment and humor. She has enlisted these three older men in her plot to make a fool of another older male, and all three seem to be all ears. Earlier she had tried to control the three older men by trying to get them to quiet down; here she controls them by revealing her plans to humiliate the figure they all now detest. Although she sits on the least-fancy chair, she is the woman in control of a group of men, including two knights, who far outrank her in conventional terms.

Sir Toby, shown from behind, seems corpulent even from this perspective, while his bald head suggests that he is far older than the young Maria, his eventual bride. He is leaning to the right, as if to hear her more clearly, while his left hand holds what looks like either an empty or a half-drained glass positioned directly in front of a huge jug of wine. There may be another, even larger jug positioned right in front of Feste, and there is definitely an empty (but once-full) wine container on the floor, in front of Sir Andrew's feet. This illustration stresses, far more than some others, that huge quantities of wine have been (and are still being) consumed at this impromptu party—a party at which Maria has not, apparently, imbibed, which may help explain how she can be so quick-witted in concocting her clever, complicated plan to humiliate their mutual enemy.

Feste, seated across from Sir Toby and wearing his fool's cap (as in many other illustrations), resembles Toby and Sir Andrew in looking like an older man who is now listening carefully (and apparently with some amusement) to Maria's plan. Interestingly, the illustrator here has drawn more attention to the pointed ears on Feste's fool's cap by juxtaposing them with two pointed candles, shown right next to him on the left (from the reader's perspective).

Feste is paying far more obvious attention to Maria than is Sir Andrew. Andrew *is* leaning forward, but his eyes look almost closed, and he is using his left fist to prop up his leaning head. He is not clearly smiling (as Feste is), and the empty glass in his right hand, as well as the empty stein at his feet, suggest that he is the character who has been consuming the most alcohol. Interestingly, his hair is not long and stringy (as the play specifies) but is instead full and curly. The bows on his shoes suggest both his wealth and his vanity, and the fact that he has not leaned down to pick up the stein from the floor suggests that he is either too lazy—or too drunk—to do so.

Conclusion

The illustrations discussed in this essay—illustrations that are far less well-known than some others from the same period—help show (literally) how a key scene in *Twelfth Night* could be (and was) imagined by intelligent people with clear gifts for visualization. Were these illustrators influenced, perhaps, by actual performances they had seen, or did their illustrations perhaps influence how the "party" scene was performed on contemporary stages? Both of these possibilities seem plausible, but what seems even more certain is that the artists who conceived and executed the many illustrated

Shakespeare editions published throughout the nineteenth century (and into the early twentieth) helped influence the ways Shakespeare's many *readers* during that period "saw" his plays in their own imaginations—on the metaphorical stages within their own minds.

Note

1. All photographs in this essay are from copies of editions personally owned by the author.

Works Cited

[Chambers Edition.] Carruthers, R., and W. Chambers, editors. *Chambers's Household Edition of the Dramatic Works of William Shakespeare*, by William Shakespeare. Illustrated by Keeley Halswelle. 10 vols. London and Edinburgh: W and R. Chambers, 1861.

[Davis Edition.] Duyckinck, George Long, editor. *The Complete Works of William Shakespeare*, by William Shakespeare. Philadelphia: Charles H. Davis, 1876.

[London Printing and Publishing Company Edition.] *William Shakespere's* [sic] *Works*. London: London Printing and Publishing, n.d.

[Scribner and Welford Edition. The Henry Irving Shakespeare.] Irving, Henry, and Frank A. Marshall, editors. *The Works of William Shakespeare*, by William Shakespeare. "With Numerous Illustrations by Gordon Browne." 4 vols. New York: Scribner and Welford, 1890.

Shakespeare, William. *Twelfth Night*. Edited by John Russell Brown. Applause Books, 2001.

[Sherwood, Jones and Co. Edition.] *The Works of Shakespeare*, by William Shakespeare. London: Sherwood, Jones n.d.

[World Syndicate Edition.] *The Complete Works of William Shakespeare*. "Illustrated with Original Designs by T. M. Matterson. Engraved by Alexander Anderson." World Syndicate, 1926.

Malvolio Deceived: Early Illustrations of the Letter and Stocking Scenes in Shakespeare's *Twelfth Night*

Jordan Bailey

Twelfth Night has long been one of the most popular of Shakespeare's comedies, and the episode in which Malvolio, the vain and self-important steward, is tricked into thinking that Countess Olivia, his employer, has fallen in love with him, has long been one of the most popular moments in the play. The same is true of the subsequent scene in which Malvolio appears before the countess, tricked out in cross-gartered yellow stockings (a style and color she detests) and trying to court her when she is still in mourning for her dead brother. Both the letter scene and the yellow-stocking episode provide plenty of opportunities for laughter, especially when they are performed on stage rather than merely read. Thus, it is not surprising that these scenes were often illustrated in various editions of Shakespeare published in the nineteenth-century, an era that produced some of the most important illustrated editions of his works.[1]

The first of these two episodes occurs in act 2, scene 5 of the play. By this point in the drama, Malvolio has aroused the combined wrath of Maria (one of the countess's servants), Sir Toby Belch (the countess's ne'er-do-well drunken uncle), and Sir Andrew Aguecheek (the hapless, ridiculous knight who hopes to marry the countess). Maria, who was especially offended by Malvolio's recent high-handed treatment of her and the two knights, has concocted a mysterious love letter, written in a convincing imitation of the countess's hand and professing the countess's supposed infatuation with Malvolio. Maria leaves the letter in a place where Malvolio is sure to find it, and she plants Sir Toby, Sir Andrew, and Fabian (a friend of theirs who also has reason to despise Malvolio) in a garden so they can watch the unsuspecting steward read the letter and interpret its hidden meanings. Vain as he is, he of course elaborately interprets it as a clear indication that the countess is smitten with him. On stage, this episode usually arouses great laughs. Nineteenth- and early- twentieth-century illustrators did their best to convey the comedy of the scene through their drawings. Some of these drawings are well known and frequently reproduced. Others, like the ones examined here, are not.

The 1904 Cassell "Leopold" Edition

The "Leopold" edition published in 1904 by Cassell and Company, for instance, includes a black-and-white drawing of this episode that clearly features all four main characters—Malvolio, Sir Toby, Sir Andrew, and Fabian. Malvolio is on the right side of the drawing, while the trio of male witnesses is on the left, hidden among some tall shrubs. Malvolio has no idea he is being watched and listened to. He holds the letter in his right hand and seems to be gesturing with his left (see fig. 1). A quotation from the play, printed directly be-

"By my life, this is my lady's hand" Figure 1. From the 1904 Cassell "Leopold" edition.

neath the drawing, has him saying "By my life, this is my lady's hand!" Maria, then, has successfully counterfeited Olivia's style of writing.

The faded, misty quality of the illustration lends a dreamy air to the scene—a fitting atmosphere given the fact that Malvolio is now indulging in his own dreams of love and power and that the three male schemers are witnessing the trick unfolding without any apparent hitch. But although most of the drawing is devoted to the tricksters and their somewhat preposterous hiding spot, most viewers' focus will almost certainly be, like that of the conspirators, on Malvolio himself. In many stage presentations of this scene, the tricksters hide *behind* Malvolio, which helps to explain why he cannot see them. Here, however, they hide in front of him, and in fact he even seems to be looking at the figure who is crouching. The whole episode, of course, is preposterous, and perhaps this is a quality the illustrator sought to convey. In "real life," Malvolio would have to be blind to miss seeing the three grown men halfheartedly crouched behind saplings. And, of course, in "real life," he could easily overhear the derisive comments they make about him. On the stage, the proximity of all four men can be made to seem ridiculously funny; on the page, the arrangement seems more obviously problematic.

Given the fact that the man crouching is the only figure who is wearing boots (a detail mentioned in the play), it seems reasonable to assume that this crouching figure is Sir Toby. He is taking the most care to conceal himself and support Maria's practical joke, showing his appreciation for Maria's wit as well as foreshadowing the devotion to her that results in their marriage at the end of the play. One of the practical jokers—presumably either Fabian or Sir Andrew—leans forward, haphazardly balancing his weight against Sir Toby's shoulder and potentially using his other hand as a brace against one of the trees (the misty quality of the illustration makes it difficult to verify the whereabouts of his left arm). Although this fellow is clearly enjoying taking part in this joke, he is not taking proper precautions to keep himself concealed from Malvolio's notice. One sneeze, one untimely twitch, could send both this figure and Sir Toby rolling straight into Malvolio's path; at the very least, it could shake the small tree, alerting Malvolio to their presence. Of the three tricksters shown, it is unsurprising that Maria chose Sir Toby Belch for marriage—he is the only one who supports her trickery with as much personal commitment as she herself does.

The men who are hiding are a mixed group, containing two knights (Sir Toby and Sir Andrew) and a man from the serving class (Fabian). Despite these differences in station, however, the men are largely homogenous. Their clothing and hairstyles are similar, and they are piled up together with seemingly no regard for which is above the other in rank. They are brought to the same level both by their love of a good joke and their disdain for Malvolio. There is no clear background behind Sir Toby Belch and company, making it clear that their whereabouts are immaterial to the story; what matters is that they are hidden. The one frustration created by the ill-defined background behind the three men is that it suggests that the wood in which they hide grows deeper just beyond them, making it inconceivable that these three would choose to hide in such a sparsely wooded area. The lack of logic makes little realistic sense, but it fits the men's personalities. The three men appear young—surprisingly so, considering that Sir Toby Belch is Olivia's uncle. They look as if they are all in their twenties, and not one appears too old for such nonsense as a practical joke.

Behind Malvolio are pictured two tall, wavy trees, looking more like the mountains or towers of a fairytale than like naturally occurring forestry. They lend a fanciful quality to the image, reminding the audience that what is pictured is all but impossible in real life—a fact that serves only to heighten the fun of the scene. Of the four men present, Malvolio is the most pompously dressed and bedecked. His facial hair is styled into an excessive, sharp moustache that must require ample amounts of gel for proper styling and professional hold throughout his numerous household duties. He is also the only fellow wearing a hat, and his clothing contains touches of frippery. One would not think, from his get-up, that he is only a steward.

Although the three tricksters are piled together in hilarity and camaraderie, enjoying their joke, Malvolio stands apart, stiff, sporting a pose of pompous self-importance. His stance implies that he is interested only in his own self-promotion, not in friendship or good fun. Moreover, although all four men are dressed in similar attire, there is something about Malvolio that is effeminate, as though he is unwilling to do anything that might bring him into contact with dirt. The other three appear quite comfortable piled together among the trees while Malvolio holds himself stiffly, even when just standing on the garden path. Meanwhile, the illustration's caption suggests that Malvolio has only just stumbled upon the planted letter and realized it resembles Olivia's handwriting, but his pose—stiff, squared shoulders, gazing into the middle distance, hand pressed against his chest—suggests that he has already assumed that it must bear lasting importance to him.

An Undated M'Phun [sic] Edition

The illustration of the "letter scene" printed in the edition published by W. R. M'Phun [sic] and Son is also in black and white (see fig. 2). It provides little background and takes a "focused" approach, presenting the characters only from the waist up. This decision leaves little space for many details save the necessary bush to hide

Figure 2. From an undated M'Phun edition.

the three tricksters. The bush itself is not very detailed, and all beyond that is just suggestion and swirl. Malvolio here appears on the illustration's left, but because he is off-centered left—almost in the middle of the image, but not quite—and because he is so close and large in contrast with all other portions of the image, he manages to keep the audience's attention and remain the focus.

Malvolio is dressed in very plain clothing. He looks like any other member of Olivia's staff: he is not dressed in any "elevated" way that might suggest he is more than just an average servant. Although he wears a hat, it is shockingly dumpy looking. It sags, as if it has lost its shape, as if it has gotten old but Malvolio has not been able to replace it yet. Moreover, nothing elevates or decorates the hat. It is surprisingly undignified and utilitarian—a strange choice for someone as pompous as Malvolio.

Malvolio's age in this illustration is nondescript, like most other things about him here. He is not terribly young, but he certainly is not old either. He is old enough that it is no shock to think he has worked his way up to being steward of a household, but he is not so old that it seems off-putting to imagine a man of his age marrying Olivia. Although he is the central subject of this image and of this very scene in the play, and although the scene itself is so absurd that he might run the risk of being more caricature than character, this depiction of Malvolio is once again quite nondescript. Nothing about him broadcasts his personality to the world. He does not seem pompous, prideful, "anal retentive," or ridiculous in any sense. Instead, he simply looks like someone who was picking up trash and stumbled upon some aristocratic gossip. This Malvolio does not look like a fellow who is jumping to the conclusion that his lady is in love with him. He looks like a man who is struggling to understand what he is reading. If anything, he seems a bit horrified by what he is reading, and what its implications could be. He does not look like a man who aspires to be the lord of a house.

Although some illustrations of this scene put the three tricksters almost in plain sight of Malvolio, here they have managed to place themselves literally behind his back, giving them an excellent vantage point for thorough spying without running the risk of drawing anyone's attention. In addition, the three have managed to choose an area with much thicker foliage than is shown in some other illustrations of this episode, covering them to a greater degree than a couple of sparse trees could manage. The fellow closest to Malvolio has beautiful eyes and thick, curly hair. Although he must be either Fabian, Sir Toby Belch, or Sir Andrew (according to the play), one might almost think that it was Maria, hiding with the other schemers after dropping the letter.

In any case, the identities of the three eavesdroppers are not easily discerned. Without being able to see who is wearing boots—a clear indicator that one fellow is Sir Toby Belch—and without being able to look at the men from top to bottom to see who is wearing clothing suited to a servant (which would identify Fabian), it is nearly impossible to know for sure which man is which. The man in the middle is dressed aristocratically, identifying him as either Sir Toby Belch or Sir Andrew. If one were forced to decide, one might assume he is Sir Andrew because he is a bit over-dressed when compared with the more earthy-looking fellow standing next to him. Beyond that, however, little headway can be made, although because Sir Toby is Olivia's uncle, it might make further sense to assume that Toby is the man on the right, who looks older than the man in the middle and who is also almost completely bald. Nonetheless, this artist, unlike some others, has not chosen to make Sir Toby Belch look very old, and so the idea of his marrying Maria is not a difficult one to imagine.

Only Malvolio and one of the aristocratic gentlemen—presumably, Sir Andrew—wear hats. The other two, perhaps for lack of propriety or lack of funds, have chosen to eschew that costume option. Funnily enough, it does seem to be both the oldest of the bunch and the youngest of the bunch who are leaving their heads uncovered, so readers are treated to a view of both luscious locks and a shining dome—a reminder that good humor is for all, regardless of age. Although these three tricksters are not falling over each other as happens in some other illustrations, they still display close camaraderie. Fabian (the presumed Fabian, at least) peeks around Sir Andrew's shoulder while he hides in the thickets, while Sir Toby, close to Sir Andrew, is turned toward him as though he is sharing a whispered joke. The three are obviously good chums brought together by good humor.

The fellow in the middle (perhaps Sir Andrew) is the least concealed of the three. In fact, he appears almost to be leaning forward, trying to get a better look while Malvolio is distracted by the letter. He is also the most ostentatiously dressed, making him easy to spot should Malvolio turn around. He clearly does not have as much respect for the joke as his two friends, adding further support to the theory that this man is Sir Andrew. Fabian and Sir Toby Belch are far too fond of pranks to risk this one's failure by such an avoidable misstep. They are also more intelligent than Sir Andrew and would not behave as foolishly as he does. Meanwhile, Fabian's eyes are smiling (an effect the artist admirably conveys!), showing that he is already giddy with the conception and present success of the prank. Fabian is not a man who has to wait until the grand finale for enjoyment; he is tickled pink from the start.

An Undated London Printing and Publishing Company Edition

If the two illustrations already discussed show the beginnings of the trick on Malvolio, the ensuing drawings show the outcome. In these illustrations, Malvolio has already taken the bait and has dressed himself up in his ridiculous gartered yellow stockings—a costume sure to offend (rather than entice) Olivia. His false assumption that she loves him makes him even more egotistical than he has already appeared, as the ensuing illustrations strongly suggest. One of these drawings, which appeared in an undated "London Printing and Publishing Company" edition, is once again in black and white (see fig. 3). It features Malvolio alone in the garden, striking a pose and living his life as the main character he has always imagined himself to be. In this depiction, however, Malvolio is not just the only character shown; he is almost *all* that is shown (save just the smallest scrape of garden behind him). His image is magnified, with the audience taking an up close, intimate look at his pomposity.

The garden here is barely shown; it is only suggested with a sparse hint of path and a short brush of trees in the background. The

Figure 3. From an undated "London Printing and Publishing Company" edition.

glimpse of the garden is so minute that it looks almost like forest or wilderness touching against a public road rather than like the private garden of a rich woman with fine, precise tastes. Nothing here is pruned, nothing coaxed or shaped, and there are no extraneous structures intended to beautify the area. Perhaps the wildness of the landscape glimpsed behind Malvolio is intended to show how wild Malvolio will soon seem to all those around him—and particularly to Olivia. While in other drawings he can look like one of the carefully pruned garden plants—not a leaf or twig out of place, and bedecked as is expected of someone associated with aristocracy—Malvolio, under the influence of the forged love letter, is here acting without the propriety or the appearance expected of a person in his role. He has grown metaphorically "wild," and just as the landscape behind him needs the taming of the gardener's shears, the tricksters will soon feel that Malvolio requires the taming of the kind of dark, locked room reserved for the mad. Because of the angle at which Malvolio stands and the width of the path he stands on, he looks like he has just made his way through the woods behind him and emerged onto the road rather than like he has made his way down the path in a respectable manner. He looks like something wild and unexpected and not wholly welcome—a sentiment shared among Sir Toby Belch and company, of course, but also spreading (in a milder manner) to Olivia.

This Malvolio wears a hat, and it is a hat serving no purpose beyond displaying style. The brim is much too short to shield the wearer's face from the sun (not that Malvolio is the sort of chap to willingly choose to labor outdoors), and nothing about the hat suggests either comfort or warmth. It is a costume to draw attention—a conclusion supported all the more by the inclusion of a ridiculous feather hanging off of the back. Its inclusion makes Malvolio look like a preening peacock.

This Malvolio seems to be firmly middle-aged. His face obviously lacks the youth to excuse (or at least make less unappealing) his pride and delusion in believing Olivia is in love with him, but it also lacks the wrinkles that could possibly hint at senility and the warped sense of reality that may also lead to such delusions. He is at a firm middle age, a point when one would expect some wisdom to have developed and to have tempered bizarre fancies. He is too old for such silliness. In favor of this assumption about Malvolio's age is the fact that his interest in Olivia (interest more in status, wealth, and power rather than interest in her as a person, of course, but such is life) is not creepy. He does not look so old that it would be as though a grandfather were marrying a grandchild, and he is not so young as to look like a teenager pursuing a grown woman. Although they are ill-matched in literally every other way, this Malvolio, whatever else he may be, is at least a reasonable contender for Olivia's affections in age alone.

This Malvolio has his chin upturned to a ridiculous degree—up and to the side, with his eyes closed. He has taken the phrase "upturned nose" to the extreme. This pose cannot be comfortable. In fact, given the age range one can suppose based on his facial features and hair choices, this man has either taken the time to stretch beforehand or has willingly subjected himself to a stiff neck (requiring the tender touch of an expert chiropractor) purely for the purpose of striking this ridiculous pose. He has not just lifted his chin and closed his eyes; it would appear that his lips are pursed together as well. He is unironically wearing the caricatured facial expression of superiority reserved typically for cartoons of tyrannical kings and oil barons. This appearance does not bode well for the man's hypothetical future as lord of Olivia's house. At best, he will make himself and the family ridiculous. At worst, he will look like a puffed-up dictator.

Malvolio here also looks like a theatre or dance instructor teaching his students how to breathe properly. His arms are held out balletically, his shoulders are high (as if he is in the midst of a deep, full breath), and his chest is puffed out as though he is demonstrating the work of the intercostal muscles in action. The tilt and upturn of his chin seems to say, "Look and emulate, dear students, as this is perfection!" Perhaps Malvolio's puffed sleeves are actually making it difficult for him to put his arms down comfortably. It may be that, in his excitement to actively pursue Olivia, Malvolio chose an outfit based entirely on style rather than comfort and is now reaping the unfortunate consequences, the first among them being that his arms must always be slightly held aloft. He looks like a young child wearing floaties in the pool. The way Malvolio has his fingers pointed in a delicate gesture suggests that he is telling the audience, "And then we stand just so, feet apart and pointed out, to attract our mate!" It is odd. This depiction of Malvolio makes him look not just arrogant or ridiculous. It is as though he is aware of an audience and aims to pass on his "wisdom." He is uncomfortably aware of the "fourth wall."

Because in this drawing Malvolio's stockings are neither obviously cross-gartered nor yellow (instead they are black), it is difficult to "place" this scene. He is, however, wearing a bold, striped shirt, as though he wanted to mirror the cross-gartered theme and create a more balanced ensemble that is striped from top to bottom.

This ostentatious, audience-aware version of Malvolio makes him seem like the sort of person who would value a "theme" in an outfit, and "stripes" is a simple one to commit to. In any case, his stance—coupled with the level of inflation of his britches—both show off all of the curves of his build. His calves are on display, the pouf of his pants lends him a shapely rear, the tightness of his shirt highlights a trim middle and (by comparison, at least) broader shoulders; he looks as though he has gone out of his way to choose his most enticing, most flattering outfit. He has put himself on full display and to the best of his advantages. This is Malvolio's version of a little black dress. Although not as heavy-handed with the frippery as he could have been, Malvolio did not shy away from adding decorative touches to his ensemble, especially the large bows to the bottoms of his britches as well as to the tops of his shoes. They do serve to balance out the excitement of the plumage in his cap, but they destroy any last traces of masculinity (or, frankly, *usefulness*) from what may have still clung to his outfit. He is all trussed up like a chicken ready for the oven.

The 1861 Chambers Edition

The depiction of Malvolio that appears in an 1861 edition published by W. and R. Chambers is also in black and white (see fig. 4). This image shows only Malvolio, who once again is depicted *after* he has read the letter but definitely just *before* he has met with Olivia. Because no one is present here besides Malvolio, readers do not witness the shock, confusion, and concern that Olivia shows when met with his apparent "insanity." Malvolio is not yet putting his plan into action; he is merely primping in preparation.

The garden in this scene is heavily pruned and shaped, making it look less like a garden one might reasonably stroll through than like something Alice might find herself trapped in after tumbling through the looking glass. There is a whimsy and a curve to every plant and construction, and this fun—while suited to the whimsy of the joke being played on Malvolio—does not seem to be in line with Olivia's style. It is particularly contrary to her current situation of being in mourning.

Figure 4. From the 1861 Chambers edition.

As in the preceding image, the background here is not the main focus, blurring and becoming nondescript just beyond Malvolio. The focus of the image is Malvolio's foolishness, not the (admittedly lavish) garden in which he makes his embarrassing debut. This Malvolio seems younger than in the previous illustration. His face is smooth, void of sharpness or wrinkle, and he wears no facial hair. His face is not just young; it is almost delicate, with a soft mouth.

Perhaps the artist chose to depict such a youthful Malvolio as a way of excusing his foolishness, explaining his quickness to believe his mistress's secret love for him by suggesting that he has not weathered enough years to be tempered by wisdom. Whereas in the preceding illustration Malvolio's pose is one of stylized elegance, this depiction shows him clearly trying to highlight his best angles. His chin is tilted high and to the side, showing a fine jawline and implying beaming confidence. This is not a man who is ready to go courting; this is a man who is ready to claim his prize and lead the parade.

This Malvolio also has one hand on his hip, lifting up a bit so as to best show off both his chest and his legs. He looks like a dancer sticking to the final move in his routine. It would, ironically, be miraculous if any woman, let alone Olivia, managed to find such an image attractive. Unlike the Malvolio in the previous illustration, this one wears no hat. Perhaps, basking in the glow of confidence afforded by Olivia's supposed love for him, he feels it would be a shame to cover his head—a sign of submission or servitude even, and something totally unbefitting to one who will soon take his place as master of this house. Perhaps he also imagines that Olivia's passion for him will be ever more stirred at the sight of his uncovered body—first hair, but who knows? Perhaps in a month or two she might even catch sight of some ankle!

This Malvolio, although he does not yet seem to be in the presence of Olivia, has already begun smiling nonstop, and it really is no surprise that Olivia's first reaction is to think that the man has fallen into insanity. His smile is full but empty, as though he smiles for no real reason except that he has forgotten how to do anything else. In fact, many people might be tempted to lock him in a dark room until he promised to find a new facial expression. Meanwhile, his outfit is excessively poofed, layered, and draped. It shows a penchant for frippery that outshines even the pins and tucks of the previous illustration. He does not simply look as though he has chosen to dress his best; he looks like a lord whose tastes run to the garish, lavishing himself in finery without the temperament of good taste.

A notable difference between the clothing worn by the Malvolio of the previous illustration and the clothing shown here is that, while both suits of clothes are finely tailored and feature decoration, this outfit is meant not just to draw attention but to occupy space. In the previous illustration, Malvolio cut a fine but slender figure; in this depiction, layers and extra cloth are used to make his body look bigger, grander than it really is. It is as though Malvolio is already beginning to grow into the idea of being lord of the house. As he begins to imagine the space around him becoming "his" space, he feels more entitled to assume as much of it as he wishes—as much of it as he can. This Malvolio also carries a cane that ironically makes him look smaller: it is a full head taller than he is and seems to have no use at all outside of aiding him in striking an impressive figure and allowing him to cosplay more effectively as lord of the house.

This Malvolio is clearly cross-gartered and (presumably, though it is impossible to say as this image is only in black and white) is wearing his yellow stockings with quite a bit of pride, positioning his legs so as to draw as much attention as possible to this ill-fated fashion faux pas. Admittedly, this Malvolio has well-shaped calves and wears the trend well, but that cannot save him. Olivia—and anyone with a sense of taste—will not be appeased by shapely calves. Where Malvolio stands, the footpath behind him widens considerably; it is as though he has just walked onto his own personal stage and is taking a moment to preen—to display his goods, as it were—before beginning his interaction with Olivia. The shape of the path is like a reverse catwalk on which Malvolio has just finished strutting his stuff and is now taking a moment to strike a pose. In the bottom right corner of the image is either a strangely bent plant or a small garden structure (perhaps a trellis?) that bears an eerie resemblance to the ribs of an animal—a strange addition to an otherwise idyllic garden scene. Perhaps this could be considered foreshadowing for Malvolio—the tricksters' joke will pick every speck of dignity from his bones, leaving him bare and embarrassed before Olivia. His own foolishness is leading him only to waste and loss.

An Undated Porter and Coates Edition

A black-and-white illustration of act 3, scene four published by the Philadelphia firm of Porter and Coates (see fig. 5) features Olivia and Maria on the left and Malvolio on the right. He is wearing a dapper outfit and yellow stockings, but the stockings are not cross-gartered. The three characters are shown together in a shadowy, intimate garden; Olivia is seated; Maria leans down on the bench behind Olivia; and Malvolio stands almost at Olivia's feet. Although all three appear on a path, trees and shadows surround the path as far as readers can see, making this appear to be a very private meeting rather than something just anyone could stumble upon. Although the trees do not look particularly pruned and the garden lacks any especially lovely or unusual plants, this illustration does make the garden

Figure 5. From an undated Porter and Coates edition.

look fine. The trees are tall and carefully mapped out, and Olivia's bench is quite large and impressive.

Maria is the least important, least impressive character in the scene. She is huddled in the darkest corner of the image, and neither Olivia nor Malvolio pays her any attention. She is present to step in if necessary—if Olivia requires her help—and to be invisible at all other times.

Helping her blend into the background is her dark clothing. Her black skirt merges with a large dark shadow, making it difficult to see where she ends, and the shadow begins. The skirt is also long and bulky, deepening the shadow and making it look as if she might have trouble walking without tripping. Maria's clothing, especially when compared with what is worn by Olivia and Malvolio, is odd. She looks like a schoolmarm or a governess, not like a lady's maid. Not only is her outfit undecorated, but she looks downright drab. This is an unfortunate costume choice for Maria in particular given how much she sparkles throughout the play. Of course, it does make sense that she is dressed in drab clothing given that Olivia has deemed it necessary for her home to be in mourning. One might, however, imagine at least a better-fitting skirt. Yet, despite the fact that Maria is largely cast aside in this illustration, her face does not look unsatisfied with her current situation. She has a small Mona Lisa smile on her face, as if she is perfectly satisfied with being a fly on the wall of this conversation—and likely she is, given that she has a front row seat to watch Malvolio make a fool of himself in front of Olivia. She is enjoying the fruit of her labors without any concern of being suspected as the mastermind behind the plot. The mastermind has earned her reward, and she is enjoying it—even if she must dress in one of the least flattering schoolteacher dresses available while doing so.

Although Olivia is supposedly in mourning throughout most of this play, this woman does not look like a woman in mourning. She is missing mourning clothes—her dress almost looks white, the exact opposite of what one would expect—and no veil covers her face. The veil may only be necessary when "outsiders" are before her; her own household, I suppose, is allowed to see her face. But the rest of the outfit is still decidedly jubilant; Cesario has managed to do quite a number on this lady. In any case, if Malvolio is attempting here to exchange secret messages with Olivia and woo her into marriage, Olivia's facial expression is odd. She does not look confused, concerned, or even angry. She looks a bit pleased, as if she would not mind hearing more of this kind of talk. She also wears a touch of a smile on her lips, and her hand rests against the base of her throat as though she is being flattered and responding with demure acceptance. One might argue that her face does seem a bit blank, as though she is trying to process what is going on and is caught off guard. Perhaps she is so surprised by Malvolio's ramblings that her face cannot even manage to express her thoughts. With so much else going on in her life, this meeting with Malvolio may be that straw that has broken the proverbial camel's back, forcing Olivia to shut down, stick a pin in it, and tell herself—like Scarlett O'Hara—"I can't think about that right now. If I do, I'll go crazy. I'll think about it tomorrow." Although Olivia is not exactly dressed in frippery and decadence galore, she does look like she has taken careful pains to look pretty. Her dress, though void of bows or any extra trimmings, is made of a fine fabric that shines in the sunshine, flatters her tones, and drapes well. She—unlike Maria—shows a touch of skin at her throat, and her hair is curled and covered very prettily. This, obviously, was not done for Malvolio's benefit; rather, she likely took care with her appearance for the sake of Cesario. Regardless, she does make a perfect picture of a woman being wooed—whether that wooing is welcome or not.

Malvolio is the strangest part of this illustration. He looks far too young to hold such an important position in Olivia's household. His skin is perfectly smooth, giving him the face of a man in his early twenties. Although he does have facial hair, it is sparse and overly styled—he looks like a young man following the latest fads and fashions. He has also clearly taken pains with his own appearance. His hair is long and lustrous—I would argue that his is the best styled, best tended mane in the image. Somehow, that detail does fit Malvolio's personality. He seems like the sort of man who would use his limited free time to pamper himself and make sure he is looking his absolute best. His clothing is also arguably the fanciest and finest in the image. It is thick, rich, full of fine textures and flattering drapes, and his outfit has more "extra" touches than anyone else's. His hat has feathers in it, there are ruffles at his throat, there are pom poms at the bottom of his britches, there are fancy buckles on his shoes—Malvolio is not just auditioning for the status of a lover, he is auditioning for admission to a new social class. His stockings are lightly colored, so they may very well be yellow, as the forged love note required. However, unless he has chosen to wear garters of exactly the same color as his stockings, it does not appear at all as though he is cross-gartered. It is strange that this part of his costume was eliminated from the drawing; after all, it is one of the most important costume requirements in the entire play. Without it, the scene makes little to no sense. Perhaps the artist is incorporating a different interpretation of what crossed garters might mean, crossing them higher up rather than keeping them focused on the calves. Many depictions of Malvolio show him dressed in striped shirts as well as cross garters; this Malvolio, however, is not dressed in anything so silly or attention-grabbing. He really does look like a fine gentleman in his outfit. Though no shrinking wallflower, he is not silly, arrogant, or pompous. He seems serious and earnest. No wonder Olivia is not making a strange face during his talk—there is nothing particularly shocking about him here. Though his speech may be odd as it mentions a note she has no knowledge of, his delivery does not seem off-putting at all.

The 1890 Scribner and Welford Edition

Another black-and-white illustration, this one from the 1890 Scribner and Welford edition, specifically illustrates act 3, scene 4, lines 28–31, where Malvolio says "Not black in my mind, though yellow in my legs. It did come to his hands, and commands shall be executed. I think we do know the sweet Roman hand" (see fig. 6).

The garden in this image is distinguished with only a touch of shading in the background, a touch of path, and one detailed tree behind Olivia. The garden is clearly not the most important part of this scene, and the artist wasted no time or effort creating detail that may draw attention away from the characters. This garden does not look like one associated with the fine estate one would expect from someone of Olivia's stature. Although it does look like a garden and not like the side of a public road (as it did in a few previous images), there is little specifically intended to beautify or even tame. The trees in the background look scraggly and wild, and there are no flowers or fine decorative pieces to spruce the area up. The scraggle

Mal. Not black in my mind, though yellow in my legs. It did come to his hands, and commands shall be executed: I think we do know the sweet Roman hand.—(Act iii. 4. 28-31.)

Figure 6. From the 1890 Scribner and Welford edition.

of the brush behind the three characters does give an air of privacy to the meeting—a blessing for Malvolio as he is currently in the midst of making a fool of himself. He, Olivia, and Maria seem to be in a small, gardened wilderness. The two benches at this garden crossroads are the only decorative touches, adding a bit of fineness and gentility to the otherwise barren scenery.

Olivia is to the far left of the image. Although her skin is delicate and smooth—suggesting youth—there is a stern, aristocratic turn to her face, as if she is used to running her own household and issuing orders with the expectation of obedience. She does not look mean or unkind—she does not even wear a look of mockery or harshness (which would be a fair expression to wear given Malvolio's strange performance before her). She looks lovely and steady, like a queen holding court. She wears no veil, and nothing about her outfit suggests mourning, as she is dressed in all light colors. In fact, as in the preceding image, she seems to be dressed all in white. In the midst of her interest in Cesario, Olivia has all but forgotten her mourning period.

This Olivia has small, delicate, feminine features, making her look all the more aristocratic and set apart as a member of a higher social class than the others in her household. She takes more care of her appearance and (supposedly) must worry over greater cares than the others. She lounges against a giant, plush cushion that someone (presumably *not* her) has carried all this way, for the sole purpose of making her more comfortable as she sits on her own bench—a bench that does not look particularly uncomfortable on its own. There also seems to be a footstool of some sort under her feet so *madame* can prop her feet up while lounging, avoiding any and all discomfort. Although Olivia's face gives the impression of one who has cares to bear, the multiple cushions cradling her body in an outdoor setting suggest that she leads not a particularly hard life.

Maria stands just to the right of Olivia, and the difference in their facial features is startling. While Olivia's face was detailed and delicate, feminine to the smallest detail, Maria's face is large and vague. Her face could just as easily belong to a man as to a woman. There is nothing particularly intelligent about her face either, especially in comparison with Olivia's. She looks very simple. Considering how intelligent Maria has shown herself to be throughout this play—organizing and implementing the prank on Malvolio—the vapid face seems inappropriate for her. Because Olivia is the one who fell in love with a woman dressed as a man, not Maria, perhaps Olivia is better suited to the simple features. But there is another strong difference between how Olivia is portrayed and how Maria is portrayed (even beyond their contrasting facial features). Olivia is wearing a rich, sumptuous, expensive gown; Maria wears only the most basic of dress, one that looks comparatively meager next to Olivia's, as if the illustrator juxtaposed a schoolteacher's dress with a coronation gown. Also, Maria is standing while Olivia is not only sitting but sitting on multiple cushions—cushions that Maria was likely tasked with carrying. Obviously, there is a stark difference between the ranks of these two women. Perhaps Maria is only wearing such a vapid, vague expression as a disguise while she watches the goings-on between Malvolio and Olivia. If she showed her intelligence, perhaps they might suspect her involvement (particularly if Olivia is aware of Maria's ability to forge her handwriting).

But at least this Malvolio is obviously wearing crossed garters! There is no doubt that he is following "Olivia's" fashion requests, and doing so with such gusto that one cannot help but notice—yellow stockings draw enough attention, but crossed garters are especially difficult to miss. Indeed, this Malvolio's attire is especially pompous; he is wearing both a full ruffled collar *and* a short cape. The cape is a fine touch for dramatic purposes; it shows off his poses and adds a touch of garishness that balances out the crossed garters. It is difficult to ascertain this Malvolio's age. He has a full head of hair (though one could not honestly call it "lustrous"), and his face is not overly lined. However, there is a sturdiness and blockiness to his features that is common for men once they have reached middle age, so it seems fair to place him at least in his forties. This is not so great an age difference as to make his interest in Olivia (or her position) uncomfortable to viewers, but it is great enough that it is astounding that he has so readily jumped to the conclusion that this woman must love him. In any case, his face and pose do not match. His pose puts him on display—showing Olivia the goods, as it were. His clothing, though not ridiculous, is a touch flamboyant (the man has gigantic rosettes on the toes of both of his shoes, like a toddler participating in a beauty pageant—not much of an everyday, "gettin' 'er done at work" look), and his stance is open and tilted back just a touch as though he is proud of what he has to offer. In contrast, his face is serious, bordering on empty. It is as though his head is not participating in the show his body is putting on. Perhaps it has washed its hands of this peacock presentation. There is little to nothing to distinguish Malvolio's face from anyone else's, and he certainly does not wear the face of a man intent on wooing a lady. He seems to be enjoying the experience about as much as Olivia is.

The 1904 Henry T. Coates Edition

The next illustration, published in the 1904 Henry T. Coates edition (see fig. 7), is once again in black and white. Its background is remarkably sparse, and it is also much lighter and much less detailed

Figure 7. From the 1904 Henry T. Coates edition.

than the two illustrations already examined. The artist for the Henry edition has done just enough to place the characters in a garden on rich grounds; beyond that, s/he felt no need to expound: the truth here is in the interaction, not the setting.

This illustration does not depict either Malvolio's stumbling upon Maria's forged love letter or his grand debut before Olivia as her would-be suitor. Rather, this image seems to pick up where the preceding image left off; Malvolio has interacted with Olivia and is now being rude and severe both with his social inferiors and with Olivia's uncle. Presumably, this drawing illustrates the episode that begins around act 3, scene 4, line 76. In this image, the three tricksters are grouped together familiarly with seemingly no regard for class or status; all three touch each other, either laying a staying hand or a steadying hand against the one closest. The common ground of a good sense of humor transcends any boundaries laid down by rules of social decorum. Fabian (at the left of the drawing) seems much older, in this depiction, than he is often imagined, as if he is a weathered, sinewy old man instead of a fun-loving rapscallion. In fact, this older Fabian seems almost too old to be a trickster, almost too old to still be in service. In fact, almost everyone in this illustration seems pitiable in some sense—or at least mean and unhappy. This illustration arguably eliminates the fun from an otherwise hilarious episode; perhaps this was not a scene that ought to have been sketched, at least by this artist.

In this illustration, Sir Toby Belch looks shockingly old, unhealthy, and unhappy. Like the other characters depicted, he, too steals from the "fun" atmosphere one would hope to find in a depiction of this scene, perhaps because of his age, perhaps just because he resembles a boulder more than a fun-loving trickster. Maria, meanwhile, looks far too young to be equally mixed up in the doings of Sir Toby Belch and Fabian. Her dimensions seem somehow "off" in relation to those of the men. She is so small and delicate that her head is nearly half the size of Sir Toby Belch's, making her almost resemble a child. This not only makes for a strange pairing in the matter of this practical joke, but it also makes for an even stranger—a downright uncomfortable—pairing when one considers that, at the end of the play, Maria and Sir Toby Belch marry. Although Maria has what seems to be a very pretty face, it is difficult to confirm that possibility with any real certainty as she has the least detailed face of the four characters depicted. Perhaps that is only due to her youth and subsequent lack of wrinkles, or perhaps it is because she has been drawn in such small proportions; regardless, more detail is devoted to her dress (a pretty affair) than to any other part of her. She is pretty, but she fades into the image among the men, who are depicted in greater detail.

Malvolio is, in some ways, the largest character in this illustration. Perhaps he was drawn to this size as a way of balancing out the grouping of three to the left of the image, or perhaps his size was meant to highlight his pomposity and visually show his elevated view of himself. Of course, there is always the chance that the artist just felt this character ought to be the tallest. In any case, Malvolio is wearing the cross-gartered look, so this scene obviously takes place after he has read Maria's forged love letter. This drawing must depict Malvolio acting unkindly toward the servants and toward Sir Toby Belch, as the bogus letter instructed him to do. This Malvolio does not just look unkind; he is also haughty, superior. He is literally looking down on the other three, both from his superior height and through his lowered, hooded eyes. He has already begun thinking of himself as the lord of the house, the rightful one to whom all report. Like the other men shown here, he seems rather old, making the idea that he might marry someone as young as Olivia seem unappealing to others, if not to him. Given this obvious age difference, it is impressive that his own self-esteem is so strong that he immediately concluded that the love letter must be addressed to him. Say what you will; Malvolio does not lack confidence. Although not necessarily ostentatious, his clothing does not fall in line with what one might expect from a servant. He broadcasts his egotism partly by the clothes he wears. He seems to consider himself at least the equal of Sir Toby, who is not only a knight but is Olivia's uncle (and who also resembles, in this drawing, conventional depictions of another famously fat Shakespearean knight: Sir John Falstaff).

An Undated Hurst and Co. Edition

Another black-and-white depiction of the scene just discussed—this one from an undated Hurst and Co. edition—again shows Malvolio lording it over Toby, Maria, and Fabian (see fig. 8). Because the characters are drawn with equal boldness and shadow to that visible in the background, the image looks fuller than some previous illustrations. Although the forestry depicted in the background is drawn with little detail, the fence and gate behind the characters as well as the ground beneath their feet seem impressively real.

Figure 8. From an undated Hurst and Co. edition.

This Malvolio obviously loves stripes—so much so that it is hard to tell if his stockings are gartered or are simple striped, like the sleeves on his arms, so that he almost resembles a bumblebee. His age is difficult to ascertain. Although he is striking a grandiose, limber pose, has managed to maintain a head of dark, wavy hair, and is entirely clean-shaven—all qualities associated with youth—he also has an incredibly deep wrinkle cupping his mouth like a parenthesis, making his face look aged. He carries (but does not wear) a hat fancifully adorned with a feather, unlike the plainer hats actually worn by the other three characters. Ironically, however, his pretentious hat actually looks like a tail—almost as if he has literally made himself look like an ass.

Not only does this depiction make Malvolio seem pompous (just look at that pose—eyes closed, nose in the air, one hand on his hip and the other held out like a king expecting a kiss!), but it also makes him look rather dandified. He seems delicate, attempting to highlight "dignity" but falling short and managing only "fancified" and anything but "manly." Cross-gartered yellow stockings were Maria's idea, but the other preposterous features of Malvolio's costume here were all *his* choices, not hers. He cannot entirely blame the tricksters for his foolish appearance—he brought most of it into the game himself.

Unlike the tricksters shown in the preceding illustration, the ones depicted here do not look terrified of (or particularly browbeaten by) Malvolio. At worst they seem unmoved, but there may also be some barely concealed gaiety running from one to the other. These tricksters seem close in age; it is not shocking that they are spending time together, nor is it horrifying that Maria and Sir Toby Belch finish the play married. Both he and she are bright and visible here, Fabian (as in previous illustrations) seems far less "present": he is fading into the shadow and lending only a silly expression to the goings on. Fabian is a fun tertiary character and an important part of the chemistry of the tricksters, but he is more a plot device than a fully developed character. At the end of the play, nobody is asking who Fabian ended up marrying. The artist who drew this illustration manages to convey Fabian's relative insignificance.

Although in previous illustrations the tricksters were very hands-on with each other—leaning against each other, touching each other's shoulders, and so on—the members of this group are maintaining their distance. The least serious of the bunch (and certainly the drunkest of the bunch), Sir Toby Belch here wears the most sober expression of any character depicted here. He upholds Maria's prank well, playing his role as a straight man with genuine heart. The two of them (who will later marry) already make an effective team and even resemble each other facially. In other respects, however, Sir Toby's appearance here is the most unfortunate thus far. His large belly is offset by skinny, shapely legs that are highlighted by boots with a touch of a heel (which also highlight his small, weirdly dainty feet). Because the image is in black and white, it looks as though Sir Toby Belch is going about with nary a stocking (yellow or otherwise) to cover his apparently bare legs. Maria, meanwhile, almost seems to be swishing her full-length dress. In many ways, she seems the most confident and self-assertive of all the characters depicted here.

Conclusion

Illustrated editions of Shakespeare's plays occupy a sort of intriguing middle ground between what might be called a "mere" reading edition (that is, one featuring nothing but text, pure and simple) and a live performance on the stage. Indeed, illustrated editions could help early readers (often physically distant from "major" Shakespearean theaters and without access to modern-day films and television broadcasts) to visualize the appearance of important characters, the ways those characters might interact, and the over-all "tone" of a key scene or episode. Illustrated editions also allow early readers to compare and contrast their own conceptions of a play's episodes with the conceptions of talented, imaginative artists who had obviously given serious thought to an episode before trying to render it visually. And these kinds of editions, full of often interesting drawings, also give early readers extra value for their money, providing them with access not only to the works of the world's most famous playwright but also to the talents of skillful contemporary visual artists.

Note

1. All photographs in this essay are from editions owned by the editor of this volume.

Works Cited

[Cassell Leopold Edition.] *The Leopold Shakespeare*, by William Shakespeare. Illustrated. Cassell, 1904.

[Chambers Edition.] Carruthers, R., and W. Chambers, editors. *Chambers's Household Edition of the Dramatic Works of William Shakespeare*, by William Shakespeare. Illustrated by Keeley Halswelle. 10 vols. London and Edinburgh: W. and R. Chambers, 1861.

[Coates Edition] Knight, Charles, editor. *The Works of William Shakespeare*, by William Shakespeare. Illustrated by Sir John Gilbert, A. R. A. Henry T. Coates, 1904.

[Hurst Edition]. *The Works of Shakespeare*, by William Shakespeare. With Illustrations. New York: Hurst Publishers, n.d.

[London Printing and Publishing Company Edition.] *William Shakespeare's* [sic] *Works*. London: London Printing and Publishing, n.d.

[M'Phun Edition.] *The Complete Works of Shakespeare*, by William Shakespeare. 2 vols. Glasgow and London: W. M'Phun and Son, n.d.

[Porter and Coates Edition.] *The Works of William Shakespeare*, by William Shakespeare. Philadelphia: Porter and Coates, n.d.

[Scribner and Welford Edition. The Henry Irving Shakespeare.] Irving, Henry, and Frank A. Marshall, editors. *The Works of William Shakespeare*, by William Shakespeare. "With Numerous Illustrations by Gordon Browne." 4 vols. New York: Scribner and Welford, 1890.

The 1998 Live Production of *Twelfth Night* at Lincoln Center: A Survey of Reviews

Eric J. Sterling

Nicholas Hytner's 1998 production of Shakespeare's *Twelfth Night* at Lincoln Center was for several reasons a particularly important staging of this play. Not only was it performed on Broadway with a cast of major stars including Kyra Sedgwick, Paul Rudd, and the Oscar-winning actress and TV star Helen Hunt, but its last performance was also filmed and broadcasted nationwide as part of PBS's prestigious "Live from Lincoln Center" series, introduced by the famous (and much-beloved) opera star Beverly Sills. Hytner's production was soon nominated for Tony Awards in various categories, including best revival of a play, best set design, best costume design, best lighting design, and best original score written for a theatrical production. Yet, published reviews for the play were largely uneven. Even critics who admired the show usually found something to dislike, especially in the major performances, although performances in the comic subplot were widely admired and practically every reviewer praised the production's set. The mere fact that the play was filmed and broadcasted in front of a "live" audience, however, makes Hytner's production a significant event in the history of Shakespeare on film. Anyone interested in how this *Twelfth Night* was actually received by its live audience need only find a copy of the television broadcast on YouTube or on other sources.[1]

Especially Negative Review

Linda Winer, in *Newsday*, wrote the most negative review of the Lincoln Center production. She called this staging "one of the most beautiful worlds ever overproduced and tricked up for such crushingly, surprisingly dull and endlessly cloying dramatics. What a disappointment." She had had high hopes for Helen Hunt as Viola/Cesario but was unimpressed, calling her performance "very boring indeed." She considered Hunt "uneasy" in her "stylized emotions" and complained that the actress's voice, usually a strength, in this case sounded "flat and unmusical" and added that Hunt's "intelligent face seems in perpetual squint." Winer also wrote that Hunt's stiffness hurt the romantic scenes, causing the talented Sedgwick to overcompensate: "Sedgwick—always a distinctive actress—overdoes the skittish charm a bit as Olivia." Winer liked the comic scenes with the fools and knaves but suggested that "a little of this unchecked horseplay goes too long a way." She did enjoy David Patrick Kelly's performance as Feste, the Fool, calling him "a pleasant combination of Rod Stewart and a leprechaun," but she added that even this performance "wears thin." She observed that this was the first production involving Hytner and designer Bob Crowley that she did not enjoy, finding them guilty, in this case, of "hyping up the visuals as a distraction." Winer concluded that the set's "winding paths," so prominently featured on stage, "miraculously come together for the final tableau. Too bad the production never does."

Negative Review

Clifford A. Ridley, of *The Philadelphia Inquirer*, believed Hytner's production failed because it was too ambitious, trying to be simultaneously a wonderful romance, a hilarious comedy, and a vehicle for showing off Shakespeare's beautiful verse. Ridley claimed that by trying to excel in all three of these categories, the production not only risked "losing point and focus" but also risked "asking actors to attempt more than they are able to deliver." He felt that both of "these potential hazards, unfortunately, bedevil[ed]" the show, calling the pace too slow and writing that because Hytner was trying "to underscore the play's lyricism" but lacked "the performers to carry it off, his lyricism often becomes languor." Ridley greatly disliked the performances of the main actors, writing that

> Hunt has about three expressions, an equal number of gestures, and a mechanical delivery. As the pouty Orsino, Rudd offers little but a well-toned body and a scraggly mass of hair; he doesn't begin to manage the poetry in the duke's

> moony ardor. As Olivia, Kyra Sedgwick is a buxom bird-brain without a trace of dignity, which quite kills the point of a part whose comic effect derives from the loss of dignity.

Ridley asserted that the lackluster performances by Hunt, Rudd, and Sedgwick made the production too dependent on the comic actors in the subplot, although he praised those actors' skills. He liked Brian Murray's performance as Sir Toby Belch but thought that Max Wright (Sir Andrew Aguecheek), Amy Hill (Maria), and David Patrick Kelly (Feste) were even better, with Kelly offering the best performance and singing beautiful songs "in a voice that blends the timeless and the contemporary." Ridley considered Philip Bosco a competent and definitely "pitiable" Malvolio, so that "his humiliation comes close to being truly tragic." Although he asserted that the comic actors played well together as a unit, he thought they did not interact smoothly with the actors in the main plot: "like the Chinese takeout food they eat in one scene, they seem out of place." Ridley ultimately decided that although the production had good intentions, it was not well executed, with something going wrong "between conception and realization." The result, he claimed, was "a production that looks all of a piece but doesn't play that way. It feels only half thought-out, slapped together," focusing more on selling tickets than on quality and, therefore, unworthy of being performed at Lincoln Center.

Negative-to-Mixed Reviews

Charles Isherwood, in *Variety*, enjoyed some aspects of what he called this "ravishingly pretty, ravishingly funny production." Although he claimed that Hunt, Sedgwick, and Rudd were good-looking actors who "please the eye more than the ear," he asserted that the comic actors in the subplot—Brian Murray, Max Wright, and Philip Bosco—performed their roles better than the actors in the main plot, writing that "surprising magic is spun from the chicanery of Sir Toby Belch, Sir Andrew Aguecheek, and Malvolio." Isherwood was impressed by set designer Bob Crowley's Illyria, calling it "a stupendously lovely, color-drenched waterworld suspended somewhere between colonial India and an imaginary Middle East." He considered Hunt "a very down-to-earth Viola...[with] a pleasingly humble, easygoing stage presence"—"a practical girl who is amusingly unflappable" but whose hand gestures he considered mechanical. Although he wrote that Hunt played the comic scenes well, he thought she struggled to speak Shakespeare's beautiful poetry "with equal artistry." Isherwood found it difficult to believe that this Viola would fall in love with "Rudd's self-dramatizing Orsino" and wrote that her attraction to the duke "must have been physical" since Rudd failed to create an interesting character: "Rudd's acting, alas, is almost as florid as his attire," and his "self-pity at countess Olivia's rebuffs should be amusing, not off-puttingly strident." Isherwood believed that Rudd was uncomfortable speaking "the rhythms of the language," compensating for this flaw by growling his words "with a forced dramatic flourish" that was possibly "an imitation (or is it parody?) of a nobly spoken, fiery Shakespearean actor" but one that in either case fell flat. Isherwood found Sedgwick's performance no better than Rudd's, adding that although both actors were quite attractive, they had trouble speaking Shakespeare's verse. He was also disappointed that Sedgwick, as Olivia, stopped mourning the death of her lost brother as soon as she lifted her veil—much too quickly. Isherwood called Sedgwick "[s]punky, histrionic and sexy in a hot pink midriff" but said that because of her exaggerated manner, she did not look or act like a countess but rather like a Barbie doll who considered Cesario her Ken. But Isherwood, like so many other reviewers, did find this production redeemed by the excellent comic performances of Murray and Wright—"actors of consummate technique, who make each comic exchange, whether ribald or abstruse, crystal clear and gut-wrenchingly funny." He felt that Wright made Aguecheek a complex "figure of affecting pathos" and that Murray made Sir Toby both complex and "explosively funny." He also enjoyed this production's Malvolio, writing that "Bosco makes it seem like Malvolio will have an aneurysm before he manages to peel his lips back from his teeth in a smile" and adding that Hytner chose not to diminish the sadness of Malvolio's embarrassment, deciding instead to stage it in darkness so that "Bosco communicates Malvolio's misery with a force that touches our sympathies, as his plight should." In general, Isherwood expressed mixed feelings about this production, writing that although it might "not touch the heart in ways we are accustomed to," on the whole, "in the beauty of its execution and the tender attention brought to the play's farcically comic corners, it finds intriguing new ones."

In another mixed review (this one for *The New Republic*), Robert Brustein greatly enjoyed Bob Crowley's beautiful set, calling it exquisite and exotic, like a court scene from *The Arabian Nights*, but also faulting it for being inconsistent in terms of "culture, place, [and] time." (He noted, for instance, that the characters in this exotic locale nonetheless wore contemporary clothes and ate Chinese take-out food.) Complaining that "Hytner's inspiration seemed to have stopped with the sets and costumes" and faulting the acting of Sedgwick as Olivia, Brustein nevertheless did enjoy the comic performances of Murray and Wright, writing that Murray's Sir Toby had "all the florid gestures of a classical ham" and that Wright became "the very embodiment of craven idiocy, of false bravado." Brustein also enjoyed Kelly's performance as Feste but suggested that he did not stress the jester's "amiable charm as [much as] his bitter foolery." Writing that Hill did not play Maria well (but was "cast against type as a buxom Amazon"), Brustein also found Bosco a "humorless Malvolio" whose arrogance might belong as much to the actor as to the character. Although Brustein believed that Hunt played Viola competently and "with considerable grace and poise," he thought "her air of sangfroid would have been more appropriate in the role of Olivia," a role instead acted by Sedgwick, whom Brustein criticized for a "brassy, squeaky hyperactivity" more appropriate to "a sitcom." Brustein claimed that Sedgwick failed to create any sense of a regal character, calling her best assets her breasts as "she emerges [from the pool] with her dress clinging to her wet body." He was also disappointed that this production ignored "the ambiguous sexuality of the relationship between Olivia and Viola."

Mixed Reviews

Ted Merwin, writing for *Theatre Journal* and focusing on the watery set, called the production "splashy" and "a very wet dream" in which water "was a constant symbol," with several pools on stage so that "the characters generally made their entrances and exits over flat bridges—curves that united at the end of the play for the two couples to make a grand exit." Merwin enjoyed the production's "Eastern motifs," such as its "China silk hangings" featuring an "exquisite blue peacock design." He also wrote that Crowley's set "provided three different perspectives of Olivia's house on different-sized drops, which nicely reminded the audience how far from that anchor-point each scene was taking place." He enjoyed Catherine Zuber's costumes, including the "Turkish harem outfits (for Olivia)" as well as the "stunning blue and white guards' uniforms." Unfortunately, Merwin did not like the allegedly "listless" performances of the main actors (observing that when watching the opening scene, he initially could not discern who spoke the famous lines connecting love with music because Orsino and his men were lying down on stage) and perceived no chemistry between Orsino "(a long-haired, bare-chested Paul Rudd) and Viola (played with low-key irony by Hunt)." Olivia, he wrote, was "played by a glamorous but shrill Kyra Sedgwick" who "bounded and lunged over the stage in increasingly revealing outfits which reduced her from supposed sexual unavailability to what seemed more like sexual desperation." Merwin was, however, pleased by the comic actors: he enjoyed Murray's Toby Belch, Wright's Aguecheek, and Bosco's Malvolio and claimed that the latter's "performance in the famous letter-reading scene was a priceless puncturing of vain glory." But he thought the best performance was Kelly's acting "as a short, hump-backed Feste."

Les Gutman began his review for *Curtain Up* by praising Crowley's highly creative set, writing that with "a pool, a pond, a moated castle and a shore with piers that disappear into the sea, it's one of the most imaginative, strikingly realized (and wet) sets I've ever seen." He thought Crowley's efforts amounted to imaginative "set design at its zenith." Gutman confessed, however, that he had major concerns about the rest of the production, suggesting that although the show struck him as "brisk, fluid, and inventive," he also found it problematic and flawed. He was ambivalent, for instance, about Hunt's acting, suggesting that she spoke "as if she is sitting in the living room of her television sitcom" and arguing that she did not deliver "a robust performance." Although he also labeled Sedgwick's performance as Olivia "unpleasantly salacious and ridiculously comic," he did not entirely blame either her or Hytner, instead laying part of the responsibility at the feet of Shakespeare himself. Calling the line delivery by Hunt and Sedgwick "contemporized," Gutman nonetheless found Hunt the more believable of the two. But he considered both actresses "little more than placeholders" until the better (comic) actors appeared on stage. Alleging that neither woman seemed "particularly inspired by Shakespeare's language," he also called Rudd so "absolutely terrorized by Shakespeare's words" and so inept in speaking that he appeared bare-chested (and once nearly nude) as part of the production's efforts to distract the audience from the weaknesses of his attempts to speak.

Like some other critics, Gutman claimed that the veterans of the New York stage who played Belch, Aguecheek, and Maria clearly outshone the celebrities—outperforming them and "stealing the show from the Hollywood interlopers" in performances he called "uniformly delicious." Gutman wrote that Murray and Wright played their roles "with almost unimaginable insight," offering performances that were both extremely funny and "poignantly complex." He thought Bosco, as Malvolio, seemed "to be straining slightly," acting well but not at the level of the aforementioned comic trio, and he also called Kelly, as Feste, "the only character who routinely has any sense," admiring his "folksy singing" (of generally mediocre songs) and finding him "endearing," particularly in the subplot rather than when "playing jester to the plotter-in-chief." Gutman called "Catherine Zuber's eclectic costume designs...particularly expressive," especially in their ability to "accentuate Crowley's sets." Thus, although Gutman generally disliked the performances of the three main actors, he considered the production still worth watching.

Ben Brantley, in the *New York Times*, expressed mixed feelings about this "spirited new production," calling it "an appetizing eyeful" that was "really as much burlesque-comic as cosmic" because it was full of "sight gags and jokes." Although he predicted that it would make audiences smile, he was nevertheless "frustrated" by what he considered "its pervasive imbalance." Like some other reviewers, he considered the set and costume designs far more impressive than the main actors' performances, which he called competent while also alleging that Hunt and Rudd "rarely suggest[ed] depths of character." Sedgwick, he thought, acquitted herself better than Rudd and Hunt, saying that the latter "has a two-dimensional flatness that keeps the audience at a distance." According to Brantley, the main plot (focusing on the two love stories) offered "laughs but little in the way of emotional nourishment."

Conceding that Malvolio is a difficult role to play, Brantley thought that Bosco did "a creditable, workman-like job with it," but he called the production's best aspects (aside from Crowley's "bedazzling sets") the comic performances by Murray and Wright, who were able to "transform the low high jinks of Toby and Andrew into a blissful vaudeville as rich in psychological detail as it is in hilarious shtick." According to this reviewer, Murray and Wright brought "a warm verisimilitude to scenes that are often treated as throwaway comic relief." Like various other commentators, he thought the comic actors performed much better than the confused lovers of the main plot, whose "misdirected passions start[ed] to look like something that might be titled 'Fast Times at Illyria High.'" Brantley wrote that the play's nobles exhibited "a quality of arrested, self-involved adolescence" and contended that Hunt's Viola distinguished herself markedly from Olivia, providing an "antidote" to the "artificiality" of the duke and countess by seeming "sane, unaffected and emotionally grounded." Although he considered Hunt's voice lovely, he added that when "hitched to Shakespeare's language, especially the poetry, it develops a singsong quality that belies her character's claim that she can speak in 'many sorts of music.'" Thus (according to Brantley), rather than getting "a Viola of lyrical feeling, we get an emotional efficiency expert," someone who "seems not so much sexually ambiguous as sexually disinterested." Although he wrote that Hytner had tried hard to create sexual tension, he concluded that the characters' lack "of chemistry robs the play of any erotic danger."

In another part of his lengthy review, Brantley wrote that Rudd did not let Orsino "grow from false love into the real thing." And although he suggested that the physically beautiful Sedgwick possessed enough familiarity with Shakespeare's language to "play inventively with line readings," he also argued that Hytner disrupted her performance with his misguided directing, making "Olivia shed her dignity in her first speaking scene and never reclaim it." Hytner, wrote Brantley, performed better when directing the "delicious physical comedy" of Murray and Wright, whom he credited with making their characters seem to be complex human beings, as when Murray located "a chilling, class-conscious viciousness in Toby" and when Wright, playing Andrew, provided "a beautifully assured picture of a heartbreakingly tentative soul." Brantley thought that Murray and Wright, while being funny, elicited "the subliminal madness and anxiety in 'Twelfth Night,' even more than this production's Malvolio." Although he believed Bosco performed well, he wrote that this Malvolio "seldom transcend[ed] the role of disapproving foil and easy target." Admiring Kelley's performance as "an unusually low-key, close-to-invisible Feste, a sort of Depression-era folk hobo type," Brantley also greatly enjoyed Tesori's music, Crowley's set, and Katz's lighting, but he found, unfortunately, that "the characters onstage don't always measure up to the ethereal charms of the land they inhabit."

Mixed-to-Positive Reviews

David Patrick Stearns, writing for *USA Today*, enjoyed this production, calling it not only "sumptuously produced and provocatively cast" but also staged with "lavish but well-considered theatricality." Although complaining about some vulgarity and "some uneven casting," Stearns thought the production offered a "freewheeling mixture of time, place, and style." He especially enjoyed Crowley's watery set and considered the production "marvelously cinematic," although he felt that act one had been "handled dryly." Stearns found Bosco, as Malvolio, "uncharacteristically buttoned up," saying that this character's embarrassing fall was played more in a tragic than in a comic vein. Stearns enjoyed the performances of Murray and Kelly, calling the latter "an unusually scruffy, outspoken court jester." He thought that Hunt, as Viola, had made good "interpretive choices" that were "sincerely executed" but that she had failed to search "deeply enough into the subtextual possibilities" of her character. Although he wrote that Sedgwick went "to such comic extremes" that audiences could not believe she was a noblewoman, he was quite impressed with the "pantherlike moves" of Paul Rudd, whose Orsino, he thought, exhibited "unstoppable sexual desires," letting him "dominate a play that keeps him offstage for long periods."

Robert Osborne, writing for the *Milwaukee Journal Sentinel*, was impressed that Hunt, a recent Oscar-winner, had taken a great chance by committing to live theatre. He found her performance as Viola "[s]incere, yes; attractive, certainly; honest, always" as well as "likable"—but not "dazzling," adding that despite her many qualities as a stage actress, she did not possess the "vocal range" necessary "to fully express Shakespearean dialogue" as well as Rudd did. Yet Osborne also felt that Rudd, despite "an interesting physicality and bravado," unfortunately spoke with "a consistently strained voice." Nonetheless, despite these alleged flaws, he considered the production "vastly entertaining to watch and a visual delight."

Positive Reviews

Don Shewey, in the LGBT magazine *The Advocate*, claimed that Hytner was reluctant to mention during interviews that his production explored "the same slipperiness of sexual identity" he had previously dramatized in his film *The Object of My Affection*. Shewey called Hytner's *Twelfth Night* "a physically ravishing production (with a show-stealing set by scenic genius Bob Crowley) that makes the case for *Twelfth Night* as Shakespeare's most direct examination of homo[sexual] love." Shewey thought, for instance, that Rudd's Orsino appeared comfortable and content while lounging on the stage with his serving boys while thinking of Olivia. Shewey, therefore, considered it "pretty clear...that this Orsino's vision of women is a romantic spasm of compulsory heterosexuality." He enjoyed the performances of all the actors except for Hunt, whom he called "too restrained—a butch-girl / femme-boy—to be much fun to watch." The acting, he asserted, proved that Americans could play Shakespearean roles admirably: he wrote that Sedgwick and Rudd "in particular pull off bold, physically daring performances." Shewey also noted that although the "cross-dressing, mistaken-identity stuff in *Twelfth Night* is usually milked for laughs,...Hytner plays it for maximum emotional disorientation." For instance, Shewey thought that when the duke kisses Cesario/Viola, believing that the page is a boy, "the tension in the theater is thick with the awkwardness, dread, and excitement of illicit sexual awakening." He also thought that the comic subplot was similarly tense because the humiliation of Malvolio "takes on darker tones than usual."

Malcolm Johnson, writing for Connecticut's *Hartford Courant*, hailed the production as "a sensuous yet eclectically tangled passage to India" and "a pictorially exquisite yet perplexing revision" of Shakespeare's beloved comedy. Yet, while calling it "[b]eautiful to look upon," he also thought it "difficult to comprehend" and "unevenly performed, with its actors working in various idioms" in a production "infused with fanciful images from an opium dream, with no necessity for logic." He did, however, admire Murray, Wright, and Bosco for putting on "effortless performances"; wrote that Sedgwick spoke her "lines with great emphasis and energy"; and said that Rudd used "a solid vocal range to offer his take on Laurence Olivier." Although he thought Sedgwick and Rudd performed much better than Hunt, at least in the first act, he suggested that Hunt's acting improved as the play progressed, so that she increasingly delivered "her lines with plainness, trueness, and utter clarity, especially in the sensitive soliloquy about her hidden, unspoken love," gradually transforming Viola "into a resourceful woman...as she skillfully navigates between the comedy of pretense and the deeper emotions that lie beneath."

Jacques le Sourd, writing for the Yonkers, New York *Herald Statesman*, enjoyed Hytner's "stellar, stately and unabridged new staging" of *Twelfth Night*, calling it (in a brief passing notice) "an exquisite-looking production on a grand scale," while Daphne Kraft, in the Passaic, New Jersey *Herald News*, especially enjoyed the show's comedy and praised this staging as "a witty, fantastical production of Shakespeare's play," one in which the characters' clothing and the skillful use of sound were instrumental in portraying "love as delirium" and "passion as contagious nightmare." Kraft was particularly impressed not only with Sedgwick's use of "modern vernacular" but also with Tesori's "original score," which she said gave Feste's famous songs and "assorted romantic moments an echoing timbre and glorious tonal accessibility that is enchanting."

Meanwhile, Jeffrey Eric Jenkins, in a column for South Carolina's *Greenville News*, particularly enjoyed the comedy of Murray and Wright, Crowley's exotic sets, Zuber's costumes, and Katz's lighting, writing that all of these factors made this production "a warming pleasure from start to finish." He praised Hytner for "accentuat[ing] the strengths of the actors" while hiding their flaws. Although he especially enjoyed Hunt's performance (asserting that "her emotional honesty is admirable"), he was disappointed by Rudd, saying he appeared to be "performing in a different version of the play."

David Sheward, in *Back Stage*, wrote that although he had seen eight previous versions of *Twelfth Night*, Hytner's was the best because the director showed "a healthy disregard for 'classicism'" and treated "the text as a vital, lively comedy on the ambiguity of sexuality rather than as a stodgy museum piece about switching wigs and codpieces." Sheward especially enjoyed the production's "sensuous design," including Crowley's "East India, red-toned dreamscape," Zuber's "harem-hedonistic costumes," Katz's "romantic" lighting, and Tesori's "haunting original score." He claimed that although Hunt acted a bit as if she were in a sitcom, she performed well as Viola. He also felt that Sedgwick did well despite sometimes exaggerating her feelings too much (as when she fell "for the disguised Viola way too fast and too hard, snapping from haughty lady to moonstruck adolescent with no transition"). Like many other critics, he thought the comic actors performed even better than the actors in the main roles, partly because they were "played as people, not stock figures of fun." Overall, he concluded that the cast had done an excellent job in a generally outstanding production.

Especially Positive Reviews

Robert Feldberg, in the Bergen, New Jersey *Record*, called this staging "sparkling," "vibrant," and "festive" and praised Hunt as "absolutely delightful." Like many other reviewers, he particularly admired Hytner's direction and Crowley's set for contributing to "a bright, capering, hilarious revival"—one faithful to the text "but not shackled by other people's ideas of how it should be presented." He wrote that the play contained "scene after scene of inspired comedy," that Sedgwick was "deliciously earthy," and that Hunt was right to call her own acting "'naturalistic, simple, [and] honest.'" He considered her a "lovely and gentle Viola"—one "spiced with wry wit and intelligence." Even Feldberg, however, agreed with many other reviewers that the hilarious comic subplot seemed to supersede and outshine the main storyline, partly because Murray, as Belch, gave "a consummate performance, using his marvelous voice and bountiful experience as a comic actor to gain every laugh imaginable and then some." But Feldberg also enjoyed Bosco's villainous Malvolio, Tesori's music, and Zuber's costumes. He ultimately found the production "a totally seductive experience, with scarcely a dull moment" and concluded that Hytner's directing made the staging "supremely entertaining" because the director did not attempt "to bend the play to his own conception or use it to illuminate some contemporary concern."

In another enthusiastic review, Fintan O'Toole, in the New York *Daily News*, wrote that although the production lasted for three hours, it seemed much shorter because it was generally so enjoyable, although he did complain about the alleged torture of Malvolio in the play's second half. Conceding that it is difficult for any director to reconcile the comic and darker elements of this play, he nonetheless praised Hytner's efforts and especially lauded Crowley's "extraordinary dreamscape of shimmering water, deep pools, Oriental carpets, and hanging lanterns," which he said all made the audience feel part "of a world where time and common sense are suspended and anything seems possible." O'Toole wrote that Hytner made everything "unfold at a stately, almost ceremonial pace," so that rather than "blurring the strangeness with speed, he lets it float beautifully to the surface."

O'Toole did, however, blame Hytner for allowing Rudd and Sedgwick to exaggerate their emotions, writing that although Orsino and Olivia are supposed to be nobles, their "necessary grandeur" was missing from this production because Rudd and Sedgwick overacted. On the other hand, he thought that Hunt had played her role "elegantly" and with restraint, showing "the real comedian's skill of always stopping just short of the obvious, allowing the audience to make the final, funny connection." Admiring the comic characters for deftly integrating the play's dark and comic elements, he called Wright "a sublimely pathetic Sir Andrew Aguecheek" and wrote that Kelly brought not only an edge of danger and disturbance to his performance as Feste but also a haunting voice. O'Toole particularly enjoyed the interplay between Bosco (as Malvolio, "who represents order") and Murray (as Belch, "who embodies anarchy"). He claimed that Malvolio went from being an object of mockery to one of sympathy while Belch transformed from being charming to acting like a bully.

Michael Kuchwara, in the *Ottawa Citizen*, loving what he called a "rapturous revival," praised Hytner and Crowley for endowing it "with blazing theatricality." He credited Crowley with creating "a fantastical, watery world made all the more bewitching by the superb collection of actors" assembled by Hytner. He particularly admired Bosco (as Malvolio) for creating "sympathy for the man all the while getting laughs." And Kuchwara was also one of the many critics who praised the comedic acting of Murray and Wright, calling them "pros" and "accomplished physical comedians, managing pratfalls as well as poetry with skill." He additionally lauded "Sedgwick's sublimely giddy performance," Kelly as the "exuberant Feste," Amy Hill's "robustness" as Maria, and Hunt's "spunky yet not overbearing" Viola. Hunt, he wrote, spoke "her lines in a clear, straightforward manner with no excessive embellishment." But he ended by giving special praise to Crowley for a set design he considered worthy of a Tony nomination. Overall, he extolled the entire production, saying it both "dazzles the eye" and "satisfies the ear, and in doing so, touches the heart."

Conclusion

All the reviewers just surveyed were greatly impressed by the talented comic actors, particularly Murray and Wright. Most also greatly enjoyed the performances by Bosco and Kelly. Assessments of the major players, however, were divided. Sedgwick and Rudd, in particular, were often criticized, sometimes for their appearance but more often for their alleged overacting and supposed problems in delivering Shakespeare's lines. Even Hunt (who had recently won an Oscar for *As Good as It Gets*) did not impress many reviewers, who sometimes found her a stiff and stilted comedian. Most reviewers, however, did praise Hytner's directing, and almost all of them extolled Crowley for having designed a spectacularly memorable set.

Note

1. For the YouTube links, see the alphabetical listing for "*Twelfth Night*" below.

Works Cited

Brantley, Ben. "FESTIVAL REVIEW; Addled Sailors in Sea of Love." Review of *Twelfth Night*. Directed by Nicholas Hytner. *The New York Times*, 17 July 1998, p. E1. www.nytimes.com/1998/07/17/movies/festival-review-addled-sailors-in-sea-of-love.html.

Brustein, Robert. "*Twelfth Night*." Review of *Twelfth Night*. Directed by Nicholas Hytner. *New Republic*, vol. 219, no. 10, 7 Sept. 1998, pp. 26–28. Rept. *Shakespeare Criticism*. Vol. 95, go.gale.com/ps/i.do?id=GALE%7CH1420068713&sid=googleScholar&v=2.1&it=r&linkaccess=abs&issn=08839123&p=LitRC&sw=w&userGroupName=avl_auburnum&aty=ip.

Feldberg, Robert. "No End of Wit in Shakespeare." Review of *Twelfth Night*. Directed by Nicholas Hytner. *The Record*, 17 July 1998, p. 96, www.newspapers.com/search/?iid=3825&query=Robert%20Feldberg%20 The%20Record&ymd=1998-07-17.

Gutman, Les. "*Twelfth Night*." Review of *Twelfth Night*. Directed by Nicholas Hytner. *Curtain Up*, 22. July 1998, www.curtainup.com/12thnigh.html.

Isherwood, Charles. Review of "*Twelfth Night*." Review of *Twelfth Night*. Directed by Nicholas Hytner. *Variety*, 17 July 1998, variety.com/1998/legit/reviews/twelfth-night-5-1200454397/.

Jenkins, Jeffrey Eric. "Bard Transcends Delivery by TV Stars." Review of *Twelfth Night*. Directed by Nicholas Hytner. *The Greenville News*, 6 Sept. 1998, p. 66, www.newspapers.com/article/the-greenville-news/125278959/.

Johnson, Malcolm. "Hunt Finds Humor, Pathos in 'Twelfth Night.'" Review of *Twelfth Night*. Directed by Nicholas Hytner. *Hartford Courant*, 17 July 1998, p. 51.

Kraft, Daphne. "Helen Hunt on Stage in Shakespeare's 'Twelfth Night.'" Review of *Twelfth Night*. Directed by Nicholas Hytner. *The Herald News*, 26 July1998, p. 53, E3, www.newspapers.com/article/the-herald-news/125278517/.

Kuchwara, Michael. "Helen Hunt Shines in Blazing Twelfth Night." Review of *Twelfth Night*. Directed by Nicholas Hytner. *The Ottawa Citizen*, 17 July 1998, p. 69.

le Sourd, Jacques. "At Lincoln Center, Its [sic] as Good as It Gets for Domestic Shakespeare." Review of *Twelfth Night*. Directed by Nicholas Hytner. *The Herald Statesman*, 17 July 1998, p. 25.

Merwin, Ted. "*Twelfth Night*." Review of *Twelfth Night*. Directed by Nicholas Hytner. *Theatre Journal*, vol. 51, no. 2, May 1999, pp. 191–92. muse.jhu.edu/pub/1/article/34610.

Osborne, Robert. "Hunt Gives (Weak) Voice to Shakespeare." Review of *Twelfth Night*. Directed by Nicholas Hytner. *Milwaukee Journal Sentinel*. 27 July 1992, p. 2.

O'Toole, Fintan. "'Twelfth Night' Makes Our Day: And We're Mad about Helen Hunt & Co." Review of *Twelfth Night*. Directed by Nicholas Hytner. *Daily News*. 17 July 1998, p. 57.

Ridley, Clifford A. "Helen Hunt as Viola in '*Twelfth Night*.'" Review of Twelfth Night. Directed by Nicholas Hytner. *Philadelphia Inquirer*. 25 July 1998, p. 48. www.newspapers.com/article/the-philadelphia-inquirer/125278569/.

Sheward, David. "*Twelfth Night*." Review of *Twelfth Night*. Directed by Nicholas Hytner. *Back Stage*, vol. 39, no. 31, 31 July–6 Aug. 1998, p. 36, www.backstage.com/magazine/article/reviews-101-33359/.

Shewey, Don. "Review of *Twelfth Night*." Review of *Twelfth Night*. Directed by Nicholas Hytner. *The Advocate*, 1 Sept. 1998, www.donshewey.com/theater_reviews/twelfth-night-LCT.html.

Stearns, David Patrick. "'Twelfth Night': Helen Hunt Isn't Its Only Star." Review of *Twelfth Night*. Directed by Nicholas Hytner. *USA Today*, 17 July 1998, p. 11E.

Twelfth Night, by William Shakespeare. Directed by Nicholas Hytner. Performances by Helen Hunt, Paul Rudd, Kyra Sedgwick, and Philip Bosco, www.youtube.com/watch?v=9cU5Py8GCmA&t=4311s; www.youtube.com/watch?v=QGDEkLqremA.

Winer, Linda. "A 'Twelfth Night' mare at." Review of *Twelfth Night*. Directed by Nicholas Hytner. *Newsday* (Nassau Edition), 17 July 1998, 90, www.newspapers.com/article/newsday-nassau-edition/125279014/.

The 2002 and 2012 All-Male *Twelfth Night* Productions at the Open-Air Globe: Their Critical Reception

Robert C. Evans

One of the most interesting and successful of all the productions of Shakespeare's *Twelfth Night* over the last several decades was first staged in 2002 at the Globe theater in London, a stunningly close replica of the original Elizabethan Globe Theater that Shakespeare himself partly owned and for which he wrote many of his very best plays. The 2002 staging was directed by Tim Carroll and starred Mark Rylance, widely recognized as one of the greatest Shakespearean actors of our era. What made this production especially interesting was the decision to use an all-male cast, with males playing all the roles, including all the female characters. This, of course, is exactly how plays were produced during Shakespeare's time: actresses did not appear on professional stages until after the 1660 restoration of the monarchy (which had been replaced by a republic following the English civil wars of the 1640s and early 1650s). The roles Shakespeare wrote for men were played by men (including Shakespeare himself), while the roles he wrote for women were played by adolescent boys, especially those whose voices had not yet "broken." The 2002 staging at the Globe did not feature male adolescents in the women's parts but instead featured men, including some young men but men, nonetheless. Yet the 2002 staging—and a highly popular revival of that staging a decade later—got us about as close as we have ever been to seeing *Twelfth Night* as Shakespeare's contemporaries saw it.

Unfortunately, the *original* 2002 Globe production was not preserved on film, but the 2012 revival definitely was. Many people consider both stagings one of the best versions of *Twelfth Night* they have ever seen; it is, for all kinds of reasons, a "landmark" production. Discussing it, however, is difficult, not only because no film of the 2002 version survives but also because the 2012 version in some cases featured actors who did not originally appear in the 2002 production. And, to make matters even *more* complicated, in 2012 the Globe refused to let professional reviewers write about the outdoor Globe production. Instead, reviewers had to wait until the play moved to one of London's professional indoor theaters. The outdoor production *was* filmed; the indoor production was not. Thus, the reviews of the outdoor production that do survive are scanty, although more reviews of the indoor production did appear. But the *film* of the outdoor production did generate a fair number of reviews, and, when the production was transferred to an indoor theater in New York, reviews abounded.

Here, however, I want to focus on the reviews generated by the 2002 and 2012 productions done at the Globe, whether those reviews were of the "live" stage version or of the excellent later *film* of the live stage version. These reviews can help us better understand not only this particular production but also the play itself.

Reviews of the 2002 Globe Production

When the Carroll-Rylance production was first staged at the Globe in 2002, it featured Rylance as Olivia, Timothy Walker as Malvolio, Bill Stewart as Sir Toby Belch, Albie Woodington as Sir Andrew Aguecheek, Liam Brennan as Orsino, Michael Brown as Viola, Peter Hamilton Dyer as Feste, Paul Chahidi as Maria, and Rhys Meredith as Sebastian. These details of casting are important because when the play was revived and filmed in 2012, some of the actors in some of the roles were not the actors who appeared in 2002. In any case, the 2002 production was enthusiastically reviewed by Ben Brantley for the *New York Times*, who saw this staging as a welcome alternative to all the "overdecorated, overeager stage productions" of *Twelfth Night* "that have been going under that name recently, all dressed up in the latest fashions and academic theories. What I'm talking about," Brantley continued, "is the simple and complicated comedy that was first performed four centuries ago and remains one of the most engaging romances ever written." That play, he wrote, "is on view again here at the Globe, the open-air theater that seeks to approximate the experience of watching Shakespearean plays as they appeared originally. For 'Twelfth Night,'" he thought, "the Globe has made its most literal bid yet for authenticity, with a production that features Elizabethan costumes, music and props, not to mention the period convention of an all-male cast." Brantley found, in this production, "none of the mustiness of the museum, none of the tourist-courting quaintness of which the Globe has periodically been accused since it opened in 1997. In frankly admitting its age, which is just over 400 years," he contended, "'Twelfth Night' has never looked younger. And in a staging that consistently calls attention to its artificiality, this play has rarely felt so real."

Brantley wrote that the typical modern "consensus seems to be that if you're going to sell Shakespeare, you need to spike it with novelty." He thought that sometimes such an approach was "illuminating" but that "often the suggestion [appeared to be] that weary old Shakespeare needs a head-to-toe makeover to appear attractive, and all the high-concept camouflage can start to smother the substance beneath." Instead, he found the Globe production "gleaming like a newly restored painting by an old master. The distinctive and complex virtues" of the play, according to Brantley, "are allowed to emerge unvarnished and unannotated." He considered it "to this production's credit that while the audience members laugh heartily throughout, there are moments when they fall into grave and wondering silences," thus reflecting the ways this staging had captured and conveyed the tonal complexity of the play itself. Brantley admired the performers for offering "stylized portraits that wind up going deeper than most naturalistic performances," adding that the "cast members bring out the actor in each of the characters," including "the poses that reflect their distorted ideas of themselves. They also do not let you forget that these actorly creatures are being portrayed by actors, whose exaggerated and mannered styles are pitched directly to their audiences."

Brantley reported that in the Globe production Duke Orsino finds himself having "a yen for his page, Cesario," an apparent male who is actually a female (Viola) who is actually being played by a young male. According to Brantley, in one scene of this staging Orsino "keeps casting furtive glances at his shy young minion and brushing against him, as if by accident. The other courtiers pretend nothing is going on." Brantley wrote that the director "stretches the scene to the breaking point, so that different levels of perception swim in and out of focus. It is," he thought, "sexy, uncomfortable and highly disorienting." He noted that the "men playing women... are not effeminate. They pitch their voices higher, but there is little mincing or swishing. And while the interpretations are funny, they always seem fully thought out, grounded not only in their characters' psychology but also as social archetypes who would have been familiar to Elizabethan audiences." He called all the actors "terrific, walking a fine line between emotional truth and comic caricature." But he added that "Mr. Rylance...is a marvel. His Olivia is hilarious in her high-born delicacy, which can assume a Monty Python-ish surrealism. She seems less to walk than to glide beneath her floor-length skirt." After discussing some more specifics of Ryland's performance, Brantley concluded, about the production as a whole, that it was quite "satisfying" to have the play's "natural, double-faced perspective brought back into focus." Rylance and his colleagues could not have asked for a better review.

Similarly positive was an assessment in *The Guardian* by Maddy Costa, who initially lamented "how few roles there are for women generally in theatre," adding that "for men to filch even these is hardly fair." But then she quickly added: "Irritation is assuaged, however, by the actual performances. Mark Rylance's stammering, fluttery Olivia is exquisite" as well as—in one crucial scene—"superbly comic and almost unbearably poignant." Costa considered "Michael Brown's wide-eyed, ingenuous Viola...a little ditsy for someone with 'a mind that envy could not but call fair,'" but added that "this dreamy quality suits the production's heart-meltingly romantic tone." She found the "dawning love between Viola and Liam Brennan's honey-voiced, wonderfully petulant Orsino...beautifully charted" and thought "the duke's shift from Olivia to Viola feels far less sudden when we have already seen the two, overcome with emotion after listening to one of Feste's love songs, falteringly embrace and almost kiss." This, Costa asserted, "is typical of [director] Carroll's ability to make even the most absurd scenes in the play feel human and real. Having stripped his production of modern accoutrements, he makes touch, close physicality, paramount," as in scenes showing characters taking each other's hands, which underline that "it is the joy of Carroll's thrilling production that each tiny gesture counts."

Finally, in another similarly positive review, Philip Fisher for the online *British Theatre Guide* wrote that "the performances from the actors playing the three female parts in Tim Carroll's production of *Twelfth Night* are so strong that the experiment seems fully justified. In fact," he reported, "the audience is soon so mesmerised by the quality of the acting that it is easy to forget that these are men playing female roles." He considered Rylance as Olivia and Brown as Viola "outstanding in a generally strong cast. The former," he suggested, "plays the Countess as a stiff, nervous innocent, possibly in homage to the Virgin Queen, Elizabeth. The scene in which she falls for Viola in the guise of Cesario is extremely funny and wholly believable. Most Englishmen," he thought, "will remember an aged maiden aunt just like this." Fisher wrote that "Michael Brown is also very strong on female body language. His walk is just right and his girlish nervousness wins over not only Liam Brennan as a very touching Duke Orsino but also everybody in the theatre." Fisher thought that in the comic subplot, "Albie Woodington makes a wonderful Andrew Aguecheek looking like an ageing rocker dressed as a hornet; while Paul Chahidi has great fun in the final female role as the scheming Maria." Fisher argued that a "slight surprise was the performance of Peter Hamilton Dyer as Feste. While fun wasn't too far away at any time and he kept things rolling along nicely, he was not a particularly comic fool, with one notably hilarious exception," while when Timothy Walker's "poor, maltreated, Malvolio...reached rock bottom, he laid his head on the stage and found a female groundling sympathetically stroking it. This," Fisher suggested, "is the Globe at its best." He also admired the "excellent period music" and the "superb costumes" and ended by calling this production "a very good introduction to both Shakespeare and the Globe Theatre for anybody, young or old, who is not already familiar with them."

Reviews of the Globe's 2012 Revived Production

When the 2002 Globe production was revived and re-staged in 2012—first at the Globe itself and then at one of London's most prominent big, indoor, "West End" theaters—it featured a cast in some ways the same and in other ways different from the first. Now, Rylance still played Olivia; Chahidi still played Maria; Peter Hamilton Dyer still played Feste; and Liam Brennan still played Orsino. But Colin Hurley had replaced Bill Stewart as Sir Toby; Roger Lloyd Pack had replaced Albie Woodington as Sir Andrew; Samuel Barnett had replaced Rhys Meredith as Sebastian; Johnny Flynn had replaced Michael Brown as Viola; and, most significantly, the much-loved actor and media personality Stephen Fry—a major box-office draw—had replaced Timothy Walker as Malvolio.

In one of the relatively few reviews of the 2012 revival actually staged at the Globe itself (before it moved to the West End), Peter Kirwan of the blog *The Bardathon* wrote that this new ensemble was "unavoidably different on account of the presence of Stephen Fry, the nation's darling," who had been absent from London theaters since 1995, when his poor reception in one play had led to his abrupt withdrawal and even to thoughts of suicide. In the meantime, however, he had become enormously popular and was now appearing in a production in which, according to Kirwan, "every actor in the immensely capable ensemble got his moment to shine." Kirwan wrote that Fry, in particular, "didn't disappoint. His slow-moving, relatively amiable Malvolio was no tyrant but an intellectual pedant, who established his studied difference to the other characters in a way befitting an actor who had joined the ensemble for a single play." Kirwan thought that Fry's "poise was careful and rarely dropped, allowing him to become a centre of gravity for his scenes that sucked the energy out of the carnivalesque, while avoiding going for cheap laughs through mugging or exaggerating." Kirwan thought that "Fry's Malvolio was, in fact, one of the most human [he had] yet seen"—a character who definitely "was no monster," so that "his cries from a barred prison jutting up from the trap and his final sloping offstage following his stuttered cry of revenge were greeted with a general sympathy."

Like almost all critics, both in 2002 and in 2012, Kirwan called Rylance's performance as Olivia "remarkable," writing that as it "progressed her unpredictability became the play's comic highlight." Kirwan thought that Rylance's movement from "the mannered to the ridiculous characterised much of the play," suggesting that "Olivia's gradual slippage of decorum increased the desire to see her fully uninhibited." Kirwan also asserted that "Paul Chahidi's Maria and Colin Hurley's Sir Toby" were "a standout partnership," and, like many critics, he claimed that "Maria stole every scene in which she appeared." He thought that "Malvolio's insults during the drinking scene" showed that "most of his disdain was reserved for [Maria], including lines normally addressed to the men." Arguing that the "carefully managed duel was a comic highlight, perhaps even more so than an amusing but straightforward box tree scene," he additionally mentioned, as another particularly funny moment, the image of "Maria hiding herself behind a tree in embarrassment and giving a pathetic 'Yay!' to back up Fabian's report of her marriage" to Sir Toby. For Kirwan, the production's general "combination of humour and affect perfectly served the reunion of the twins, where for the first time ever I heard suppressed shrieks of delight as they came together. It was, finally, a moment of wonder that defined the play." He considered this group of actors "the most capable ensemble the Globe has seen in some years," adding that this staging, while "not the most out-and-out hysterical version of the play," made "a powerful claim for good verse speaking, simple comedy and a festive ensemble as the Globe's most important ingredients." By avoiding "the obvious traps of the celebrity production and instead celebrating the creation of theatrical community between actors and audience," this version, according to Kirwan, "was fully invested in...creating an entirely wonder-full production."

Also positive (if not as positive as Kirwan) was an anonymous reviewer for the "There Ought to Be Clowns" theater blog (see "Anonymous"), who began by confessing that s/he was "not really a fan of Mark Rylance, just so you know" but who seemed to enjoy most of the production. This reviewer especially admired "the incredible level of detailed work that has gone on here at all levels.

Liam Brennan," s/he thought, "imbues Orsino with a much greater deal of personality than is often granted to this lovesick Lord, making him a constant point of interest," while "Colin Hurley's Sir Toby Belch reins in the [usual] boisterousness to construct a much more interesting character." According to this reviewer, "Feste's presence possesses an intriguing ambivalence in Peter Hamilton Dyer's hands," while "James Garnon makes one notice Fabian more than I've ever done before." But the "unexpected star of the show" for this writer (and many others) was "Paul Chahidi's Maria, a warmly wry, comic performance that brims with such a natural confidence that he completely transcends the cross-gender casting to a point where one forgets [quite] quickly that he's a man in a dress and instead his [is] just one of the funniest performances currently in London." Calling Rylance-as-Olivia "almost Kabuki-inspired as he skitters around the stage in white-face," this review commended Rylance for "playing up the effects of [Olivia's] sheltered existence as a distinct lack of social skills and pulling out humour from some unexpected places. It was a performance of his," the reviewer wrote, "that I did actually warm to for once," thanks to Rylance "blending into the ensemble in a way I haven't seen before, though he may have erred a little close to scene-stealing in the final section." Like other commentators, this writer "did have difficulties with Johnny Flynn's Viola," calling his acting "a stylised mode of performance" (perhaps deliberately so) unfortunately "characterised by a thin, reedy vocal delivery, a kind of stiffness in the way that he carries himself and a consequent lack of variation in his acting." This reviewer was not "alone in wishing that Sam Barnett—an excellent Sebastian here—had been cast as Viola instead," and, in fact, when the production eventually moved to New York, Barnett did indeed replace Flynn as Viola and won a Tony nomination for his efforts.

The reviewer for "There Ought to Be Clowns" asserted that "Claire Van Kampen's music captures the lightly reflective, almost melancholy tone of the production," a tone "further epitomised by Stephen Fry's Malvolio, a steward of more avuncular warmth than gruff edges," making "him a sadder figure and somehow more endearing to the audience. It's a different take," this writer continued, "but one which largely works even if it leads to something of an uncertain tone at the end," with "the post-imprisonment darkness robbed of some of its context and sitting a little more uneasily amidst the rest of the comedic unfolding." Ultimately, "Anonymous" thought that this Globe production offered "some exceptionally great character work" but produced "an overall effect that is partially muted. Maybe," s/he suggested, "this is partly due to the [more than three hours'] length," or "maybe it is partly due to a staging which rarely makes use of the opportunities offered by the venue"—"perhaps an acknowledgement that it was always destined to end up in a West End theatre." The review ended by asserting that "a lack of vibrancy does not however mean a lack of quality, and there is no doubting that there is some seriously impressive acting on display here."

Even more impressed was Alex Needham, writing for *The Guardian*, whose review was published under a headline proclaiming that "Stephen Fry's *Twelfth Night*" was anything but a "One-Man Show." Needham began by asserting that "no single actor dominates this radical yet perfectly balanced production" and continued by proclaiming that "it is difficult to imagine that *Twelfth Night* could be performed more effectively than it currently is at the Globe theatre"—where, he oddly reported, critics "have been forbidden to review the show until it transfers to the West End in November." But Needham humorously advised his readers that his article would not be an official review because he had actually paid for his ticket months ago rather than waiting to receive free seating as a pre-approved reviewer. He suggested that although this "*Twelfth Night* is performed in Jacobean costume, with traditional instruments accompanying its various songs," it was "nonetheless a radical production that makes Shakespeare seem completely contemporary. The Bard's sexual fluidity," he thought, "runs particularly free in the powerfully homoerotic scene" in a production in which "for once, the gender confusion is convincing." He noted that when Olivia (Rylance) says "most wonderful! when both [twins suddenly] appear on stage, the inference is that she would like a threesome with the pair of them—which is greeted by riotous cheers from the audience."

Commenting on Rylance's performance in general, Needham suggested that in other productions he had seen, "a young, often beautiful woman plays Olivia. Played by Rylance, she could easily seem grotesque, but in a performance of incredible finesse and intelligence, he creates a character that exerts her power through wit and intelligence, not looks." He also, like many critics, observed that while "Maria is often just a sidekick to Andrew Aguecheek and Sir Toby Belch,...here she is the motor of the plot to trick Malvolio, as well as enjoying, in her lingering kiss with Sir Toby, the suggestion that she has another story away from the action of the play." Needham wrote that Fry, as Malvolio, "plays the role with considerable subtlety," offering "not a showy star turn" but instead a performance that "rebalances the play." According to Needham, while "Belch and Aguecheek are uproarious," Malvolio's "parting shot 'I'll be revenged on the whole pack of you' is the cry of a broken man, greeted with guilt from the other characters and sympathy, rather than derision, from the audience." Needham concluded that the "reason such complexity is pulled off is ultimately down to the whole cast working at such a high level of accomplishment that no single actor dominates. If anyone," he thought, "pulls the play together, it is ultimately Feste, whose songs cast a final spell over an audience which has been rapt with attention from the start. It's a show in which the proportions of comedy to melancholy have been measured out with forensic attention."

Finally, one more—if very brief—assessment, this time from an uncredited writer for *Glasgowtheatreblog.com* (see "Review") called this *Twelfth Night* "the most magical ever—as close to perfection as anything I've ever seen on stage." This writer felt that "Fry as Malvolio...in a nicely tuned performance...never lets the character fall into cheap farce" and termed the Globe staging "theatrical perfection and the ultimate example of an ensemble cast."

The 2012 Globe Production on Film

Given the high praise this Globe production routinely received—wherever and whenever it was performed, including not only at the Globe but also in the West End and in two American tours—we are quite lucky to have the 2012 production preserved on film, both through streaming and on DVD. Unfortunately, the filmed version seems to have attracted even fewer reviewers than the initial performances at the Globe, although some reviewers of the film have gone into quite a bit of detail when discussing the production.

One of those commentators was Joel Reid, writing for a website completely devoted to "costume dramas"—films set in previous centuries. This website, *Frockflicks.com,* is in fact particularly interested in costumes and clothing, and so Reid spent much of his very lengthy (and witty) essay discussing precisely these issues. But he also made intriguing comments about the 2012 Globe production as a whole. He noted that the Globe *Twelfth Night* had originally appeared in 2002 and had then toured abroad before being revived in 2012. He reported that he had had "the benefit of having seen both the live and filmed versions to compare. Largely," he said, "they are indistinguishable from each other, with the exception that the tour utilized a traveling set that recreated the play-space at Blackfriars ([an] indoor theater space of Shakespeare's time) instead of the larger-scale Globe setting," which "was harder to recreate in the variety of theaters they would be presenting the production in on the tour." Reid then listed some major costuming errors often found in plays or films set in the past. These included:

- Improperly worn corsets/incorrect period corsets
- No shifts under corsets
- Hair undone/modern hairstyles paired with period clothing
- Clothing worn without proper under layers
- Visible zippers/snaps/metal grommets
- Clothing from disparate periods mixed together in the same production
- Modern makeup styles worn with period clothing
- Lack of appropriate head wear/accessories
- Obvious lack of practice/rehearsal, moving naturally [i.e., in modern or recent movements?] in period clothing so [that the costumes] read like foreign costumes to the wearer

Reid judged the Globe staging "guilty of NONE of the usual pitfalls and foibles that trip up a period production and earn it the ire of Frock Flicks in large or small measure." He did, however, feel that the team at the Globe had got one thing wrong "despite a wealth of good intent and solid scholarship." After admiringly discussing in detail the actual look of the costumes at the Globe, Reid eventually got to his main complaint: that the kinds of clothing worn by the actors in 2002 and 2012 were very convincing examples of the kinds of *everyday clothing* worn by people in Shakespeare's time but were, for that very reason, not as exotic or interesting enough for a play set in the mysterious, lyrical setting of Illyria. Therefore, "to an audience from 1600, seeing this production of *Twelfth Night* would look rather boring as the characters all wear average everyday clothing that the audience could see out on the street for free." According to Reid, when theatergoers in Shakespeare's day went to a play set in an exotic location, they would expect to see exotic costumes, not standard Elizabethan clothing.

Reid then offered one visually illustrated example after another of surviving costume designs from the Renaissance to make his point, remarking that in general these designs are a "far cry from the very staid and safe image that The Globe's modern production of *Twelfth Night* puts forward." He argued that "there is a wide gap between how the culture of the era would have likely addressed fantastical or whimsical costuming and how The Globe has chosen to represent it," adding that

> the play purports to take place in a foreign ancient land and therefore one would think some effort might have been taken to help convey that fact in the way that the characters in the play are dressed, since their mode of dress was really the only visual cue the audience would be afforded to support the references in the text about time and place.

He thought that "what the actors wear, by rights, should look more theatrical than like everyday Elizabethan street wear that the audience could exit The Globe and see walking about on passers-by."

Nevertheless (and most importantly for our present purposes), Reid stressed that he wanted

> to reiterate that I loved this production, both live and on film. I think it does an amazing job of engaging its audience with a concept of period manner and behavior that you don't often see on stage or on film. I think its stewardship to the styles of dress at the time [is] virtually unparalleled, and the clothing seen on screen could easily be displayed in a museum as an example of styles and construction techniques from the period, and I think the actors uniformly inhabit those clothes with a truth and naturalness that make them seem as normal as jeans and T-shirts are to us today...all of which are truly commendable attributes that we should applaud and celebrate. But I also think it's important to be cognizant of how it diverges from true historical accuracy in its method of presentation so we can always have something more to reach for and aspire to when creating pieces like this.

He then concluded his generally very favorable review by mentioning (without explaining) some "other ways I think that The Globe misses the mark" but said that these matters "have less to do with the fundamentals of the clothing and more with other aspects of the mechanics of how a play would have been presented then as opposed to how we can viably do so now to a modern audience." All in all, then, Reid offered a quite positive review.

Also enthusiastic (with just a few reservations) was Eric Minton, a reviewer for *Shakespeareances.com*, who began by asserting that "If there's any fault with the DVD version of Shakespeare['s] Globe's 2012 production of William Shakespeare's *Twelfth Night* it is this: the production improved after it was filmed. By the time this production reached Broadway" in 2013 "the performances were keener, the ensemble tighter, and the action funnier." Nonetheless, Minton wrote that what "is most refreshing" about the Globe's "text-centric rendering" of the play

> is that some of the characters, unencumbered by 400 years of portrayal traditions, emerge into whole new lights. This is especially true of Fry's Malvolio. He is no villain; he is no obnoxious clown. He is, merely, "a kind of puritan," serious, self-centered, holier-than-thou even to his lady, yes, but quite a good administrator of her household, too. His tragic flaw is not any of these qualities; rather, it is his fantasizing the possibility that his lady might love him.

"I have never before," Minton added, "seen a Malvolio I've so identified with," partly because "Fry's portrayal is so simply honest," as when he speaks the lines "I do not now fool myself, to let imagination jade me; for every reason excites to this, that my lady loves me,"—a statement, according to Minton, that Fry concludes "with such incredulous wonder that you can hear sympathy in the audience. 'I am happy,' he says with innocent wonder. This," Minton thought, "is funny, and this is sad, too, and the audience just melts for him. If you know what's coming, your own heart will ache."

In Minton's opinion, because "Malvolio is clearly not a villain, Toby Belch becomes something of a villain. On Broadway," he reported, "Hurley had rounded the character into a genial yet mischievous jokester, but in the DVD version his Toby has a much sharper edge." Minton wrote that "Dyer's Feste keeps his psychological distance, if not a physical separation, from Toby." Instead, it "is Fabian (played with slick slyness by James Garnon) who serves as Toby's cohort in mischief." Minton thought that the "measured pace" of Roger Lloyd Pack's Sir Andrew contrasts with "Hurley's uninhibited energy," so that "much of Aguecheek's humor grows in this gap between the two, thanks to Pack's timing." Meanwhile, Minton felt that in the Globe production, "Maria's loathing of Malvolio comes off as jealousy rather than reaction to abuse," partly because "Olivia clearly has greater regard for and gives higher rank to the steward than for the waiting woman." Like almost every reviewer of this *Twelfth Night*, Minton extolled Chahidi's performance *as* Maria, just as he also found Rylance's Olivia in the DVD "marvelous in its own right but more so for the memory of his New York performance."

Minton noted that Rylance, moving around on stage in a long black gown, "seems to glide like a wound-up porcelain doll on wheels. The first time he crosses the stage," he reported, "the audience laughs, and everything about his movements and expressions is so painfully reserved it's hilariously funny." Minton also thought that Liam Brennan, as Orsino, "acts with [great] subtlety of movement and inflection" and that "his increasing bafflement at the end is sublimely played."

Minton did feel that

> [this] production's one blemish—and it is only so relative to the New York staging—is in the casting of Johnny Flynn as Viola. This is not a slam on his acting abilities or performance, for he exhibits Viola's discomfort in her absurd situation with nervous ticks and breaking voice. His best moment comes in the faux fencing scene with Aguecheek where Flynn's physical comic skills are put on display.

But Minton felt that "Flynn was too tall for the role" and that "even in playing Viola in her 'woman's weeds' he looks and moves" in ways that struck Minton as "too masculine. You thus," according to Minton, "don't feel the confusion on the scale as we did in New York when Barnett [who played Sebastian at the Globe] shifted to Viola and near look-alike newcomer Joseph Timms took on Sebastian." Finally, praising "John Paul Connolly as Antonio" by saying that "he presents what might well be a definitive portrayal of this minor role," Minton ended by calling this presentation of *Twelfth Night* "one of those stage productions that will be talked about for ages."

Conclusion

As if all the success and acclaim outlined above were not enough for Carroll, Rylance, and their talented ensemble, the revived Globe production soon moved from that very distinctive outdoor theater into a major indoor theater—the Apollo—in London's West End. In some ways, this move was quite appropriate, because *Twelfth Night* was definitely performed in various indoor venues during its day, including a famous performance at the so-called "Middle Temple," one of the "Inns of Court" where young men prepared for future careers in the law and other forms of public service. The play was also performed indoors at the royal court, and, after the Restoration, it moved to indoor theaters almost entirely until relatively recently. Therefore, moving from the Globe (whether the Globe that existed in Shakespeare's day or the Globe that now exists in our own) made great theatrical sense and had great theatrical precedent. In a "sequel" to the present essay, I will discuss how the play was received by critics when it was performed not only at the Apollo but also in a comparable indoor theater when the whole production moved to New York.

Works Cited

Anonymous. *There Ought to Be Clowns*, Review of *Twelfth Night*. Directed by Tim Carroll. *There Ought to Be Clowns*, 26 Sept. 2012, oughttobeclowns.com/2012/09/review-twelfth-night-shakespeares-globe-2.html.

Brantley, Ben. "Theater Critic's Notebook: Boys Will Be Girls in Pure Shakespeare." Review of *Twelfth Night*. Directed by Tim Carroll. *The New York Times*, 29 Aug. 2002, p. E1, www.nytimes.com/2002/08/29/theater/critic-s-notebook-boys-will-be-girls-in-pure-shakespeare.html.

Costa, Maddy. Review of *Twelfth Night*, by William Shakespeare. Directed by Tim Carroll. *The Guardian*, 24 May 2002, www.theguardian.com/stage/2002/may/24/theatre.artsfeatures1.

Fisher, Philip. "*Twelfth Night*." Review of *Twelfth Night*. Directed by Tim Carroll. *British Theatre Guide*, n.d., www.britishtheatreguide.info/reviews/twelfthnightglobe-rev.

Kirwan, Peter. "Twelfth Night @ Shakespeare's Globe." Review of *Twelfth Night*. Directed by Tim Carroll. *The Bardathon*, 30 Sept. 2012, blogs.nottingham.ac.uk/bardathon/2012/09/30/twelfth-night-shakespeares-globe/#:~:text=As%20part%20of%20this%2C%20Fry,ensemble%20for%20a%20single%20play.

Minton, Eric. "What Achieved Greatness Was Born Great." Review of *Twelfth Night*. Directed by Tim Carroll. *Shakespeareances.com*, 22 May 2014, www.shakespeareances.com/willpower/onscreen/Twelfth_Night-Globe13.html.

Needham, Alex. "Stephen Fry's *Twelfth Night*: This All-Male Affair is No One-Man Show." Review of *Twelfth Night.* Directed by Tim Carroll. *The Guardian*, 1 Oct. 2012, www.theguardian.com/stage/2012/oct/01/stephen-fry-twelfth-night-all-male.

Reid, Joel. "*Twelfth Night* by the Globe Theater." *Twelfth Night.* Directed by Tim Carroll. *Flockflicks.com*, 6 Apr. 2021, www.frockflicks.com/twelfth-night-by-the-globe-theater/.

"Review: Twelfth Night, Shakespeare's Globe, London with Mark Rylance and Stephen Fry." Review of *Twelfth* Night. Directed by Tim Carroll. *Glasgow Theatre Blog*, 20 Oct. 2012, glasgowtheatreblog.com/2012/10/20/review-twelfth-night-shakespeares-globe-london/.

The 2012-13 All-Male *Twelfth Night* at Two Indoor Theaters: Its Critical Reception

Robert C. Evans

When Director Tim Carroll and actor Mark Rylance staged an all-male production of William Shakespeare's *Twelfth Night* at the modern recreation of Shakespeare's Globe Theatre in 2002, reactions from critics and audiences were especially strongly positive. Rylance, then the artistic director of the Globe, himself starred in the work, playing the role of Olivia in one of the most memorable and most hilarious performances imaginable. No wonder, then, that the 2002 production soon embarked on a multi-city tour in the United States, where the play was now staged not in venues comparable to the open-air Globe but in more conventional, indoor theaters where the production was made to look as if it were taking place in the kinds of indoor theaters also available in Shakespeare's day. Indeed, *Twelfth Night* was definitely performed in such theaters during and after Shakespeare's lifetime, including performances in schools of law as well as the royal court.

Thus, when this exceptionally memorable production was revived in 2012 and performed at the Globe once more, it made perfect sense for it to then move to an indoor theater (the Apollo) situated in London's West End. Once more, both at the Globe and at the Apollo, the play was a major critical and popular success—so much so that even when it was being staged at the Globe its movement to the Apollo was already planned. Fortunately, the Globe performance, in all its tragicomic (but mostly quite comic) splendor, was preserved on film and will be permanently available via DVD and streaming sources for future generations to watch and love. No films survive, unfortunately, of the indoor performances in London and New York, but those stagings were widely reviewed and almost always celebrated. This essay, then, functions as a sequel to an earlier essay in which I discussed reviews of the Globe productions.

Here I will focus on critics' reactions to the way the play was staged in London's West End.

Negative Reviews of the Apollo Theater Production

One of the few mostly negative reviews of the Apollo staging came from David Benedict, writing for *Variety*, the prominent entertainment magazine. Benedict began on a positive note, calling Rylance's "dazzlingly watchable antics" as Olivia "nothing short of a star turn" but finding Rylance's performance "both the production's strength and its weakness" and arguing that "Rylance's unfettered show-stealing...overbalances the proceedings," resulting in an "inconsistent production that makes the play itself feel only fitfully convincing." Benedict did think that the Apollo's "largely unchanging lighting...keeps much of the auditorium more brightly lit than is usual, which tends to keep audiences more engaged," and he also suggested that Stephen Fry's "combination of nice timing and patrician manner perfectly suit the pompous steward" Malvolio, although Benedict wrote that Fry "lacks energy and emotional depth," suggesting that his Malvolio's strained attempt at forced smiling "is funny for being unexpected" while finding "the rest of his performance...predictable." Benedict thought that "[s]ince [Fry] reveals vicious high-handedness only at the very end, the stakes remain low even during his wrongful imprisonment, which should be much more upsetting than it is here."

Benedict thought that this production had missed a "huge potential for dramatic tension and sight gags," that it suffered from "slack pacing," and that the decision to cast men rather than boys in the women's roles was "understandable" but "at odds with the 'self-styled authenticity'" of the staging. He termed Paul Chahidi, as Maria, "almost the only person who makes auds [sic; typical *Variety* lingo] recognize his character's crucial rank within Olivia's household," crediting Chahidi for using "his own voice rather than the disconnected, high head-voice Johnny Flynn adopts for Viola." According to Benedict, Flynn, "[s]ounding like a cartoon idea of a woman," thereby distanced himself "from both the action and the audience. Worse," Benedict thought, "his lack of vocal power undermines [Flynn] whenever the emotions run high." Benedict found Liam Brennan's Orsino "gruff," said that most of Rylance's "laughs come from additions to the lines rather than the text itself," claimed that such "interpolations are strikingly funny but at odds with the 'original practices' principle," and concluded by lamenting the production's alleged "lack of breadth and depth."

Only a bit more positive than Benedict was a blogger identified only as "nick730," who almost immediately began with complaints. He wrote that he was "disappointed by [Flynn's] Viola," especially for using a "high reedy voice which borders on parody," adding that "keeping it throughout the show doesn't leave much room for subtlety of performance." This reviewer also described the voice of Rylance's Olivia as "quite high-pitched" but said that Rylance "gets away with it (of course, getting away with performances nobody else could pretty much sums up his career.)" This, he continued, "is a rather vulnerable Olivia, eliciting both laughs and sympathy" and he found that although this Olivia was somewhat older than usual, "there's something quite childlike about her, like she's been sheltered by the father and brother she suddenly lost." Like many critics, "nick730" called special attention to Chahidi's "strong" Maria but warned that at "at times this becomes The Maria Show," although he did credit Colin Hurley for offering a "very understated Sir Toby" and for "mining every bit of comedy in the role, something that sadly can't be said of everyone."

This reviewer wrote that Fry's

> Malvolio is not the most vicious take on the puritanical steward you'll ever see, more self-important than mean-spirited. His warmth means his gulling is sad much earlier than it usually is, and although I do like a bit more vitriol in my Malvolios it's a different take that works well enough and, along with Rylance and Chahidi, Fry is the person who seems to "get" the little details in which opportunities for humour can be found, and whose presence livens up proceedings.

He called Fry "one of the few" actors in this production who tried "to engage with the groundlings, such a familiar feature of Globe productions that it's notable here for its absence."

Summing up his misgivings, he wrote that there were "lots of little things like this that made this overall a rather under-powered *Twelfth Night* for me. It's entertaining enough but never raucous, or anything close to it." He suggested that this production seemed to be taking the melancholy aspects of the script "very much to heart," making the pace too "leisurely, although picking up energy in the second half, especially in the 'well-done' duel episode." He concluded: "There's not much to actively dislike here, but I did feel that if this was the signature production of Rylance's tenure [at the Globe, where it was first staged in 2002], perhaps I didn't miss much by skipping those years."

Positive Reviews of the Apollo Theater Production

Somewhat more positive than Benedict and "nick730" was Philip Fisher, writing for the *British Theatre Guide*, who (1) praised Rylance's "convincing" performance as a "stately, Edith Evans-like Olivia"; (2) noted that in the move to the Apollo the production remained "much the same, including gorgeous period costumes and music"; but (3) observed that "Jenny Tiramani's setting has now changed quite significantly." Fisher called the move "a mixed blessing," explaining that while the Apollo "offers creature comforts that cannot even be dreamt of at [the Globe's] Bankside [location], the atmosphere and young, tourist audience that are the Globe's major selling points cannot be replicated." Fisher thought that although the "polymath" Fry "acquits himself adequately, early on it is hard to forget that this is Stephen Fry, so close is he to playing himself." But he added that "as the actor relaxes into the role, the performance grows." According to Fisher, there was "much ribald laughter available, as Carroll retains the ironic Globe tone, allowing actors to play off the audience and making the most of stage business, including the unforgettable, undersized box tree that takes such a key role in an exceedingly funny letter scene." However, he considered the "cross-dressing...a mixed blessing, sometimes overwhelming the drama but at other times enhancing it so that, for example, Johnny Flynn makes a good Viola/Cesario, shy and timid whatever the gender." And, as so often, Chahidi was praised for "taking the role of Maria so convincingly that one frequently has to do a double take before accepting that this is a man in drag—and a consistently funny one at that—rather than a desperate matron." Practically every time and everywhere the play was staged, Chahidi was singled out for enthusiastic commendation.

Writing for *The Guardian*, renowned theater critic Michael Billington awarded the Apollo production four-out-of-four stars, claiming that Jenny Tirimani's "permanent set—a decorated oak screen, with some of the audience seated in on-stage galleries—suits *Twelfth Night* especially, and recreates the collegiate atmosphere the play must have had when seen at the Inns of Court in 1602." Calling Stephen Fry's Malvolio the production's "big draw," he asserted that Fry "acquits himself extremely well. He is suitably grave, dignified and overbearing. My only reservation," he remarked, "is that Fry has such natural lordliness and is so handsomely bearded that you feel he would be a catch for any Olivia," adding that "[c]lass revenge, which [often] motivates the plot against the presumptuous steward, is less a factor in this version than is the idea of passion breaking through a stonewall surface." Billington promised readers that they would see, in Rylance's Olivia, "the stylised movements and white face of the *onnagata* (female impersonator) from Japanese kabuki theatre being shattered by uncontrollable sexual desire." Billington wrote that he generally opposed "the idea of adult males playing Shakespeare's women: it is hardly authentic, as the parts were written for teenage boys." But he thought that in this production it did "yield a very funny performance from Paul Chahidi, who turns Maria into a plumply roguish figure forever eyeing Sir Toby with lascivious enthusiasm." Ultimately, he called the Apollo *Twelfth Night* "a very good production that reflects the shifting, opal-like colours of Shakespeare's mysterious comedy."

A reviewer identified only as "Londonist" began by asserting that "Stephen Fry may steal the headlines, but Mark Rylance steals the show." This writer felt that although the Apollo staging "feels like a production transplanted rather than adapted, and no doubt worked better in the period venue for which it was conceived," the "bravura acting still makes for a hugely enjoyable evening." "Londonist" suggested that Rylance's "performance requires a double suspension of disbelief—not only is he a man, but he is also middle-aged. Yet this," the author continued, "only adds to the comedy," for although "it's hard to imagine why Orsino would be in love with this Olivia," in the "emotionally mercurial world of *Twelfth Night* that hardly matters. Instead we get a performance exquisitely calculated for laughs—and who'd say no to that?"

"Londonist" thought

> Johnny Flynn's Viola—a man playing a woman playing a man—was, ironically, the most feminine. His distracted looks towards Liam Brennan's Orsino were meltingly believable, and the erotically charged scene in which they both listen to the fool singing Come Away Death [sic] was a priceless exercise in how to conjure theatre out of thin air.

"Londonist" wrote that "Paul Chahidi played Olivia's housekeeper Maria very effectively as a pantomime dame—a welcome addition to the more slapstick scenes, which can otherwise seem dated," but this writer considered Fry's Malvolio "a little flat," suggesting that "Fry can act superior, but he cannot manipulate emotions with the facility of a Rylance or Flynn." This review concluded, however, that such an objection was merely "a minor niggle when the overall standard of acting is so high. And good acting is what makes all that poetry we read at school leap out of the book and sound spontaneous and funny. Period performance has rarely felt so up-to-date."

Similarly positive was an anonymous review in the London *Evening Standard* (see "*Twelfth Night* – Apollo Theatre"), which praised Rylance's "white-faced, flustered, delicate Olivia," saying "[o]ne moment he resembles Queen Elizabeth I; the next he's a vulnerable geisha." The reviewer thought that "Fry plays Malvolio as more of a patrician, scholarly figure than a fussy parvenu or joyless puritan," remarking that "he's confident, if not perhaps the most fluent mover, and his voice is generously mellow." Meanwhile, this writer found Liam Brennan's "lucid Orsino...more interesting than most interpretations I've seen" and enjoyed Johnny Flynn's Viola, calling her "a picture of shy embarrassment." Although the reviewer wrote that the pacing "is a bit too slow" and that "at times the tone tilts towards pantomime," the *Standard*'s assessment concluded that "the sense of ensemble is strong, the play's peculiarities come across vividly, and Rylance is once again a marvel."

Julie Carpenter, in the London *Express*, wrote that this *Twelfth Night* "works like a dream," calling it "a must-see production that is as deliciously funny as it is scrupulously authentic." She admired its "brilliantly comic" tone, mentioning that "Paul Chahidi makes Maria a far more comical character than I ever remember" and asserted that she was not sure how the play "could have been done better." According to Carpenter, "At the frozen heart of the production is Rylance's imperious, icy, but ever-so-slightly overplayed Olivia. Thawing from a start that suggests real damage in her past to a giggling, girlish nymph," Carpenter continued, "Rylance dominates." Partly for that reason, she added, "Liam Brennan's Orsino doesn't stand much of a chance in his tripping, gliding thrall, and Johnny Flynn's unforgivably blank Viola gets swallowed up whole. Only a neat bit of homoerotic dumbshow," she thought, "saves that particular partnership from nullity." But she concluded that this version "lives in the comedic moment," resulting in a "production that sees no damage done that cannot be undone with a kiss and a final caper."

Matt Wolf, writing for *The New York Times* under a headline reading "A Libidinous Frenzy That Is Hard to Resist," noted that Rylance's 2002 performance in *Twelfth Night* had "suggested itself as the stuff of legend," but Wolf then added that with the new 2012 staging "the legend has only been enlarged." Describing Rylance in his black-gowned, white-faced get-up as Olivia as resembling "a geisha gone lustfully gaga," Wolf found the Apollo production "hard to resist," although he did feel that Rylance's acting overshadowed that of others on stage, writing that Rylance's talent "tends to leave behind those in the cast who don't possess either Mr. Rylance's technique (Johnny Flynn as an unusually blank Viola) or his innately comic cut-and-thrust (Roger Lloyd Pack's rather strenuous Andrew Aguecheek). But the ensemble players who fall into line with their star," Wolf continued, "don't just keep up with Mr. Rylance, they at times outpace him," such as Paul Chahidi as a "bosomy wonder" of Maria, "here configured afresh as a cunning, low-down figure of malice as well as mirth." Wolf also admired Fry's "dignified, excellently spoken account" of a Malvolio who suggested "a hint of sweetness behind the bluff facade."

Sarah Hemming, in the *Financial Times*, wrote that at the Apollo "Jenny Tiramani's candle-lit, honey-coloured set, with some spectators housed in wooden galleries on stage, creates a festive mood" and that "Carroll's affectionate production emphasises the playacting," so that "both the lovesick Orsino and the grieving Olivia are playing roles that crumble once they both fall for Cesario." Hemming thought that Rylance made Olivia's "battle between controlled modesty and flustered infatuation very funny" and that if "Fry's Malvolio is not the funniest you will see," he was all "the more touching for that: this is a pedantic man whose pomposity isn't enough to earn him the cruel treatment" he suffers. Hemming called Chahidi's Maria "a wonderful, roguish, matronly figure" and ended with overall praise of this "warm, mellow staging of Shakespeare's mysterious comedy."

Alexandra Coghlan, in a long assessment for *The Arts Desk*, praised the Apollo production for having made every effort "to preserve or recreate those elements that make the Globe so special." She found Fry's performance as Malvolio "unexpectedly gentle, a supporting rather than scene-stealing comedic turn that seeks out the humanity in this well-intentioned pedant." Coghlan considered his final, revenge-filled exclamation "the exasperated cry of one we know will forgive, rather than the threat of one turned feral through mistreatment." The result, she thought, was "a substantial rebalancing of the play. With the Malvolio thus muted there's space for Paul Chahidi's charmingly sadistic Maria to shine," adding that Maria's "[d]ry little asides and plenty of freedom with Shakespeare's lines invest her with a vivid inner life."

Writing for the London *Telegraph*, Charles Spencer announced that he could "think of no living actor who takes to the stage with such ease and spontaneity as Mark Rylance," who, according to Spencer, "makes the theatre feel like the place that he calls home." Spencer praised Rylance's performance as Olivia "virtuosic" and "fresh-minted"—one that created "pure comic delight" by offering a "sublime" Olivia who was a "sad but also absurd figure waking to the wonder of love." Fry, meanwhile, struck Spencer "as a solid rather than an inspired Malvolio, comically capturing the puffed-up conceit and pomposity of the man, but largely missing the character's poignancy." But he considered Pack "a deliciously absurd and poignant Sir Andrew Aguecheek" while writing that Johnny Flynn, Samuel Barnett, Paul Chahidi, and James Garnon "all excel." He ended by calling *Twelfth Night* a "lovely" production "lifted to greatness by Rylance's glorious star performance."

Especially Positive Reviews of the Apollo Theatre Production

An anonymous reviewer for LondonTheatre.co.uk (see "*Twelfth Night*—Review") was strongly impressed by the set at the Apollo, writing that "you might be forgiven for thinking that the Globe had been squashed and miraculously trundled indoors for the winter" but then eventually shifting attention to the performances, noting that Rylance's Olivia "seems to be floating rather than walking" and then saying that in "many productions of this play, I have been disappointed with rather camp portrayals of Sir Andrew Aguecheek. But Roger Lloyd Pack sensibly avoids that," while "Mr Hurley's Sir Toby," despite being a drunk, "is nevertheless an intelligent man shot-through with an ample streak of bitterness and resentment. And Stephen Fry," this reviewer continued, "is in fine form as the detested Malvolio who, in spite of his overbearing demeanour, we come to feel some semblance of sympathy for at the end of the play. In general," the review concluded, "I found all the performances hugely impressive and enjoyable" in what the reviewer called an "astute and meticulous production."

Peter Viney, in a lengthy and quite enthusiastic assessment, noted that when the production moved to the West End, it featured an Elizabethan "Inns of Court/Whitehall indoor theatre setting (based on Wadham College, Oxford). That's probably more authentic," Viney felt, "if as legend has it the play was first produced on Twelfth Night [the holiday in January, when], it would certainly have been in an indoor theatre." Viney noted that the Apollo's "programme proudly informs us that 10 to 20 people worked on each costume, [that] only authentic fabrics are used (knitted silk stockings!) and that the cast all wear authentic Elizabethan under garments." Viney wrote that the production also featured "authentic music with sackbuts, lute, cittern, recorders, pipes, tabor, cornetto (the first ever use of authentic Elizabethan instruments in the West End theatre), and dozens of candles lit above the stage" while the theater's electric lights stayed lit. "This," Viney commented, "is Shakespeare in Shakespearean costume. At last, you might say. And so do I." He felt that when compared to the Royal Shakespeare Company's recent presentation of *Twelfth Night*, "this one is better in every single role on the stage."

Like many others, Viney admired what he called "a superb Maria from Paul Chahidi," whose "facial expressions and reactive acting" he considered "hilarious." He added that "Maria has to be a powerful figure" partly because "Sir Toby's too drunk and Sir Andrew too thick to develop the letter trick against Malvolio." Viney considered Rylance "a very, very different Olivia. She is tremulous, nervy rather than nervous, stuttering at times, [and] likely to do sudden panicky unexpected things." He noted that "Rylance has to take tiny, tiny steps (maybe it's the Elizabethan underwear), and is constantly turning, with his full dress, like a Dalek on wheels, so that every manouevre is back and forth, round and round, like trying to park a large car in a small space. His timing," Viney added, "is impeccable," and in general this critic called Rylance, in 2012, England's greatest living actor. He found "a definite touch of (knowing) drag" about Rylance's Olivia, suggesting that the "female fluttering and indecision" offer "a male perspective" on the character.

Turning to other actors, Viney observed that although Sebastian and Viola appear "in identical costumes with identical hair," observers "can always tell which is which, but only just." He also praised this production's "perfect Feste" and called Fry's performance "quite wonderful," especially in "presenting Malvolio sympathetically," thereby making him a "Malvolio you genuinely feel sorry for" even "while maintaining a powerful sense of the actor's own personality." Viney felt that Fry "even carries off that very difficult cellar/prison scene respectably." Ultimately, he called the Apollo *Twelfth Night* "a prime example of ensemble playing" and "the best of the half dozen *Twelfth Nights* we've seen in the last few years." He gave the production five stars out of five.

Writing for *The Independent*, Paul Taylor asserted that "Mark Rylance and Stephen Fry stand at opposite ends of the acting spectrum. The former is a protean genius who can lose himself unrecognisably in his roles. The latter performs subtle clever variations on the Stephen Fry persona." He found the Apollo production "gloriously successful" and Fry's performance "intelligently pondered, generous to the other actors, and almost studiedly not a 'star turn' by a celebrity guest artiste," saying it "restores balance to a play in which Malvolio's scenes can hog the limelight. Fry's steward," he continued, "is a scholarly type with a mandarin accent and air of finger-wagging snootiness," while he added that "Rylance reprises his wondrously funny Olivia" in acting that "is a marvel of fluttery, brilliantly timed panic" featuring "bouts of stammering disarray and slapstick consternation." According to Taylor, "Rylance brings this woman's emergence from the stately safety of mourning to absurd and absurdly touching life." He called the other actors "superb" and said it was "remarkable how deftly a sense of the Globe's atmosphere has been conjured in an indoor proscenium arch theatre."

Also especially positive was a review for *TheStage.co.uk* by Ben Dowell, who called "this beautifully judged transfer...memorable and heartfelt," with Fry managing "to convey a deep sense of pathos beneath the pompous absurdity" of Malvolio, whose "delusional exultation following his gulling" this critic considered "both a triumph of comic timing and an intelligent study in human failure." This "Malvolio's final, prophetic cry at the end," Dowell thought, is one "of broken, bellowing hurt." Dowell admired the way "Jenny Tiramani's interior wood panelled set" offered an unusual "closer, more domesticated feel" in the indoor theater, adding that the "sense of ungloomy homeliness is helped by the addition of lots of candlelight on stage" and also saying that the "boisterous...carousing" of Toby and Aguecheek had the effect of really "waking up a packed house." Dowell commended the "beautiful tenderness as well as hesitancy beneath the vanity" of Rylance's Olivia "as he glides around in her mourning weeds almost as if on wheels." He praised "Johnny Flynn's soft and vulnerable Viola" and wrote that "Hurley's Belch shows quite what a cruel and exploitative character he is beneath all the booze-fuelled jollity." Dowell added that although he had "seen Aguecheek with a bit more life, personality and comic brio than Lloyd Pack musters, I have never seen a Feste who manages to combine this weight of sardonic melancholia with such beautiful singing" in a voice that "casts a genuine spell." He found the whole production "an exceptionally fun and joyous" staging of "this most poignant and enjoyable of plays."

Reviews of the New York Production

Given all the enthusiasm that the Globe/Apollo production aroused in London, it is not surprising that it quickly moved, in 2013, across the Atlantic to New York, where it was now presented in another indoor, proscenium-arch venue: Broadway's Belasco Theatre. In the Belasco production, several new actors appeared in roles previously played by others in London. Most significantly, Samuel Barnett, who had played Sebastian in London, now played Viola in New York, perhaps because several reviewers had complained about Johnny Flynn's performance of that role in London. The actor now playing Sebastian in New York was Joseph Timms, while Angus Wright had now assumed the role of Sir Andrew Aguecheek.

Reviews of the New York staging were, with a few exceptions, just as positive as those for the London production. One of those exceptions came from Christopher Hoile, writing for *Stagedoor.com*, who began by acknowledging that the Belasco staging had "received extraordinarily rapturous reviews." Hoile, however, found director Tim Carroll's "idea of 'original practices'...a severely flawed approach" but wrote that "[l]uckily for Carroll, everyone in the troupe of *Twelfth Night* tries to do his best even if he doesn't succeed." He then returned to his major complaint, writing that "[i]f 'original practices' were not really just a system a director can invoke or dismiss at will, Carroll should really have boys, not men, play the female roles since that is how it was done in Shakespeare's day." The fact that almost no director, almost anywhere, in recent centuries seems to have tried such an approach (for obvious reasons) did not seem to bother Hoile. In any case, he wrote that of the three men playing women in the Carroll production, "Chahidi is by far the most successful. He does not attempt a falsetto but rather a rich matronly tone that well suits Maria." But Hoile thought that Barnett worked "so hard at speaking in falsetto that he loses all subtlety of speech, rather a deficit in a central character." Yet Hoile contended that both "Chahidi and Barnett are much better at playing women than Rylance," who, he noted, "does not glide as the other two men do, but takes odd mincing steps that cause his costume to bounce with ridiculous rigidity. Olivia," Hoile thought, "is the character who ought to have the most dignity of the three women, but this mode of locomotion only makes her appear comic." He noted that Liam Brennan, as Orsino, "is alone in using a north-country accent even though his accent should be the same as Olivia's and the other 'Illyrians,'" adding that he "also makes little sense of what he says." Hoile commented that Colin Hurley, as Sir Toby, "has very little presence, which means that the so-called 'kitchen scenes,' in an unusual turn, are consistently dominated by Maria—but then Chahidi has stage presence enough for two." According to Hoile, "Stephen Fry's slightly dim Malvolio is funny but there is more to the role than he finds there," and he also wrote that although "Feste can become a kind of genius of the play,...Peter Hamilton Dyer's hangdog character never takes on that role and his songs never seem to sum up the action."

Hoile did think that "Carroll's cast amongst themselves do bring out insights in the text simply by communicating it as clearly as possible," suggesting that finally audiences "understand why Olivia so consistently defends Malvolio throughout the play—he represents the kind of severity she wishes she could maintain." He also praised

Chahidi for giving "Maria the motivation of using the trick on Malvolio as the way to win Sir Toby as a husband, thus a way to join the aristocracy she serves. Indeed, this Maria," Hoile thought, "chuffs Malvolio with the same desire for social climbing that she is guilty of. Chahidi makes this brilliant angle so dominant that it completely eclipses the Toby-Aguecheek plot." Hoile ended, somewhat ambivalently, by stating that this production might perhaps "be the best *Twelfth Night* ever seen on Broadway, or even off-Broadway, but it certainly does not live up to the immoderate encomiums critics have heaped on it." So: maybe the best ever but not the very best production it might be possible to imagine.

Another fairly negative review of the New York production came from Scott Klavan, writing for *Escapeintolife.com*. According to Klavan,

> while the production is meticulously, beautifully mounted and thoughtfully and amiably performed, it remains low-key. Here, Count Orsino is an older, somewhat dispirited courtier, rather than the dashing younger man often associated with the part; Sir Toby is short, petulant and red-faced, not the large and lusty Falstaffian fellow we expect; and Olivia, as played by Rylance, is something of a monstrosity, a repressed and spoiled woman driven into a passive-aggressive hysteria by her lust for Cesario. Even Feste is quiet and bummed-out.

Klavan sought a production in which "a transcendent love is a powerful inner fantasy that overcomes the drab physical reality in front of our faces." He therefore wrote that "the panache-free style" of the Belasco staging, as well as a "lack of charisma among the performances causes the show to lack a certain size and spirit: outrage, desolation, exultation and joy are mostly absent." For Klavan, the "concept of a Shakespearean show with unadorned, historical verisimilitude is admirable, but the result is that our patience is tested in the three-hour running time and when our laughter comes, it is sporadic, and strained."

Klavan was also disappointed by this production's conclusion, writing that "Malvolio's ending, fist-shaking vow to take revenge has little impact; he doesn't seem capable of it. The same is true of Sir Toby's final rejection of Sir Andrew. This moment," according to Klavan, "doesn't make all that much sense in the original text, but here, it comes out of nowhere and passes without notice. If the characters are kept small and somewhat weak, any kind of big emotional expression seems unjustified." He wrote that Ryland did "give Olivia an inventive, wacked-out [sic] exuberance, a departure from the rest of the cast," but he thought that this "Olivia is never fully vulnerable, and real"; he found it "not believable for a moment that Sebastian would be taken with this kooky Countess." Klavan also thought that because almost "everyone on stage stays grounded and dispassionate (or exaggerated and easily dismissed), the audience is kept safe, spared from self-reflection, self-deprecatory laughter and the self-knowledge that might follow. If nothing is ventured, nothing is lost, and gained." He found it "not enough to see men move about in corsets and gowns, however comic. Like the production as a whole, they've got the outside of the women down; but the inside is unexplored, up in the air." He did end, however, on a few positive notes, remarking that "Barnett and Timms, playing the twins, often scale the heights of the text; the audience actually believes that these two parts are played by one person, an acting (and directing) feat." He also wrote that "Hamilton Dyer brings affecting world-weariness and beautifully nuanced singing to the role of Feste the Fool." Ultimately, however, Klavan concluded that this *Twelfth Night* was "tremendously adept, but shie[d] from the ether, the hearts and souls of its script and characters. We visit the Elizabethan theater, but get stuck to the wooden floor."

Finally, in a brief and somewhat mixed assessment, Richard Zoglin, in *Time* magazine, found Rylance's Olivia "sensible and appealing," "often very funny," and "the strong center of a very good, mostly straightforward production"—one, however, unfortunately handicapped by "too many gimmicks." Zoglin considered Olivia's odd way of walking "nothing but a visual stunt, bearing no relation to the character" and thought that "most of the time" Rylance merely seemed "to be pandering for laughs."

Mostly Positive Reviews

Hoile, Klavan, and Zoglin, however, were very much in a minority among critics, most of whom found the New York production either mostly impressive or exceptionally impressive. Thus, Linda Winer, in *Newsday*, called the Bellasco production "Big-Event Theater at its most deeply satisfying," praised it for its "fascinating and eye-opening all-male" staging, lauded the production as a whole as "exhilarating," and called Rylance a "preposterously gifted acting chameleon and showman" who created "an irresistibly self-possessed yet vulnerable Olivia." She felt that "Shakespeare's language, as well as his meanings, have seldom been as clear," admired Fry's "noble Malvolio," and added her voice to those of the many previous reviewers who thought that "Paul Chahidi turns Maria, Olivia's gentlewoman in 'Twelfth Night,' into a genuine star turn."

Similarly enthusiastic (if much briefer) was Elysa Gardner, writing in *USA Today*, who awarded the Belasco production three-and-a-half stars out of a possible four and who wrote that this *Twelfth Night* was, "under Carroll's robust guidance, a joy—sly and bawdy and finally touching, without ever losing its glorious naughtiness." Similarly brief, but also similarly enthusiastic, was an assessment in the *New York Post* by Elisabeth Vincentelli, who called Carroll's production "a feast for the senses," even if she initially found the idea of men playing women "particularly troubling" in such a "gender-bending" play. She nonetheless admired this production's "enchanting" and "very funny" atmosphere, praised Barnett's "winsome Viola, as eloquent as she is romantic," but thought that Stephen Fry did not completely "sell his oddly demure Malvolio," although she did think that Fry "looks so noble that the idea of Olivia falling for him isn't entirely preposterous."

Jonathan Mandell, in another brief but mostly positive review for NewYorkTheatre.me, wrote that the Belasco production offered "electrifying theater...at least half the time," adding that "this *Twelfth Night* is actually less confusing than past productions, requiring less suspension of belief during the bulk of the play when Viola is disguised as a man. No actress I have ever seen portraying Viola," Mandell continued, "has been very convincing as a man. Samuel Barnett is—which also makes the constant mistaking of Viola/ Cesario for his identical twin-brother Sebastian (Joseph Timms) far more plausible now that the two actually do look identical." Mandell thought that if Barnett, "in his period-white makeup and falsetto," is "less convincing as a woman, that matters less, since he is only portraying Viola as a woman for the briefest of times during the beginning and the ending of the play." But for Mandell, the "real standout here" was "Mark Rylance as Olivia, who glides as if a cartoon character with wheels for feet beneath her bulbous black dress" and who "does pratfalls like Lucille Ball and double-takes that rival Jackie Gleason's, but who somehow nevertheless is never less than persuasive as a countess." He ended by calling this staging "full-throttle entertainment."

Exceptionally Positive Reviews

Even more numerous than the mostly positive reviews were ones that were exceptionally positive, including an assessment by Ken Ludwig for his own blog. Ludwig felt that "the actors who played... women didn't try to impersonate women but rather played the truth of the human beings in question, regardless of their gender." He wrote that the "audience forgot about the gender of the actors because the truthfulness of the acting was so paramount," adding, "I have seen literally dozens of productions of *Twelfth Night* over the years (it may well be my favorite play in the canon), but last Tuesday night I was, more than ever, wrapped up in the theatricality" of the drama. He thought that "if any play could be enhanced by all-male casting, *Twelfth Night* is the prime candidate" and added that "The Globe's all-male casting makes this freedom-of-gender aspect of the play clearer than I have ever seen it." Ludwig concluded by remarking that "Rylance and his director Tim Carroll have created a *Twelfth Night* that gives all of us a new appreciation of Shakespeare's many-leveled intentions, and they have done it by using genuine Shakespearean casting. I, for one, have been changed by the experience."

Equally impressed was Mark Kennedy, a drama writer for the Associated Press whose review was syndicated in various papers across the country and who called Rylance's Olivia "wonderfully mad with passion," adding that this "darkish comedy" had been given "the lightest of stagings." He reported that in the Belasco production the stage was "illuminated by chandeliers packed with real dripping candles" and noted that theater-goers who arrived early would be able to "witness the pre-show ritual of actors dressing and preparing their makeup onstage," while some would "actually be seated on the stage in towers on either side, a nod to the intimate theaters of The Bard's age." He found Rylance as Olivia, "gliding about like a Kabuki character," a special "highlight" of the production.

Hilton Als, in *The New Yorker*, called the Belasco production "grand and unsurpassable," writing that Orsino was played by "the fantastic and sexy Liam Brennan," who, according to Als, played the duke as "a straight drama queen, the kind of guy who wouldn't know what to feel without an audience to play to." He found the whole effort "one of the best-designed productions out there, both vivid and otherworldly, like an Elizabethan drawing." He admired the "lovely Samuel Barnett as Viola"; praised Colin Hurley's Toby Belch as "charming and physically loose"; but also, like many other reviewers, especially extolled Paul Chahidi, as Maria, for giving "one of the greatest performances" Als had ever seen. He even suggested that the director had allowed "Chahidi to upstage Rylance, the show's ostensible star." Als praised Chahidi's "near-Kabuki-like control over his face and body" and said that "Chahidi adds his own mysteries—about the art of performance—to Shakespeare's."

Ben Brantley, in *The New York Times*, called the Belasco staging "a peerless production," commenting that "the bewilderment of the characters onstage floods us with pure, tickling joy." Brantley said that he could not "remember being so ridiculously happy for the entirety of a Shakespeare performance" since he had seen the very first version of this production, at The Globe, way back in 2002. He wrote that Rylance's performance "makes you think, 'This is how

Shakespeare was meant to be done.'" He regretted that "[s]o many interpretations of the canon now are tricked out in the condescending, high-concept garb of anachronistic settings, with comedy that exaggerates the (yuck, yuck) bawdy parts with broad, illustrative gestures," but he promised his readers that "even if you're an inveterate bardolator, you may find [in this new production of *Twelfth Night*] lines that you never fully grasped before making sense." He thought that Viola had been "splendidly embodied by Samuel Barnett," that Angus Wright had done a fine job as the "blissfully slow-on-the-uptake Sir Andrew Aguecheek," and that Rylance's Olivia was the best he had ever seen. He observed that in contrast to "most versions" of *Twelfth Night*, in this production the "foibles" of the play's "characters are never exaggerated into grotesqueness, just as the men playing women do not speak in falsettos or flounce about. Even the Puritanical Malvolio, usually an ugly gargoyle, is refreshingly embodied by Mr. Fry with the complacency and affectation of someone you might recognize from your own office," so that when "he becomes the target of a sadistic revenge plot, for once you feel for the guy."

Reviewing the Belasco production for *Variety*, the "Bible" of the entertainment industry (with its odd ways of using words), Marilyn Stasio called the New York staging "a stroke of genius" and wrote that "these amazing thespians faithfully observe the theatrical rituals and customs of Elizabethan times, including the tradition of playing broad comedy directly to the rowdy groundlings in the cheap seats." She found elements of tragedy in this comedy, largely thanks to "the compassionate view that Stephen Fry takes of the melancholy Malvolio," writing that "Fry dares to acknowledge the feelings of inadequacy that make this gloomy fellow such an easy victim." More generally, she thought that the "delight" audiences took in this production derived, in part, from "the fun of watching grown men squeezing themselves into women's clothes and mincing around in pretty little shoes. But it has far more to do," she added, "with the psychological validity of their performances," interestingly suggesting that it was "no wonder that Rylance's Olivia, who is [like Viola] also in deep mourning for a beloved brother, would respond to the womanly side of this supposed boy." Stasio ended by praising the play's "astonishing actors" and obviously took pleasure in the whole experience of having witnessed their performances.

In a review for *Vulture.com*, Jesse Green, often a writer for *The New York Times*, urged readers to "gallop," not "trot," to the Belasco production, humorously reporting that Rylance, as Olivia, moved around the stage like "a Geisha hovercraft" and joking that audience members "immediately perceive how difficult it would be for any man to touch such a woman; he could hardly get at her." He thought that in this staging "the opportunities of period authenticity as a *modern* experience emerge" and wrote that in the scene in which Orsino and Viola sit right next to each other, the "sexual tension builds to an explosion of what we would now call homosexual panic. As moderns," he continued, "we can read this moment with double vision, or as a palimpsest: funny once, though now something more. This," he thought,

> is typical of the way the Globe's methods enhance the experience of *Twelfth Night*. But it would be an excellent production anyway. It is...beautifully spoken and perfectly audible throughout the theater without a single microphone. With so little in the way of trickery to fall back on, the actors' choices are especially clear and sometimes novel. Samuel Barnett...is a touching Viola and a game Cesario; Liam Brennan makes Orsino's melancholy unusually manly; Angus Wright's Aguecheek is somehow dignified in his imbecility. And Stephen Fry, in his first Broadway appearance, makes a smart and original case for Malvolio. Usually a grotesque prig and egomaniac, he is here nothing much worse than a stuffy manager-type; it is only the vicious baiting of the court rowdies that exposes his repressed self-delight and gaudy inner fop.

Then, of course, there's Rylance, whom we should not be surprised to find a superb comedian. His slightly manic but fresh way with verse makes its language feel new and exigent; he's always *doing* something with it, usually something funny and revealing.... The grieving Olivia, of all characters, thus becomes, in Rylance's performance, the comic engine of the play.

Writing for *TheHollywoodReporter.com*, under a headline reading "Mark Rylance Cements His Place among the Greatest Living Stage Actors in This Ridiculously Entertaining" play, David Rooney found the production, "rather than being reverential or scholarly," instead "rip-roaring, user-friendly entertainment for the people." He considered it "one of the major New York cultural events of the season," called Rylance a "crazed genius" and "simply astonishing," and asserted that "every single member of this magnificent company more than holds his own," so that what "could happily have been The Mark Rylance Show turns out to be so much more." Rooney promised readers that this *Twelfth Night*, along with the *Richard III* with which it was paired, "might be the most lucid and engrossing Shakespeare productions you will ever see" and noted that "the actors all perform without amplification, now a rarity on Broadway." He thought *Twelfth Night* had never, in his experience, been "funnier or more enchanting" and observed that the "fact that Rylance's Olivia is no beauty makes the ardor with which Orsino pursues her more amusing, just as her grave earnestness makes an even bigger joke of her obliviousness to Cesario's true identity as the nubile Viola. This," he continued, "is comic acting of the highest order," and he considered it "a particular delight to watch Fry deploy his erudition alongside a willingness to play the dupe; he makes Malvolio's humiliation quite touching."

Even the relatively "minor" characters appealed to Rooney, who wrote that the "antics of the drink-sodden pranksters Toby Belch and Andrew Aguecheek can grow tiresome in lesser productions, but Colin Hurley and Angus Wright wring riotous humor from the roles, blending goofy slapstick with winking subversiveness. Wright's braying guffaw is a classic," and he called Barnett's Viola/Cesario "the sublime essence of sweetness and grace." In light of the "dizzying heights of the comedy," he found "the moments of poignancy... unexpectedly lovely." But his strongest praise was for Rylance, asserting that what makes him "such a dynamic performer to watch is that no matter how eccentric his choices—and many of them are way out there—they are never made selfishly or without logic. He is in full command of his character at all times, but what's equally important is that he never performs in a star vacuum. His connection to the entire ensemble is unquestionable." It would have been hard for Rylance and his colleagues to ask for a more enthusiastic review than this.

In the mass-circulation magazine *Entertainment Weekly*, Thom Geier called the new production "fascinating," "unforgettable," and "as close to Elizabethan-era performances as one can hope to find in the 21st century." Reporting that audience members sometimes got "drawn into the action (to hold a flask for the tipsy Sir Toby Belch in Twelfth Night, for instance)," he hailed the "costumes, designed by Jenny Tiramani," as "wonders" and praised director Tim Carroll for "bend[ing] over backwards to make these Shakespearean classics broadly accessible."

Geier wrote that "several of the comical performers stand out: Stephen Fry as the ultimately sympathetic spoilsport Malvolio, Peter Hamilton Dyer as the quick-witted fool Feste, and Paul Chahidi as Olivia's mischievous maid Maria," and he ended by calling the production "a triumph." Similarly enthusiastic was David Finkle, for the *Huffington Post* website, who wrote that Rylance's "imagination is so unbounded that anyone who relishes superlative acting can't take his or her eyes off him for fear of missing what unexpected subtle or broad gesture or inflection will occur next." But he also asserted that the entire company of actors was "as accomplished an ensemble as has been seen locally in a long while," finding none of them "weak." He even praised the final jig, commenting that "[t]here's method to the theatrical madness, which is reminding the audience as it prepares to leave that no matter how high or low the evening's spirits have soared or sunk, there's still something to be said for merriment. With this evening's list of triumphs, it's not only the actors who want to join in the jig. The audience is in the let's-all-jig mood as well."

Finally, awarding the production five stars out of a possible five, David Cote of *Timeout.com* found the Globe staging "utterly enchanting," said it "render[ed] the text lucid and the action transparent," and called it "a spectacle of surpassing elegance and buoyancy." Asking himself (and his readers), "What's gained and what's lost by thus historicizing the scene?," he answered: "To my mind, a great deal of clarity and textual innocence is gained, while the only thing lost is four centuries of directorial and academic humbug." He wrote that the "actors' vocal approach acknowledges the poetic nature of the language: There's an increased formality and a concomitant decrease of psychological innuendo. We are reminded that these plays are very old, as are their social codes, gender roles and narrative devices." Cote said he could not "remember a performance of Shakespeare that so beguiled me with its simplicity and lyric vibrancy" and wrote that the "performances are all pitched perfectly between light comedy and pensive melancholy, which is precisely where *Twelfth Night* lives. Rylance," he continued, "tempers his typical eccentricities for Olivia, who is vain and impetuous, but adorable and demure." And he also found "something touchingly plaintive in Peter Hamilton Dyer's deadpan clown, Feste, who speaks truth to power, but seems just as bemused by more common foibles and frailties of those around him. This fool knows he's one wrong joke away from prison. All in all," Cote concluded, "it's a marvelous cast, and no one tries to 'act' Elizabethan; they just serve the words and the words serve them."

Conclusion

It seems safe to say that few stagings of *Twelfth Night* have been as well received as the 2012–13 productions starring Mark Rylance and Stephen Fry. Of course, the fact that Rylance and Fry *were* the stars helps, in part, to explain this immensely positive reception. After all, Mark Rylance—now *Sir* Mark Rylance—is widely recognized as one of the greatest actors of his generation, and Stephen Fry has long been one of the most popular figures in British culture, both as an actor in films and on television and as an author and media personality. But the success of the London and New York productions cannot be attributed entirely to Rylance and Fry; almost everyone else in the company was hailed for their excellent acting, especially Paul

Chahidi for his truly memorable performance as Maria, a role that rarely gets much attention from either audiences or critics. The fact that this production was performed entirely by males in period costumes and looked like the sort of thing Shakespeare's own audiences might have experienced during Shakespeare's lifetime added to the interest these productions created, although it is important to remember that this "original practices" staging might easily have failed if not done as well as it was done by Rylance and his colleagues. Anyone seeking a real insight into how a Shakespearean comedy can be staged in ways that are genuinely funny as well as deeply illuminating might want to buy or rent the filmed version of this production. If the testimony of most critics is any indication, the small cost will pay valuable dividends indeed.

Works Cited

Als, Hilton. "The Mirror Has Two Faces." Review of *Twelfth Night*. Directed by Tim Carroll. *The New Yorker*, 17 Nov. 2013, www.newyorker.com/magazine/2013/11/25/the-mirror-has-two-faces.

Benedict, David. "Mark Rylance's Dazzlingly Watchable Antics as a Reproving Olivia Overturned by Lust in Shakespeare's Globe's All-Male 'Twelfth Night' Constitute Nothing Short of a Star Turn." Review of *Twelfth Night*. Directed by Tim Carroll. *Variety*, 19 Nov. 2012, variety.com/2012/legit/reviews/twelfth-night-2-1117948779/.

Billington, Michael. "*Twelfth Night/Richard III* Review." Review of *Twelfth Night*. Directed by Tim Carroll. *The Guardian*, 18 Nov. 2012, www.theguardian.com/stage/2012/nov/18/twelfth-night-richard-iii-review.

Brantley, Ben. "Boys Will Be Boys (and Sometimes Girls)." Review of *Twelfth Night*. Directed by Tim Carroll. *The New York Times*, 10 Nov. 2013, www.nytimes.com/2013/11/11/theater/reviews/twelfth-night-and-richard-iii-with-mark-rylance.html.

Carpenter, Julie. "First Night Review: Twelfth Night, Apollo Theatre, London." Review of *Twelfth Night*. Directed by Tim Carroll. *Express*, 20 Nov. 2012, www.express.co.uk/entertainment/theatre/359244/First-night-review-Twelfth-Night-Apollo-Theatre-London.

Coghlan, Alexandra. "*Twelfth Night. Richard III*, Apollo Theatre." Review of *Twelfth Night*. Directed by Tim Carroll. *TheArtsDesk.com*, 19 Nov. 2012, theartsdesk.com/theatre/twelfth-nightrichard-iii-apollo-theatre.

Cote, David. "Twelfth Night and Richard III." Review of *Twelfth Night*. Directed by Tim Carroll. *TimeOut.com*, 7 Nov. 2013, www.timeout.com/newyork/theater/twelfth-night-and-richard-iii.

Dowell, Ben. "*Twelfth Night*." Review of *Twelfth Night*. Directed by Tim Carroll. *The Stage*, 19 Nov. 2012, www.thestage.co.uk/reviews/twelfth-night-review-at-apollo-theatre-london.

Finkle, David. "First Nighter: Mark Rylance and Company's Superb *Richard III* and *Twelfth Night*." Review of *Twelfth Night*. Directed by Tim Carroll. *Huffpost.com*, 10 Nov. 2013, www.huffpost.com/entry/first-nighter-mark-rylanc_b_4252632?ec_carp=719821025005580153.

Fisher, Philip. "Twelfth Night." Review of *Twelfth Night*. Directed by Tim Carroll. *British Theatre Guide*, n.d., www.britishtheatreguide.info/reviews/twelfth-night-apollo-shaftes-8269.

Gardner, Elysa. "Mark Rylance Romps through Two New Shakespeare Stagings." Review of *Twelfth Night*. Directed by Tim Carroll. *USA Today*, n.d., eu.usatoday.com/story/life/theater/2013/11/10/broadway-review-twelfth-night-richard-iii/3455249/.

Geier, Thom. "Twelfth Night Stage." Review of *Twelfth Night*. Directed by Tim Carroll. *Entertainment Weekly*, 10 Nov. 2013, ew.com/article/2013/11/10/twelfth-night-stage/.

Green, Jesse. "Theater Review: Say What You Will About Twelfth Night and Richard III." Review of *Twelfth Night*. Directed by Tim Carroll. *Vulture.com*, 10 Nov. 2013, www.vulture.com/2013/11/theater-review-richard-iii.html.

Hemming, Sarah. "*Richard III/Twelfth Night*, Apollo Theatre, London." Review of *Twelfth Night*. Directed by Tim Carroll. *Financial Times*, 19 Nov. 2012, www-ft-com.ezp.lib.cam.ac.uk/content/6eb0e2f6-3250-11e2-916a-00144feabdc0.

Hoile, Christopher. "Elsewhere." Review of *Twelfth Night*. Directed by Tim Carroll. *StageDoor.com*, 22 Dec. 2013, www.stage-door.com/Theatre/Elsewhere/Entries/2013/12/22_New_York,_NY__Twelfth_Night.html.

Kennedy, Mark. "Review: Mark Rylance Shines in 2 Shakespeare Parts." Review of *Twelfth Night*. Directed by Tim Carroll. *San Diego Union Tribune*,10 Nov. 2013, www.sandiegouniontribune.com/sdut-review-mark-rylance-shines-in-2-shakespeare-parts-2013nov10-story.html.

Klavan, Scott. "*Twelfth Night or What You Will*." Review of *Twelfth Night*. Directed by Tim Carroll. *EscapeintoLife.com*, n.d., www.escapeintolife.com/theatre/twelfth-night-or-what-you-will/.

Londonist. "Theatre Review: Twelfth Night @ Apollo Theatre." Review of *Twelfth Night*. Directed by Tim Carroll. *Londonist.com*, n.d., londonist.com/2012/11/theatre-review-twelfth-night-apollo-theatre.

Ludwig, Ken. "A Discussion of *Twelfth Night* on Broadway." Review of *Twelfth Night*. Directed by Tim Carroll. *KenLudwig.com*, 16 Dec. 2013, www.kenludwig.com/posts/2013/12/16/a-discussion-of-twelfth-night-on-broadway.

Mandell, Jonathan. "Twelfth Night and Richard III Review: Mark Rylance Brings Shakespeare to Broadway." Review of *Twelfth Night*. Directed by Tim Carroll. *New York Theatre*, 10 Nov. 2013, newyorktheater.me/2013/11/10/twelfth-night-and-richard-iii-review-mark-rylance-brings-shakespeare-to-broadway-that-would-be-familiar-to-shakespeare/.

Nick730. Review of Twelfth Night. Directed by Tim Carroll. *Partially Obstructed View*, 25 Sept. 2012, partially-obstructed-view.blogspot.com/2012/09/theatre-review-twelfth-night.html.

Rooney, David. "Twelfth Night/Richard III." Review of *Twelfth Night*. Directed by Tim Carroll. *Hollywood Reporter*, 10 Nov. 2013, www.hollywoodreporter.com/news/general-news/twelfth-night-richard-iii-theater-654931/.

Spencer, Charles. "*Richard III/Twelfth Night*, Apollo Theatre, Review." Review of *Twelfth Night*. Directed by Tim Carroll. *The Telegraph*, 19 Nov. 2012, www.telegraph.co.uk/culture/theatre/theatre-reviews/9687579/Richard-III-Twelfth-Night-Apollo-theatre-review.html.

Stasio, Marilyn. "Broadway Review: 'Richard III/Twelfth Night.'" Review of *Twelfth Night*. Directed by Tim Carroll. *Variety*, 10 Nov. 2013, variety.com/2013/legit/reviews/broadway-review-richard-iiitwelfth-night-1200816666/.

Taylor, Paul. "Fry's Reined-in Malvolio Defers to the Brilliant Rylance." Review of *Twelfth Night*. Directed by Tim Carroll. *Independent*, 18 Nov. 2012, www.independent.co.uk/arts-entertainment/theatre-dance/reviews/first-night-twelfth-night-richard-iii-apollo-theatre-london-8327354.html.

"Twelfth Night, Apollo Theatre, W1—Review." Review of *Twelfth Night*. Directed by Tim Carroll. *Evening Standard*, 5 Jan. 2013, www.standard.co.uk/culture/theatre/twelfth-night-apollo-theatre-w1-review-8328778.html.

"*Twelfth Night*—Review." Review of *Twelfth Night*. Directed by Tim Carroll. *London Theatre*, 16 Nov. 2012, www.londontheatre.co.uk/reviews/twelfth-night.

Vincentelli, Elisabeth. "Mark Rylance Leads All-Male Casts in New Shakespeare Shows." Review of *Twelfth Night*. Directed by Tim Carroll. *New York Post*, 10 Nov. 2013, nypost.com/2013/11/10/mark-rylance-leads-all-male-casts-in-new-shakespeare-shows/.

Viney, Peter. "Twelfth Night—Apollo 2012." Review of Twelfth Night. Directed by Tom Carroll. *Peter Viney's Blog*, n.d., peterviney.com/stage/twelfth-night-apollo-2012/.

Winer, Linda. "'Twelfth Night' and 'Richard III' Review: Top-Notch Event." Review of *Twelfth Night*. Directed by Tim Carroll. *Newsday*, 11 Nov. 2013, www.newsday.com/entertainment/theater/twelfth-night-and-richard-iii-review-top-notch-event-theater-i29511.

Wolf, Matt. "A Libidinous Frenzy That Is Hard to Resist." Review of *Twelfth Night*. Directed by Tim Carroll. *The New York Times*, 27 Nov. 2012, www.nytimes.com/2012/11/28/arts/28iht-lon28.html.

Zoglin, Richard. "Now Is the Rylance of Our Discontent." Review of *Twelfth Night*. Directed by Tim Carroll. *Time*, 27 Nov. 2013, entertainment.time.com/2013/11/27/now-is-the-rylance-of-our-discontent/.

Playing Shakespeare's *Twelfth Night* for Laughs in Four Major "Live" Productions

Robert C. Evans

William Shakespeare's *Twelfth Night* is often considered one of his funniest and most appealing comedies and has frequently proven successful on stage. The play is widely performed and often revived, and one indication of its popularity with playgoers is the fact that performances of this work at the revived Globe Theatre in London have been recorded and released on video on three separate occasions (2012, 2017, and 2021), an achievement equaled only by another Shakespearean comedy (*A Midsummer Night's Dream*), which also had three distinct videotaped performances (2013, 2016, and 2021). Apparently, the Globe and the video makers (who also profit from such productions) considered these two comedies popular enough to have warranted being both staged and filmed on three separate occasions. And the 2012 Globe production of *Twelfth Night* was *so* popular—both with audiences and critics—that it was quickly staged at another London theater (this one inside rather than open-air) before then moving across the Atlantic to be staged (again to huge critical and popular success) in the United States.

Of all of Shakespeare's various kinds of plays, his comedies, in particular, benefit from being performed (and filmed) before live audiences. Few things are more contagiously funny than the laughter of a large crowd, and such laughter also shows us when, how, and why particular moments in the comedies actually *work* in the intended way. Whereas audiences watching history plays, problem plays, romances, and especially tragedies are likely to be mostly silent (except in the comic moments within those works), comedies uniquely *invite* responses in sound, whether that sound involves laughter, cheering, applause, whistling, or some of the other kinds of raucous reactions one can hear and see in filmed versions of the comedies. Filmed comedies that do not include audiences are far less likely to provoke laughter in viewers, partly because they are usually witnessed, at least when they are available on DVD or television, within the privacy of individual homes. But the best onscreen productions of Shakespearean comedies that include audiences can provoke riotous laughter when viewed even under such private circumstances. This is usually not the case when a comedy is filmed without an audience present.

For all these reasons, this essay examines various scenes from four different filmed *stagings* of *Twelfth* Night. These stagings include an acclaimed 1998 production performed at New York's Lincoln Center, a 2011 production performed at Canada's Stratford Festival, a 2012 production performed in London at Shakespeare's Globe, and a 2017 production performed at London's National Theatre. In all four productions, some lines and situations provoked uniform and predictable laughter, but in some stagings certain lines were played for laughs (and won them) while provoking little or no laughter in other productions. By comparing and contrasting responses to all four productions, I hope to suggest, both to critics and to future directors and actors, when and how some episodes from *Twelfth Night* can work especially well on stage in generating the laughter its author obviously hoped to produce. I hope that this essay will also be valuable to people (including critics) reading the text of the play who do not have ready or convenient access to the various ways the text can be successfully *staged*. Merely reading Shakespeare can be a powerful experience, but that power can be magnified when we read his plays with actual "live" audience reactions in mind.[1]

Laughter in Act 1

Most of the laughter in act 1 begins (and then continues) when Toby and Maria arrive on stage in scene 3. At the Globe, Maria won some laughter when she urged Toby to come in "earlier" (1.3.3); at Lincoln Center, people laughed at Toby when he announced that his clothes were "good enough to drink in" (1.3.10), when he asserted that other people could "hang themselves in their own straps" (1.3.10), when he remarked that Sir Andrew could speak three or four languages "word for word" (1.3.23), and when he said that he was drinking "healths to [his] niece" (1.3.34) when he was obviously drinking for his own benefit. But the biggest of his early laughs at Lincoln Center came when he proclaimed that he would drink to her "as long as there is a passage in my throat" (1.3.35). The Toby in the Globe production won laughs when, later in line 35, he pulled out a drinking bottle from a place where he had carefully hidden it, while both in the National Theatre production and at Lincoln Center Toby also won laughter when discussing his boots (1.3.10–11).

The entrance of Sir Andrew Aguecheek at 1.3.39 won laughter in all four productions, partly because, at Stratford, he arrived in a golf cart and partly because, at the National, he was not only dressed in a ridiculous pink suit but spoke his line "How now Sir Toby Belch" in a particularly funny way, as also happened at Lincoln Center. At the Globe, at Stratford, and especially at the National his reference to Maria as a "fair shrew" (1.3.41) made people laugh, while his question "What's that" (1.3.44) when urged to "accost" Maria generated laughter both at the Globe and at Stratford. His subsequent address to Maria as "Good Mistress Accost" (1.3.46) made the audiences at Lincoln Center, Stratford, and the Globe all laugh, and the same thing happened again when, at Stratford and the Globe, he next called her "Mistress Mary Accost" (1.3.49). Audiences in Stratford and at the National laughed at 1.3.51–52 when Sir Toby urged Sir Andrew to "front [Maria], board her, woo her, assail her," with the Stratford Sir Toby mimicking sexual thrusts while speaking. When Sir Andrew responded that he would not "undertake her in this company" (1.3.52–53), he won laughter at the Globe by gesturing toward that theater's famous "groundlings," while people laughed at Lincoln Center and at Stratford when he asked Toby "Is that the meaning of accost?" (1.3.53). People laughed at Lincoln Center and at Stratford when Andrew asked Maria if she thought she had "fools in hand" (1.3.60), while they laughed at the Globe when Maria replied, "Sir, I have not *you* by the hand" (my emphasis; 1.3.60).

A good bit of laughter occurred at Stratford, the Globe, and the National when Maria told Andrew "I pray you bring your hand to the buttery bar and let it drink." At Stratford, as she was saying this, she put his hand on her breast; at the Globe, Andrew seemed confused by her meaning; at the National he looked at Toby as if Maria had just sexually propositioned him. Meanwhile, when Toby replied that he thought he was not the kind of ass that did not know how to keep his "hand dry" (1.3.67), the audience at Lincoln Center laughingly interpreted his comment as a reference to masturbation. The audience at Lincoln Center laughed again when Sir Toby called Andrew a "knight" (1.3.72); the audience at the Globe laughed when, at this point, Toby pulled out yet another bottle of wine he had stashed on stage; the audience at Lincoln center laughed once more when Sir Andrew conceded that he had "Never" before been so "put down," when he called himself a "great eater of beef," and when he remarked that he did not think this habit had damaged his wit (1.3.77–78). That last assertion provoked especially hearty laughs at the National, with Sir Toby's sarcastic response ("No question"; 1.3.78) meanwhile getting real laughs at Lincoln Center. At both the National and the Globe, people laughed at Sir Andrew's assertion that he believed he had "no more wit than a Christian, or an ordinary man has" (1.3.76). It was Andrew, then, who so far provoked the most laughs in act 1, scene 3, and he provoked still more laughs at all four theaters when he, the supposed master of various languages, had to ask Toby the meaning of "Pourquoi" (1.3.82). His reference to spending too much time watching "bear-baiting[s]" (1.3.84) generated laughter at both the Globe and the National. When Andrew asks Toby if his hair did not become him (1.3.88), the actor playing him in Stratford shook his hair, provoking laughs, while Toby's reply that Andrew's hair looked "Excellent" made people at the National laugh, and his ensuing comment that Andrew's hair hung "like flax on a distaff" (1.3.89) provoked laughs at Lincoln Center. People both in Stratford and at the Globe laughed at Toby's "hope to see a housewife take thee between her legs, and spin it [i.e., his hair] off."

Lincoln Center's Andrew provoked laughter merely by saying the word "Faith" (1.3.91) and then later by dancing when later mentioning his love of "masques and revels" at 1.3.99–100—lines the audience at the National also found funny, just as the National audience also laughed when Andrew said that he would "not compare" his dancing skills with those of "an old man" (1.3.102-03). Later, when he said that he thought he had "the back-trick" (a style of dancing) "as strong as any man in Illyria" (1.3.107–08), the Andrew at the National received hearty laughs by incompetently dancing backwards, while the Stratford Andrew received somewhat lesser laughs by "moonwalking" ala Michael Jackson.

At the National, people laughed after Sir Toby asked Andrew "Wherefore are these things [i.e., his alleged dancing talents] hid?" (1.3.109); at Lincoln Center, it was Toby's next question ("Wherefore have these gifts a curtain before 'em?" [1.3.109–10]) that made people laugh; while at both Lincoln Center and at Stratford the audience laughed when Sir Toby got to Shakespeare's reference to a "sink-a-pace" (1.3.114), partly because in Lincoln Center that phrase was replaced with the word "horn-pipe" and partly because, at Stratford, Toby at this point pretended to urinate into a golf hole on a golf course. Toby and Andrew both generated laughter at the Globe by dancing together when Toby praised the "excellent constitution" of Andrew's leg (1.3.115-16), while the actor playing Andrew at the National won laughter by showing off his "dun-colored stock[ing]" (which was actually bright red in this production [1.3.118]) and then dancing and spinning. The same actor did a particularly ridiculous dance when Sir Toby asked him to "Let me see thee caper" (1.3.122), creating so many good feelings that the audience not only laughed but applauded as this scene came to its end. At the Globe, Andrew generated laughs at this same point by walking off the stage as if he had hurt his leg.

What do all these particular moments of laughter suggest? First, they suggest that only a few lines in act 1, scene 3 are guaranteed laugh-lines—lines to which audiences always and everywhere respond with mirth. Sir Andrew's entrance into this scene generated laughter at all four of the productions surveyed here, and the same thing happened again when he had to ask Toby the meaning of "Pourquoi" (1.3.82). Otherwise, however, the moments of laughter varied from production to production, with only a few other lines generating laughter in more than one staging. One of these moments occurs when Sir Andrew addresses Maria as "Good Mistress Accost" (1.3.46), which provoked laughter at Lincoln Center, at Stratford, and at the Globe. But the firm conclusion to be drawn from this survey of 1.3 is that Andrew is its comic star—the character who generates the most laughs partly because of his foolishness, partly because of his apparently limited intelligence, and partly because Toby enjoys making him the butt of Toby's jokes and other comments.

Act 1, Scene 5

Strong and consistent laughter did not return to the stage in the four productions surveyed here until the latter two thirds of act 1, scene 5, when the obviously inebriated Sir Toby enters Olivia's garden, where Olivia has just been talking first with Feste and then with Maria. In the Globe production, Toby, quite drunk, inspired laughter merely by trying to walk (unsteadily), while in the Stratford staging the audience laughed at Feste's words "here he comes" (1.5.99). The Globe audience laughed at Olivia's first words on seeing Toby ("By mine honor, half drunk"; 1.5.101), while strong laughter arose when Toby, badly slurring his words, announced that a visitor outside Olivia's gates (the disguised Viola) was "a gentleman" (1.5.105). His subsequent belch earned laughter at Lincoln Center, Stratford, and the Globe; in the latter theater he belched as if he was having a heart attack, causing Olivia to exclaim (in some lines added to Shakespeare's text), "Oh no! Toby! Help! Help!," at which point Toby then seemed to release a massive fart that sent the other, nearby characters scurrying while waving their noses. This bit of stage business provoked enormous laughter at the Globe, as did Toby's exclamation "A plague o' these pickle-herring" (1.5.105–06), which likewise generated major laughter in Stratford and at the National, where Toby walked unsteadily as he said these words.

At Lincoln Center, people laughed when Toby mistook Olivia's reference to "lethargy" as a reference to "lechery"; at the National they laughed when he promised to "defy" lechery; while at the Globe a big laugh came from his promise to defy "lechery"

(1.5.110). Thus, just four simple words ("Lechery? I defy lechery") generated different moments of laughter: laughter at Lincoln Center in response to "Lechery?"; laughter at the National in response to "defy"; and massive laughter at the Globe in response to the final reference to "lechery." This example illustrates how different productions (and actors) can use the very same words to provoke significantly different reactions—something readers of Shakespeare may wish to keep in mind as they "produce" the plays silently, in their own minds. On stage, the play's words—even three quite simple words ("I"; "defy"; "lechery")—can be accentuated and pronounced in different ways and can also be accompanied by different particular kinds of stage business. The Stratford Toby, for instance, won a big laugh when, after saying "Lechery? I defy lechery," he waved at Maria, while his next words—"There's one at the gate" (1.5.110)—made people laugh at the National because he seemed to have forgotten (and then suddenly recollected) that Viola was still waiting outside.

Toby's next few words—when he says "Give me faith, say I. Well, it's all one" (1.5.112–13)—similarly provoked laughter at different points from different audiences. At Lincoln Center, people laughed at the words "Give me" (when Toby seemed to look up toward the heavens); at the National they laughed at the word "faith," especially when Toby seemed tired of talking; and there was laughter in Stratford when he said "Well, it's all one," apparently because the actor seemed to fart. Meanwhile, back at Lincoln Center there was enormous laughter when the drunken Toby, having spoken these words, noticed (and seemed startled by) one of Olivia's waiting ladies, who all were dressed entirely in black. Thus, comparing and contrasting different productions of a Shakespeare play can not only suggest the different ways the dramatist's individual particular words can be "put across" but also the different kinds of stage business directors can inject into a show to win laughter.

Scattered laughter appeared in different theaters in response to various ensuing moments in act 1, scene 5. Thus, at Stratford, people laughed when Feste spoke the words "drowns him" (1.5.117); at the National they laughed when Feste said the words "the madman"

(1.5.122); people at the Globe laughed when Malvolio entered the scene (apparently finding his walk funny; see 1.5.125), just as they laughed at the National when the character employed a humorous hand gesture when telling Olivia that a visitor had come "to speak" with her (1.5.127), and just as they laughed again when Olivia replied "Tell him, he shall not *speak* with me" (1.5.129; my emphasis). When Malvolio replied that the visitor insisted that he *would* "speak with [her]" (1.5.132), he once again made the funny hand gesture, this time earning even greater laughter from the National Theatre audience.

When Olivia asked, "What kind o'man is he?," Malvolio's answer—"Why, of mankind" (1.5.133–34)—provoked laughter at all four theaters, but apparently for different reasons. At Lincoln Center, Malvolio spoke his reply as if assuming that Olivia might be stupid; at Stratford he accentuated each syllable of the word ("man-kind"); at the Globe he spoke as if he were confused by Olivia's question; and at the National Malvoli*a* (played by a woman) accentuated *man*, as if to imply that Olivia did not like men. Thus, one word was delivered by four different actors, in four different productions, in four different ways, with all four ways earning the desired laughter.

When Olivia asked Malvolio "Of what personage, and years is he [i.e., the visitor]?" (1.5.138), Malvolia at the National generated unusual laughter, partly by making another small hand gesture when replying "as a squash is before 'tis a peascod" (1.5.140), then by using more hand gestures when saying "between a boy and man" (1.5.142), then by pronouncing "speaks" in a funny way (after a hesitation and as if repulsed) in the phrase "he speaks very shrewishly" (1.5.143), and then again when concluding with the final words of this brief reply. People laughed a bit at the end of this reply when it was delivered at Lincoln Center, but the National's female Malvolia worked this reply for all it was worth. No other version of the reply, in the other three productions, generated nearly as much laughter. The National production, set in modern times, was often quite inventive not only in its casting but in its stage business. Thus, when Olivia asked that a veil be placed over her face (1.5.147), she and all her ladies also put on sunglasses and the ladies stood behind her, defiantly, as if to intimidate the visitor. And when Viola entered after this bit of funny business, she was carrying a guitar. Admirers of Shakespeare who prefer more "traditional" productions (such as the "original practices" one at the Globe) might find the National's approach initially off-putting, but by the end many of them might be won over by the sheer success of the National's efforts. (This, for whatever it is worth, was my own reaction.)

At the Globe, great laughter arose when Viola, mistaking Maria for Olivia, called her "Most radiant, exquisite, and unmatchable beauty," and laughter arose again when Maria replied to this compliment with an awkward smile. (The fact that Maria was played at the Globe by a middle-aged man probably had something to do with this audience reaction.) At the Globe, once more, people laughed when Viola said that she had taken "great pains" to learn her speech (a speech intended for Olivia) and Maria repeated those words, and this same announcement also generated laughter at Lincoln Center. At the Globe, Olivia won laughs when asking Viola if Viola was a "comedian" (1.5.162); at Lincoln Center, a bit of laughter followed Viola's reply "I am not that I play" (1.5.164); and, again, at Lincoln Center there was a bit of laughter when Viola later said "Alas, I took pains to study it [her speech]" (1.5.172). But particularly great laughter broke out when, at the National, Viola then said that her speech was "poetical" and began playing her guitar (1.5.172). At the Globe, people laughed when Olivia tried to dismiss Viola by emphasizing the word "skipping" in the phrase "so skipping a dialogue" (1.5.177). Moments in Viola's reply at 1.5.179–81 generated bits of laughter at Lincoln Center, but real laughter did not return again in any of the versions of this scene until Olivia, at 1.5.200, said that she had "read" the "chapter" of Orsino's heart and considered it a "heresy." In the National's production, people laughed heartily at the word "read" (because it picked up on Viola's earlier reference to the "chapter" of Orsino's heart at 1.5.198), but at the National they laughed at the word "heresy"—a word that generated even stronger laughter at the Globe, where Olivia spoke that word while scooting around the stage in the extremely funny walk used by the Globe's Olivia (Mark Rylance) throughout the play. Finally, when Olivia removed her veil and asked Viola if her face was not appealing, laughter broke out at Lincoln Center, in Stratford, and at the Globe when Viola replied that Olivia's appearance was excellent "if God did all" (i.e., if Olivia was not wearing cosmetics; 1.5.206).

Other moments of especially vigorous laughter in the conclusion of act 1, scene 5 came at various points. Thus, people at Lincoln Center, at the Globe, and at the National all laughed heartily when Olivia told Viola that Orsino should send no more messengers "Unless, perchance, you come again" (1.5.250). Indeed, people at the Globe found Olivia's next two lines funny as well, partly because of the stumbling awkwardness Rylance exhibited when saying them. When Olivia later regrets having asked Viola "'What is your parentage?'" (1.5.258), the reaction at both the National and the Globe was especially raucous, particularly when Rylance, at the Globe, put Olivia's hand to her head and shook it, as if she feared that she had made a complete idiot of herself. At the National, laughter ensued during Olivia's next three lines, especially at the words "art," "actions," and "soft, soft," and when Olivia tried to calm herself down ("Not too fast; soft, soft!"), audiences at all four theaters burst out laughing, especially when the Olivia at the National patted down her dress while saying so. A few lines later, when Olivia removes her ring to hand it to Malvolio, instructing him to give it to Viola, an especially huge laugh arose at the Globe as Rylance struggled frantically to get the ring off of his finger, even sticking his finger in his mouth to wet the ring wet and make it easier to remove. People also laughed enthusiastically when Rylance's Olivia almost screamed the words "Hie thee, Malvolio" (1.5.275) when urging her steward to pursue Viola as quickly as possible. At the National, the audience laughed when Olivia smacked "Malvolia" to get her moving right away, and particularly when "Malvolia" then trotted off the stage, holding her butt. There was spontaneous applause both at Lincoln Center and at the National when this whole scene ended.

Act 2, Scene 2

More laughter—often hearty—occurred in various productions when Mavolio/a caught up with Viola. Both at Lincoln Center and at

Stratford, Malvolio was humorously confused when, coming on stage, he saw Viola also entering the stage when he had just seen her "twin" brother, Sebastian (introduced in act 2, scene 1) leaving it. At the National there was huge laughter when "Malvolia" used her hands to gesture back and forth to indicate the distance she had travelled when trying to catch up with Viola, telling the latter "You might have saved me my pains" (2.2.5). At the Globe, laughter arose when Malvolio said that Viola might "have taken it [i.e., the ring] away yourself" (2.2.5). People laughed at the National when "Malvolia," having given the ring to Viola, took it back again while saying "And one thing more" (2.2.7). And people laughed (twice) at Stratford when Malvolio referred to the ring by saying "this" and then again when Malvolio said "Receive it so" (2.2.9). When Viola refused the ring, "Malvolia" at the National won massive and continual laughter when s/he said, in a deep and melodramatically threatening voice, "Come sir," as well as when she equally melodramatically tossed the ring onto the ground, and also when, saying "there it [the ring] lies," s/he dropped to her knees and pointed back and forth from the ring to Viola's eyes. More gestures between "Malvolia" and Viola won even more laughter at the National, and anyone who had doubted the wisdom of casting a woman (Tamson Greig) to play Malvolia would have begun to abandon those doubts by this point. Here and throughout the National's production, Greig did a splendid and often hilariously funny job.

But the actresses (or, at the Globe, actor) playing Viola also generated much laughter during this scene. There was laughter at Lincoln Center, at the Globe, and especially at the National when Viola spoke the line "Fortune forbid my outside have not charmed her [i.e, Olivia]" (2.2.15), and there was laughter again at the Globe and particularly at the National when Viola, in shock, realized that "She [Olivia] loves me sure" (2.2.19). People at Stratford laughed when Viola said, "I am the man" (2.2.22) as she realized the implications of her predicament, but that statement generated an even bigger laugh, at the Globe and at the National, when Viola spoke the words fearfully, adding "ooo, ooo" to imply her apprehension. Meanwhile, her next line, referring to Olivia as a "Poor lady!" (2.2.23), won strong laughter at Lincoln Center, and the Lincoln Center audience laughed a bit once more when Viola later asked, "What will become of this?" (2.2.33), a question that generated especially hearty laughs at the National. People at the National also laughed at Viola's later comment "O Time, thou must entangle this, not I" (2.2.37), partly because the National's Viola strongly emphasized the word "I."

Act 2, Scene 3

The third scene of the second act of *Twelfth Night* has long been regarded as particularly funny and was, for that reason, often the subject of artists' illustrations during the nineteenth century, the heyday of illustrated editions of Shakespeare.[2] This is the scene in which Toby, Sir Andrew, and Feste create so much noise during a bout of boisterous drinking that they at first alarm Maria and then arouse the strongly censorious Malvolio. Feste's opening words in this scene—"How now, did you never see the picture of We Three" (2.3.14–15)—generated laughter at Stratford, at the Globe, and at the National, but especially at Stratford, whose Feste showed his buttocks to his two friends while saying those words, while the actor playing Feste at the Globe held up two dead rabbits (tied with ropes) next to the sides of his head. A few lines later, Sir Andrew won laughs from the Lincoln Center audience by seeming to get sick from some Chinese food he had been eating (2.2.20); people at Stratford laughed heartily when Andrew referred nonsensically to "the equinoctial of Quebus" (2.2.20); and at Stratford they laughed again when Feste said "I did impeticos thy gratillity" (2.3.24)—a comment neither the audience nor the other characters could comprehend.

Because Toby, Andrew, and Feste are all drinking in act 2, scene 3, there is plenty of room here for funny stage business, as when, at Lincoln Center, the audience laughed as Toby, requesting "a love song" from Feste, was just about to eat some spoiled food that Sir Andrew had previously found rancid (2.3.31), or when Andrew, while listening to Feste's song, began (at 2.3.38–39), to "slow dance" with himself at the National, or when (again at the National) a sentimental Andrew began to hug a surprised Toby from behind at around lines 2.3.44–45). At the end of Feste's song, both Toby and

Sir Andrew at the Globe seemed comically stupefied, and there was spontaneous applause of the song both at Lincoln Center and at Stratford. Andrew won laughter at the Globe when calling the song "Very sweet" at 2.3.50 (the Globe Andrew was a humorously sad drunk), while the Andrews at both Stratford and Lincoln Center generated laughs when Andrew called the song "contagious" (2.3.50). (At Lincoln Center they laughed at that word partly because of the running gag about spoiled food.) Meanwhile, laughter resumed a bit later in the scene when Andrew asks Feste to sing a song titled "Hold my peace" and Feste replies, "I shall never begin if I hold my peace" (2.3.61–62)—a reply that generated laughter at the National and strong laughter at Stratford (where Feste grabbed his crotch) and at Lincoln Center, with the Lincoln Center Toby cracking up at the fool's reply. At Stratford, it took the dim-witted Andrew a second or two to "get" the joke, making the audience laugh again, while at Lincoln Center a dance broke out as Feste sang and, at Stratford, the trio began chaotically but playfully hitting each other while dancing. Indeed, at Stratford the singing and dancing became especially boisterous (and thus particularly funny), with the audience clapping along with the merry trio. Also at Stratford, when a censorious Maria arrived on the scene and shouted "Hold!!!" (not in Shakespeare's text), more laughter ensued when everyone except Andrew suddenly ceased singing and dancing.

When Andrew abruptly realized that he was now the only one still making noise, he became hugely embarrassed, causing even more laughter. Although some viewers of the filmed Stratford production may initially have been skeptical of the director's decision to "modernize" the play (as I admit I was), by this point many viewers probably will be won over by the sheer goofiness of the performances (as I admit I was). The Stratford Sir Andrew was particularly and memorably humorous, especially in moments like the one just described. He won laughter again when saying that Toby "does it [i.e., fooling] with a better grace, but I do it more natural" (2.3.73), a line that also generated laughs both at the Globe and the National. Indeed, Toby's "fooling" with Maria at this point created particular laughter at the Globe, while the ensuing singing and dancing at Lincoln Center (inspired by Feste's line "'O the twelfth day of December'"; 2.3.74) made people laugh, just as it made them laugh especially heartily at the Globe, where Sir Andrew sang in a high falsetto while swinging the two dead rabbits, tied to a rope, around his head —until all the singing abruptly stopped upon the entrance of a disgusted Malvolio, at which point the Globe audience broke out into boisterous laughter as a chastened Andrew pitifully began to pet one of the dead rabbits.

At Stratford, Malvolio entered in his pajamas; at the National (where there had just been raucous applause for all the noise and dancing) he came in and turned off a roaring boombox; and at all four theaters his opening question—"My masters, are you mad?" (2.3.76)—provoked instant laughter, particularly at the National, where Toby quickly draped a black cloth over Feste and where "Malvolia's" reaction to the entire scene seemed especially indignant. When, at Stratford, Malvolio asked the revelers "Is there no respect of place, persons, nor time in you?" (2.3.80–81), laughter broke out when some bread, which had been inserted into a toaster a few seconds earlier, popped out of it at exactly the moment Malvolio finished this line, while further laughter occurred (and was especially strong at Lincoln Center and the Globe) when Toby replied, "We did keep time, sir" (2.3.82), referring to their singing. When the disgusted Malvolio finished his attack on the revelers by bidding them "farewell" (2.3.88), Toby won laughter at Lincoln Center (and particularly at the Globe, where he walked unsteadily), by quickly starting a new song beginning "Farewell, dear heart, since I must needs be gone" (2.3.89–90).

Conclusion

If there were space available, one could easily go on, detailing all the ways in which these four distinct productions brought out the laughter inherent in some of Shakespeare's lines (or created additional laughter through clever stage business). But, alas, space is not available, and, in any case, by now the point is clear: Shakespeare's comedies are especially funny when seen (and sometimes filmed) *on stage in front of laughing audiences*; they are likely to seem less funny when simply read or when merely filmed, with no audience present. Laughter, to use a word emphasized in the play itself, is often "contagious" (2.3.50), and it is always helpful to remember that Shakespeare's plays were above all written to be staged, not merely read. Reading, it is true, can give one time to ponder the skill of Shakespeare's phrasing and the depths of his meanings, and a strong case can be made that his plays were *meant* to be read as well as seen and heard.[3] But when reading the comedies, in particular, it is helpful to imagine how they might have been staged originally and how they have also been staged more recently, in venues such as Lincoln Center, the Stratford Shakespeare Festival, Shakespeare's Globe, and the National Theatre in London. Reading the plays *in conjunction with* an essay such as this one can remind readers of how variously the dramas can be imagined by particular directors, how differently they can be brought to life by specific actors, and how distinctly they can provoke responses from specific audiences in specific performance spaces.

Notes

1. One could, of course, try to find and watch DVDs or other video recordings of the productions discussed in this essay, but then one would have to take notes about the various "laugh lines" in order to remember them all. That, essentially, is what I have done here, thus saving readers time and trouble.

All citations from *Twelfth Night* in this essay come from John Russell Brown's "Applause" edition (see below), which offers useful but necessarily very brief notes about how the play can be (and has been) staged. The present essay can afford to go into much more detail about such matters than Brown was able to offer. Likewise, the present essay is much more detailed than the notes provided in the nonetheless very valuable "Shakespeare in Production" edition edited by Elizabeth Schafer.

2. I deal with illustrations of this scene in another essay in the present volume.

3. On this matter, see (especially) the book by Lukas Erne cited below, particularly the second edition.

Works Cited

Brown, John Russell, editor. *Twelfth Night*, by William Shakespeare. The Applause Library. Applause Theatre Books, 2001.

Erne, Lukas. *Shakespeare as Literary Dramatist*. 2003. 2nd ed. Cambridge UP, 2013.

Schafer, Elizabeth, editor. *Twelfth Night*, by William Shakespeare. Shakespeare in Production. Cambridge UP, 2009.

Shakespeare, William. *Twelfth Night*. Edited by John Russell Brown. The Applause Library. Applause Theatre Books, 2001.

Twelfth Night, by William Shakespeare. [Lincoln Center, New York]. Directed by Nicholas Hytner. Performances by Helen Hunt, Philip Bosco, Paul Rudd, and Brian Murray. PBS, 1998, www.youtube.com/watch?v= 9cU5Py8GCmA; www.youtube.com/watch?v=QGDEkLqremA.

Twelfth Night, by William Shakespeare. [National Theatre, London] Directed by Simon Godwin and Robin Lough. Performances by Tamsin Greig, Daniel Rigby, Tamara Lawrance, and Oliver Chris, www.ntathome.com/products/ twelfth-night.

Twelfth Night, by William Shakespeare. [Shakespeare's Globe, London] Directed by Tim Carroll. Performances by Mark Rylance, Stephen Fry, Paul Chahidi, and Samuel Barnett. BBC/Opus Arte, 2013.

Twelfth Night, by William Shakespeare. [Stratford Festival, Stratford, CA.] Directed by Des McAnuff and Barry Avrich. Performances by Andrea Runge, Mike Shara, Sara Topham, Brian Dennehy, and Tom Rooney. Stratford/eone, 2012.

RESOURCES

Chronology of William Shakespeare's Life

1564 William Shakespeare is born in Stratford-upon-Avon in April, 1564. He is baptized in the local church on April 26. His date of birth is usually assumed to have been April 23. His parents are John and Mary Shakespeare. John is a successful glove-maker who, in the years preceding and following William's birth, is a respected member of the local government, although later he suffers financial and social reversals. In addition to giving birth to William, Mary bears seven other children. William almost certainly attends the local grammar school.

1582 William marries Anne Hathaway, daughter of a prominent local farmer. Anne is three months pregnant at the time of the wedding and eight years older than William. In 1583, Anne gives birth to a daughter (Susanna). In 1585, the couple has twins (Hamnet and Judith). Hamnet dies in 1596.

1585–92 Details of Shakespeare's life during this period are unclear and have been the subject of much speculation. One legend (now widely doubted) suggests that he had to leave Stratford to escape the law after he allegedly poached deer from the property of a prominent local landowner. Other writers have speculated that during his time in Stratford Shakespeare may have worked for a lawyer and/or may have taught school. Some recent scholars have suggested that during part of this period Shakespeare may have been living, teaching, and (as an amateur) acting while part of the household of a prominent Catholic family in Lancashire. Numerous other theories abound concerning these "lost years." The idea that Shakespeare taught in some capacity seems plausible to many.

1592 An allusion this year by the London writer Robert Greene seems to mock Shakespeare as an "Upstart Crow" and implies that by this time Shakespeare was living in London, acting in plays, and writing blank verse, presumably for

	the professional theaters that were increasingly being founded at this time. Greene's attack also alludes to one of Shakespeare's plays (now known as *Henry VI, Part Three*). Most scholars assume that by 1592 Shakespeare had already written a number of his earliest plays.
1594	In 1593, plague forces the closing of London's theaters. Shakespeare is often assumed to have written some of his most important nondramatic poems during the period when the theaters were closed. These poems (especially the popular *Venus and Adonis*, which was followed by *The Rape of Lucrece*) seem to have been partly intended to attract the patronage of powerful persons. The earliest sonnets are also often dated to this period. Some scholars believe that Shakespeare was also writing plays during the time when the theaters were closed, with an eye either toward private performance, future public performance, or both. *Venus and Adonis*, *Lucrece*, and some of the sonnets were publicly praised in 1598, although the sonnets were not printed until 1609. In the period following the reopening of the theaters in 1594, Shakespeare's theatrical career once again flourished. He wrote plays, acted in them, and profited from the sales of tickets. These profits eventually made him a rich man.
1594–99	During this period, Shakespeare is productive as an actor, writer, and, in 1599, part owner of the newly constructed open-air, octagonal-shaped Globe Theater, one of the most important public theaters in history. He earns 10% of the profits of the new theater. He is a member of the so-called "Chamberlain's Men," an acting company sponsored by one of the most powerful political figures in the kingdom. By 1597, Shakespeare is able to purchase a substantial home in Stratford, where his wife and surviving children apparently still live while he lives and works in London.
1603	With the death of Queen Elizabeth in this year and the accession of King James I (who remained King James VI of Scotland), the name of Shakespeare's acting company is changed from "The Lord Chamberlain's Men" to "The

King's Men." Their patron is now the most important person in the entire now-united kingdoms. Both before and after Elizabeth's death, Shakespeare's plays are performed at the royal court. The actor/playwright is now both increasingly wealthy and increasingly well known. In 1602 he buys more property in Stratford, and in ensuing years he makes further investments in his home town.

1608 In this year, Shakespeare's company, in addition to performing at the Globe (in Southwark, across the River Thames and south of London), begins performing in a much smaller, more elite indoor theater inside the city of London itself.

1611 Shakespeare is often assumed to begin retiring from full-time involvement in the stage in this year, although some collaborative plays post-date this period. This is the year of his last great "romance" (a modern term), *The Tempest*, which is often seen as a valedictory work.

1616 Early in this year, Shakespeare amends his will, providing generously for his daughter, his sister, and the local poor and remembering various friends, including old theatrical colleagues. The will mentions his wife only briefly, which may or may not be significant. He dies on April 23 (that is, supposedly 52 years to the day of his supposed birth date). He is buried in the same local church where he had been baptized.

1623 In this year, friends of Shakespeare oversee the publication of the famous "First Folio," the massive book that contains most of his works (although many of his writings had previously been individually published in small, affordable, "quarto" editions).

Note: Much of the information cited here was helpfully assembled by Terry Gray and published on one of the many splendid pages of his generally impressive website "Mr. William Shakespeare and the Internet" (web.archive.org/web/20111025081356/http://shakespeare.palomar.edu/life.htm). See, in particular, web.archive.org/web/20111007131108/http://shakespeare.palomar.edu/timeline/timeline.htm.

Works by William Shakespeare

For an exceptionally detailed discussion of the chronology of Shakespeare's works (including discussion of the many disputes about the chronology) see William *Shakespeare: A Textual Companion*, by Stanley Wells and Gary Taylor (Norton, 1997), pp. 69–144. See also the similarly detailed discussion by David Bevington, editor, *The Complete Works of Shakespeare* (Longman, 1997), pp. A1–A21. Bevington helpfully gives the full titles of quarto (small format) printings and also makes their dates of publication quite clear.

Plays were usually first performed not long after they were written. In some cases we have evidence of first (or at least early) performances; in some cases we do not. Whereas dates of first printings are usually solid, dates of first performances are often conjectural.

Even the best experts often disagree about the dates of probable composition of Shakespeare's works. In the listing below, Bevington's suggestions are cited alongside those of G. Blakemore Evans (in *The Riverside Shakespeare*, 2nd ed., Houghton Mifflin, 1997, pp. 77–87) and Wells and Taylor. The frequent variances will give some idea of how often even the best students of these issues can disagree.

Love's Labor's Lost (Bevington: c. 1588–97; G. B. Evans: 1594–95 ["revised 1597 for court performance"]; Wells and Taylor: 1593–95; comedy; first known printing, 1598).

The Henry the Sixth Plays (Bevington: c. 1589–92; G. B. Evans: 1589–90 [revised 1594–95 for Part One; 1590–91 for Part Two; 1590–91 for Part Three]; Wells and Taylor: Part Three, 1590–92; Part Two: 1590–91; Part One: 1591–92 [with other authors]. Three history plays; the second part was first printed in 1594; the third part was first printed in 1595; the first part [perhaps the last written of the three] was first printed in 1623).

Titus Andronicus (Bevington: c. 1589–92; G. B. Evans: 193–94; Wells and Taylor: 1590–91; tragedy; first known printing, 1594).

The Comedy of Errors (Bevington: c. 1589–94; G. B. Evans: 1592–94; Wells and Taylor: 1592–94; comedy; first known printing, 1623).

The Two Gentlemen of Verona (Bevington: c. 1590–94; G. B. Evans: 1594; Wells and Taylor: 1589–93; comedy; first known printing, 1623).

The Taming of the Shrew (Bevington: c. 1590–93; G. B. Evans: 1593–94; Wells and Taylor: 1590–93; comedy; first known printing, 1623).

Venus and Adonis (Bevington: 1592–93; G. B. Evans: 1592–93; Wells and Taylor: 1593; narrative poem; first known printing, 1593).

Richard the Third (Bevington: c. 1592–94; G. B. Evans: 1592–93; Wells and Taylor: 1592–93; history play; first known printing, 1597).

The Rape of Lucrece (Bevington: 1593–94; G. B. Evans: 1593–94; Wells and Taylor: 1594; narrative poem; first known printing, 1594).

The Sonnets (Bevington: 1593–1603; G. B. Evans: 1593–1609; Wells and Taylor: 1598–1609; sonnet collection; first known printing, 1609).

King John (Bevington: c. 1594–96; G. B. Evans: 1594–96; Wells and Taylor: 1594–96; history play; first known printing, 1623).

Romeo and Juliet (Bevington: 1594–96; G. B. Evans: 1595–96; Wells and Taylor: 1594–95; tragedy; first known printing, 1597).

A Midsummer Night's Dream (Bevington: c. 1595; G. B. Evans: 1595–96; Wells and Taylor: 1594–95; comedy; first known printing, 1600).

The Merchant of Venice (Bevington: c. 1596–97; G. B. Evans: 1596–97; Wells and Taylor: 1596–97; dark comedy; first known printing, 1600).

Richard the Second (Bevington: c. 1595–96; G. B. Evans: 1595; Wells and Taylor: 1594–96; history play; first known printing, 1597).

Henry the Fourth, Part I (Bevington: 1596–97; G. B. Evans: 1596–97; Wells and Taylor: 1596–97; history play; first known printing, 1598).

Henry the Fourth, Part II (Bevington: 1597–98; G. B. Evans: 1598; Wells and Taylor: 1597–98; history play; first known printing, 1600).

The Merry Wives of Windsor (Bevington: 1597–1601; G. B. Evans: 1597 ["revised c. 1600–01"]; Wells and Taylor: 1597; comedy; first known printing, 1602).

Much Ado About Nothing (Bevington: 1598–99; G. B. Evans: 1598–99; Wells and Taylor: 1598–99; comedy; first known printing, 1600).

As You Like It (Bevington: 1598–1600; G. B. Evans: 1599; Wells and Taylor: 1599–1600; comedy; first known printing, 1623).

Henry the Fifth (Bevington: 1599; G. B. Evans: 1599; Wells and Taylor: 1599; history play; first known printing, 1600).

Julius Caesar (Bevington: 1599; G. B. Evans: 1599; Wells and Taylor: 1599; tragedy; first known printing, 1623).

The Phoenix and the Turtle (Bevington: finished by 1601; G. B. Evans: c. 1601; Wells and Taylor: 1601; allegorical poem; first known printing, 1601).

Hamlet (Bevington: c. 1599–1601; G. B. Evans: 1600–01; Wells and Taylor: 1600–01; tragedy; first known printing, 1603).

Twelfth Night (Bevington: 1600–02; G. B. Evans: 1601–02; Wells and Taylor: 1602–03; comedy; first known printing, 1623).

Troilus and Cressida (Bevington: c. 1601–02; G. B. Evans: 1601–02; Wells and Taylor: 1602–03; "problem play?"; first known printing, 1609).

A Lover's Complaint (Bevington: c. 1601–05; G. B. Evans: 1602–08; Wells and Taylor: 1598–1609; narrative poem; first known printing, 1609).

All's Well That Ends Well (Bevington: c. 1601–05; G. B. Evans: 1602–03; Wells and Taylor: 1603–05; comedy; first known printing, 1623).

Measure for Measure (Bevington: 1603–04; G. B. Evans: 1604; Wells and Taylor: 1604; dark comedy; first known printing, 1623).

Othello (Bevington: 1603–04; G. B. Evans: 1604; Wells and Taylor: 1603–04; tragedy; first known printing, 1622).

King Lear (Bevington: 1605–06; G. B. Evans: 1605; Wells and Taylor: 1605–08; tragedy; first known printing, 1608).

Timon of Athens (Bevington: 1605–08; G. B. Evans: 1607–08; Wells and Taylor: 1604–07 [with Thomas Middleton]; tragedy; first known printing, 1623).

Antony of Cleopatra (Bevington: 1606–07; G. B. Evans: 1606–07; Wells and Taylor: 1606–07; tragedy; first known printing, 1623).

Macbeth (Bevington: 1606–07; G. B. Evans: 1606; Wells and Taylor: 1606; tragedy; first known printing, 1623).

Pericles (Bevington: 1606–08; G. B. Evans: 1607–08; Wells and Taylor: 1608–09 [with George Wilkins]; comedy or "romance"; first known printing, 1609).

Coriolanus (Bevington: c. 1608; G. B. Evans: 1607–08; Wells and Taylor: 1608; tragedy; first known printing, 1623).

Cymbeline (Bevington: c. 1608–10; G. B. Evans: 1609–10; Wells and Taylor: 1610–11; comedy or "romance"; first known printing, 1623).

The Winter's Tale (Bevington: c. 1609–11; G. B. Evans: 1610–11; Wells and Taylor: 1609–10; comedy or "romance"; first known printing, 1623).

The Tempest (Bevington: c. 1611; G. B. Evans: 1611; Wells and Taylor: 1610–11; comedy or "romance"; first known printing, 1623).

King Henry the Eighth (Bevington: 1613; G. B. Evans: 1612–13; Wells and Taylor: 1613 [with John Fletcher]; history play; first known printing, 1623).

The Two Noble Kinsmen (Bevington: 1613–14; G. B. Evans: 1613; Wells and Taylor: 1613–15 [with John Fletcher]; tragicomedy; co-written with John Fletcher; first known printing, 1634).

The listing above follows Bevington's suggested order of possible composition; here, on the other hand, is the order suggested by G. B. Evans: *1 Henry VI*; *2 Henry VI*; *3 Henry VI*; *Richard III*; *Venus and Adonis*; *The Comedy of Errors*; *Sonnets*; *The Rape of Lucrece*; *Titus Andronicus*; *The Taming of the Shrew*; *The Two Gentlemen of Verona*; *Love's Labor's Lost*; *King John*; *Richard II*; *Romeo and Juliet*; *A Midsummer Night's Dream*; *The Merchant of Venice*; *1 Henry IV*; *The Merry Wives of Windsor*; *2 Henry IV*; *Much Ado about Nothing*; *Henry V*; *Julius Caesar*; *As You Like It*; *Hamlet*; *The Phoenix and the Turtle*; *Twelfth Night*; *Troilus and Cressida*; *A Lover's Complaint*; *All's Well That Ends Well*; *Measure for Measure*; *Othello*; *King Lear*; *Macbeth*; *Antony and Cleopatra*; *Coriolanus*; *Timon of Athens*; *Pericles*; *Cymbeline*; *The Winter's Tale*; *The Tempest*; *Henry VIII*; *The Two Noble Kinsmen*.

Here is the order of possible composition suggested by Taylor and Wells: *The Two Gentlemen of Verona*; *The Taming of the Shrew*; *3 Henry VI*; *2 Henry VI*; *Titus Andronicus*; *1 Henry VI* [with other authors]; *Richard III*; *The Comedy of Errors*; *Venus and Adonis*; *Sonnets*; *The Rape of Lucrece*; *Love's Labor's Lost*; *A Midsummer Night's Dream*; *Romeo and Juliet*; *Richard II*; *King John*; *The Merchant of Venice*; *1 Henry IV*; *The Merry Wives of Windsor*; *2 Henry IV*; *Much Ado about Nothing*; *Sonnets, A Lover's Complaint*; *The Passionate Pilgrim*; *Henry V*; *Julius Caesar*; *As You Like It*; *Hamlet*; *The Phoenix and the Turtle*; *Twelfth Night*; *Troilus and Cressida*; *Measure for Measure*; *Othello*; *All's Well That Ends Well*; *Timon of Athens*; *King Lear*; *Macbeth*; *Antony and Cleopatra*; *Pericles*; *Coriolanus*; *The Winter's Tale*; *Cymbeline*; *The Tempest*; *Henry VIII*; *The Two Noble Kinsmen*.

Bibliography

Anderson, Linda. *A Kind of Wild Justice: Revenge in Shakespeare's Comedies*. U of Delaware P, 1987.

Arlidge, Anthony. *Shakespeare and the Prince of Love: The Feast of Misrule in the Middle Temple*. Giles de la Mare, 2000.

Atkin, Graham. Twelfth Night: *Character Studies*. Continuum, 2008.

Barber, C. L. *Shakespeare's Festive Comedy: A Study of Dramatic Form and Its Relation to Social Custom*. 1959. Meridian, 1963.

Bate, Jonathan, and Eric Rasmussen, editors. *Twelfth Night, or, What You Will*, by William Shakespeare. Modern Library, 2010.

Bloom, Harold, editor. *William Shakespeare's* Twelfth Night. Chelsea House, 1987.

Booth, Stephen. *Precious Nonsense: The Gettysburg Address, Ben Jonson's Epitaphs on His Children, and Twelfth Night*. U of California P, 1998.

Cookson, Linda, and Bryan Loughrey, editors. *Critical Essays* on Twelfth Night. Longman Group, 1991.

Davies, Stevie. *Twelfth Night*. Penguin, 1993.

Donno, Elizabeth Story, editor; Introduction by Penny Gay. *Twelfth Night, or, What You Will*, by William Shakespeare. Cambridge UP, 2017.

Draper, John W. *The* Twelfth Night *of Shakespeare's Audience*. Stanford UP, 1950.

Edmondson, Paul. *Twelfth Night*. The Shakespeare Handbooks. Palgrave Macmillan, 2005.

Elam, Keir, editor. *Twelfth Night, or, What You Will*, by William Shakespeare. Arden Shakespeare, 2003.

Findlay, Alison, and Liz Oakley-Brown, editors. Twelfth Night: *A Critical Reader*. Bloomsbury Arden, 2014.

Ford, John R. Twelfth Night: *A Guide to the Play*. Greenwood Press, 2006.

Giese, Loreen L. *Courtships, Marriage Customs, and Shakespeare's Comedies*. Palgrave Macmillan, 2006.

Hotson, Leslie. *The First Night of* Twelfth Night. Macmillan, 1954.

King, Walter N., editor. *Twentieth Century Interpretations of* Twelfth Night. Prentice-Hall, 1968.

Leech, Clifford. Twelfth Night *and Shakespearean Comedy*. U of Toronto P, 1965.

Lothian, J. M., and T. W. Craik, editors. *Twelfth Night*, by William Shakespeare. Methuen, 1975.

Massai, Sonia, editor. *William Shakespeare's* Twelfth Night*: A Sourcebook*. Routledge, 2007.

Minton, Gretchen E., editor. *Twelfth Night*, by William Shakespeare. The Arden Shakespeare, 2020.

Novy, Marianne. *Love's Argument: Gender Relations in Shakespeare*. U of North Carolina P, 1984.

Osborne, Laurie. *The Trick of Singularity:* Twelfth Night *and the Performance Editions*. U of Iowa P, 1996.

Palmer, D. J., editor. *Shakespeare:* Twelfth Night*: A Selection of Critical Essays*. Macmillan, 1972.

Pennington, Michael. Twelfth Night*: A User's Guide*. N. Hern Books, 2000.

Potter, Lois. *Twelfth Night*. Macmillan, 1985.

Schiffer, James, editor. Twelfth Night*: New Critical Essays*. Routledge, 2011.

Wells, Stanley, editor. Twelfth Night*: Critical Essays*. Garland Press, 1986.

Wells, Stanley, and Roger Warren, editors. *Twelfth Night, Or What You Will*, by William Shakespeare. Oxford UP, 1994.

White, R. S., editor. Twelfth Night*: Contemporary Critical Essays*. MacMillan, 1996.

About the Editor

Robert C. Evans was I. B. Young Professor of English at Auburn University at Montgomery, where he taught since 1982 and was awarded emeritus status upon his retirement in 2021. In 1984, he received his PhD from Princeton University, where he held Weaver and Whiting fellowships as well as a University fellowship. In later years his research was supported by fellowships from the Newberry Library (twice), the American Council of Learned Societies, the Folger Shakespeare Library (twice), the Mellon Foundation, the Huntington Library, the National Endowment for the Humanities, the American Philosophical Society, and the UCLA Center for Medieval and Renaissance Studies.

In 1982, he was awarded Princeton's G. E. Bentley Prize and in 1989 was selected Professor of the Year for Alabama by the Council for the Advancement and Support of Education. At AUM, he received the Faculty Excellence Award and was named Distinguished Research Professor, Distinguished Teaching Professor, and University Alumni Professor. Most recently he was named Professor of the Year by the South Atlantic Association of Departments of English. In 2020, he won the Eugene Current-Garcia Distinguished Scholar Award presented annually by the Alabama College English Teachers Association.

He is a contributing editor to the John Donne *Variorum Edition*, senior editor of the *Ben Jonson Journal*, and is the author or editor of over eighty books (on such topics as Ben Jonson, Martha Moulsworth, Kate Chopin, John Donne, Frank O'Connor, Brian Friel, Ambrose Bierce, Amy Tan, early modern women writers, pluralist literary theory, literary criticism, twentieth-century American writers, American novelists, Shakespeare, and seventeenth-century English literature). He is also the author of roughly six hundred published or forthcoming essays or notes (in print and online) on a variety of topics, especially dealing with Renaissance literature, critical theory, women writers, short fiction, and literature of the nineteenth and twentieth centuries.

Contributors

Melissa Anderson earned a PhD in comparative literature from the University of Chicago and an MLIS from San Jose State University. She is currently associate professor in Hannon Library at Southern Oregon University in Ashland, Oregon. Her most recent scholarly publications focus on nineteenth-century literature, the literature of climate change, pedagogy, and information literacy. She is currently working on a book on Jane Austen and information history.

Jordan Bailey is an independent scholar whose research interests center around education in the United States, especially the historical development of the public education system and its responses to changing political and social environments. She is also interested in and concerned with education in general, including teaching reading, writing, and literature across developmental stages. Her areas of literary research are the development of children's and young adult literature in the United States. Previously published essays have dealt with feminism, Martin Luther King, Jr., greed in literature, *The Odyssey*, Abraham Lincoln, and many other topics. Her recent work has involved the detailed analysis of illustrations of major literary texts.

Christopher Baker is professor emeritus of English at Georgia Southern University, where he taught English renaissance literature as well as mythology and the Bible as literature. Twice president of the South Central Renaissance Conference, he is author of *Religion in the Age of Shakespeare* (Greenwood, 2007) and editor of *Absolutism and the Scientific Revolution 1600–1720: A Biographical Dictionary* (Greenwood, 2002). His essays have appeared in *Milton Studies*, *Comparative Drama*, *The Ben Jonson Journal*, *Studia Neophiloligica*, the *Journal of Modern Literature*, and elsewhere.

James Hirsh, professor emeritus of English at Georgia State University, is the author of *The Structure of Shakespearean Scenes* (Yale UP); *Shakespeare and the History of Soliloquies* (which won the 2004 South Atlantic Modern Language Association Book Award); articles in *Shakespeare Survey*, *Shakespeare Quarterly*, *Shakespeare*, *Medieval and Renaissance*

Drama in England, *Cahiers Élisabéthains*, *Ben Jonson Journal*, *South Atlantic Review*, *Papers of the Bibliographical Society of America*, *Studies in the Literary Imagination*, *Essays in Theatre*, *Modern Language Quarterly*, and other journals; as well as chapters in books published by Cambridge UP, Bloomsbury, Routledge, Continuum, Salem Press, Publications des Universités de Rouen et du Havre, and other presses. Hirsh is the recipient of the Georgia State University Distinguished Honors Professor Award, the Beverly Rogers Literary Award, and the Discoveries Award conferred by the editorial board of the *Ben Jonson Journal*.

Brandon Schneeberger is an assistant professor of English at Montreat College. His research explores etymology, conversation, and religion in early modern and eighteenth-century British literature. He has published on a variety of British authors including William Shakespeare, Samuel Johnson, and Jane Austen. He serves as managing editor for *The Ben Jonson Journal* and is the author of the Ben Jonson page for the Oxford University Press series *Oxford Bibliographies in British and Irish Literature*. Forthcoming publications include an examination of how Dante's *Divine Comedy* influences our reading of Coventry Patmore's *The Unknown Eros* and an exploration of the liturgical elements in G. K. Chesterton's *The Man Who Was Thursday* (*Religion and Literature*).

Eric J. Sterling earned his PhD in English at Indiana University in 1992. He is distinguished research professor of English at Auburn University at Montgomery, AL, where he has taught since 1994. He is also director of the Master of Liberal Arts program. He has published dozens of refereed articles on the Holocaust, and his book *Life in the Ghettos during the Holocaust* was published by Syracuse University Press.

Matthew M. Thiele is an associate professor of English at Glenville State College in Glenville, WV. He has published several recent articles on the influence of plague on early modern English literature, including two articles in the *Ben Jonson Journal*. His other scholarly interests are comedy as a genre and domestic abuse. He has published humor writing in *McSweeney's Internet Tendency*, *Points in Case*, *Slackjaw*, and elsewhere, and he publishes a blog on literature through *Medium*.

Nicolas Tredell has published 25 books on literary and cultural topics and over 450 essays and articles in peer-reviewed academic journals such as

American, British, and Canadian Studies, *The Review of Contemporary Fiction* and *Victorian Poetry*, and in major literary magazines like the *London Review of Books*, *PN Review* and the *Times Literary Supplement*. He formerly taught at Sussex University. He is the co-founder and co-director, with Angela Tredell, of Tredellian Press, which produces pamphlets of quality fiction and nonfiction. He gives frequent lectures, seminars and readings, in person and online, at a wide variety of venues across the globe.

Edwin Wong is the founder of The Risk Theatre Modern Tragedy Playwriting Competition. His publications include: *The Risk Theatre Model of Tragedy: Gambling, Drama, and the Unexpected* (2019) and *The Harmony of Fixed Fate and Free Will in the Iliad* (2002). A critic and director, he specializes in the intersection between probability and drama. He has been invited to present his theory of tragedy at annual conferences held by the National New Play Network, the Canadian Association of Theatre Research, the Society of Classical Studies, and the Classical Association of the Middle West and South. He was educated at Brown University and the University of Victoria, where he read ancient theatre. His next projects include working with playwrights to produce risk theatre tragedies and a series of readings of canonical plays from the perspective of probability, chance, and the random element.

Index